THE MUSICAL WORLD OF
Boublil & Schönberg

The Creators of
Les Misérables, Miss Saigon,
Martin Guerre, and The Pirate Queen

Margaret Vermette

APPLAUSE THEATRE & CINEMA BOOKS ♦ NEW YORK

AN IMPRINT OF HAL LEONARD CORPORATION

The Musical World of Boublil and Schönberg: The Creators of Les Misérables, Miss Saigon, Martin Guerre, *and* The Pirate Queen
Margaret Vermette
Copyright © 2006 Margaret Vermette, except for Chapter 5: *Master of the House: Producer*, which is © 2006 Cameron Mackintosh, Ltd.

Book design by Mark Lerner; front cover design by Hal Leonard Creative Services

Photo credits for color insert: *Les Misérables, Miss Saigon, Martin Guerre*: Photographer: Michael Le Poer Trench; *The Pirate Queen*: Photographer: Joan Marcus. All color insert photos are © Cameron Mackintosh Ltd.

Library of Congress Cataloging-in-Publication Data:
Vermette, Margaret.
 The musical world of Boublil and Schönberg : the creators of Les misérables, Miss Saigon, Martin Guerre, and The pirate queen / Margaret Vermette.
   p. cm.
 Includes bibliographical references (p.) and index.
 ISBN 978-1-55783-715-8
 1. Boublil, Alain. 2. Schönberg, Claude-Michel. 3. Lyricists--France--Biography. 4. Composers--France--Biography. 5. Musicals--History and criticism. I. Title.
 ML385.V398 2006
 782.1'40922--dc22
 [B]
                         2006036897

Applause Theatre & Cinema Books
19 West 21st Street
Suite 201
New York, NY 10010
Phone: (212) 575-9265
Fax: (212) 575-9270
Email: info@applausepub.com
Internet: www.applausepub.com

Applause books are available through your local bookstore, or you may order at www.applausepub.com or call Music Dispatch at 800-637-2852

Sales & Distribution

NORTH AMERICA:
Hal Leonard Corp.
7777 West Bluemound Road
P. O. Box 13819
Milwaukee, WI 53213
Phone: (414) 774-3630
Fax: (414) 774-3259
Email: halinfo@halleonard.com
Internet: www.halleonard.com

EUROPE:
Roundhouse Publishing Ltd.
Millstone, Limers Lane
Northam, North Devon EX 39 2RG
Phone: (0) 1237-474-474
Fax: (0) 1237-474-774
Email: roundhouse.group@ukgateway.net

CONTENTS

ACKNOWLEDGEMENTS

I would like to thank all those who gave so generously of their time in talking to me at great length and answering my endless questions. Without them this book would not have been possible. First and foremost, of course, I thank Alain Boublil and Claude-Michel Schönberg, but also Herbert Kretzmer, Richard Maltby, Stephen Clark, Trevor Nunn, Nicholas Hytner, Conall Morrison, Cameron Mackintosh, John Dempsey, Frank Galati, Mark Dendy, Moya Doherty, and John McColgan. Thanks also to Colm Wilkinson for the insights and personal experiences he shared in the Foreword.

I would like to acknowledge the efficiency and patience of Rosy Runciman, archivist at Cameron Mackintosh Ltd, who gave me invaluable assistance in compiling the Fact File in Chapter Seven; my grateful thanks. Thanks also to Sue Coombes, personal assistant to Alain Boublil, for her unstinting help throughout, to Paula Burke, executive manager at Abhann Productions, more recently, for her very prompt and helpful replies to all my *The Pirate Queen* queries, and to Jane Austen, personal assistant to Cameron Mackintosh. I am indebted to Michael Le Poer Trench and Joan Marcus for the use of their wonderful color production photographs and to

Roger Wemyss Brooks, photograph librarian at Cameron Mackintosh Ltd. for his patience and expertise.

My thanks to all those at Applause Books for their expertise and enthusiasm, which has made the publication process such a rewarding experience: Michael Messina, Brian Black, Kay Radtke, Mark Lerner, and Richard Slater, and to my agent, Janet Glass.

My thanks also for much practical help and encouragement from: Simon Bowman, Bill Brohn, Phil Chandler, Hal Luftig, Elaine Paige, Susan Wallace, and David White. Friends and family alike have shown continuing interest and great support for what has been a lengthy project, and without the constant support and encouragement of my husband Mike, I could not even have begun.

Photo by Margaret Malandruccolo

FOREWORD

Music expresses that which cannot be said
and on which it is impossible to be silent.
—VICTOR HUGO (1802–1885)

I am delighted that Margaret Vermette has decided not to be silent and to write this wonderful book on the musical works of Alain Boublil and Claude-Michel Schönberg. In it she reveals the personal thoughts and work methods of these two people and their many collaborators, who together have created some of the greatest musical theatre of our time, from *Les Misérables, Miss Saigon*, and *Martin Guerre* to their new show *The Pirate Queen*.

As one who has to a large extent made his living in musical theatre, the book is a fascinating read; to also have been fortunate enough to be the original Jean Valjean in *Les Misérables*—and to have had the beautiful song "Bring Him Home" written for me—gives this book a special meaning in my life. Herb Kretzmer captured the essence of that song with his perfectly-crafted lyrics.

People often ask me did I ever tire of playing Jean Valjean, and I try to explain that the emotional truth and honesty of Boublil and Schönberg's music and lyrics would sweep you away, show after show, to that utterly realistic world they created of nineteenth-century Paris. You never *played* Valjean, you *were* Valjean, because that's where their work placed you. Granted, you were physically and emotionally exhausted after the show, but very rarely during a performance.

So if you have ever wondered about the process involved in creating these great shows and finally putting them on stage, this book will take you on this often frustrating but amazingly passionate journey. Enjoy.

Colm Wilkinson
September 2006

COLM WILKINSON created the role of Jean Valjean in *Les Misérables*, both in London and then on Broadway.

Claude-Michel Schönberg and Alain Boublil at the opening night party at Tavern on the Green in New York's Central Park, following the Broadway premiere of the revival of *Les Misérables* on November 9, 2006.

Photo by Charlotte Schönberg

INTRODUCTION

This book has been written for all those who love the musicals of Boublil and Schönberg and also for those who have a more general interest in the creative process of musical theatre. Alain Boublil and Claude-Michel Schönberg have achieved phenomenal worldwide success with their musicals and won many awards. But what is especially remarkable is the public devotion to their work. From the very beginning, with the opening of *Les Misérables* at the Barbican Theatre in London in October 1985 and the generally dismal critical reviews that followed, the public have chosen to make up their own minds and vote with their feet, often going to the shows not just once but many times. Audiences are the lifeblood of the theatre, and by the end of 2005 over 53 million people all over the world had seen *Les Misérables* alone. In Summer 2005, *Les Misérables* was voted Best Musical by the listeners of Elaine Paige's BBC Radio 2 program, scooping an amazing 41 percent of the vote, and on October 8, 2006, *Les Misérables* reached its twenty-first birthday and became the longest-running international musical ever with over 42,000 professional performances worldwide. Boublil and Schönberg may not be the most famous writers of musical theatre today, but they may well be the most appreciated. It is, perhaps, because of their emotional and theatrical understanding of what people really want from a major musical that their work has not only captured the hearts and minds of audiences so completely, but has continued to hold them and create new generations of fans.

Musicals in general are sometimes disdained by "serious" theatregoers and critics alike. But musical theatre is the most demanding of all collaborative theatre art because it requires the bringing together of so many disparate elements. The last few decades of the twentieth century saw a change in the scope of musical theatre that began in England with the musicals of Andrew Lloyd Webber and was taken further still with the advent of *Les Misérables, Miss Saigon*, and *Martin Guerre*. These three musicals have pushed back the boundaries of what was considered possible or even desirable in musicals and have changed forever the public perception of what a musical is. They are not light, frothy, song-and-dance musicals with superficial, predictable story lines interrupted by songs with catchy tunes and happy endings in the tradition of musical comedy. That, of course, is not everyone's cup of tea. The late Jack Tinker of London's *The Daily Mail* famously christened *Les Misérables*, "The Glums," while Jane Edwardes in *Time Out* reviewed *Miss Saigon* with the comment: "Quite why such a melodramatic, weepy story line is so popular is a mystery to me. Whatever happened to musicals with jokes?"

But Boublil and Schönberg have taken the genre and reinvented it. Their shows do not allow one to sit back passively and simply be entertained because they demand a high level of emotional engagement from the audience. They deal with individual stories set in a historical context at a moment of crisis, and handle themes that are at once universal and personal to every audience. They create multidimensional characters that the audience really cares about and invest them with recognizable truths with which the audience can identify. Although intricately structured, their musicals have a cohesive narrative sweep and emotional clarity with stories that carry the audience along with them. The realism of their subject matter is well suited to the sung-through form, which never denies the dramatic impulses and the structural and thematic unity that characterize their work.

Boublil and Schönberg are musical dramatists with a mastery of the sung-through form, which allows them to tackle serious subjects of epic dimensions. Their musicals are driven by the narrative rather than led by the music, and the rich texture of their storytelling is enabled in great part by Schönberg's extraordinary gift for writing melodic and rhythmic recitative. Boublil and Schönberg have a unified vision whereby words and music are fused together in a mutually dependent and organic way to meet the dramatic requirements of the story. The lyrics are not intended to dazzle you with wit and cleverness, as they traditionally do in many wonderful Broadway-style musicals. They are written so as not to call attention to themselves but to convey in a very natural way the thoughts and emotions of the characters. Likewise, the scores are not designed to highlight individual hit songs because their primary purpose is to engage the audience in the narrative and to tell the story in their own way. They are marked by a musical sincerity and are full of variety and vitality, with soaring and often heart-rending melodies that make you love them more each time you hear them. Music can heighten and reinforce emotion in a drama because music is heard on a different emotional level than dialogue. Music enriches a drama by raising the ordinary to the exceptional, and it has a way of making it seem more real than reality.

Musical theatre is unifying because it allows an audience to feel together those emotions that are usually only felt alone. And it is notable in Boublil and Schönberg's musicals that, whether in the UK, the United States, or in all the differing parts of the world where they play, audiences respond in the same way at the same moment to the same part of the performance because the emotions evoked are understood and embraced by all cultures. These musicals are not sentimental, but they touch people's hearts in a unique way and they are accessible on many levels. They make you sad, they make you happy, and they help you to reinterpret your own life. The stories evoke emotions in the extreme so that the audience leaves the theatre with that wonderful heady mix of trauma and euphoria. If Boublil and Schönberg's musicals are so often likened to opera, it is because while owing a great deal to the pleasure of the tragic form, they have the scale, seriousness, and intensity of opera, and because they are entirely sung-through.

Each new show that Boublil and Schönberg have written has been consciously and determinedly different from its predecessors. With *Les Misérables* they took the genius that was Victor Hugo's story and made it their own. But however good the source, it still had to be adapted and reinvented musically. It was indeed a remarkable feat of compression to turn such a long and complex novel into three hours of musical theatre that capture the very essence and passion of Hugo's masterpiece. *Les Misérables*, affectionately known by many as *Les Mis*, is a musical of the people and for the people. Hugo himself said of his novel, "I do not know whether it will be read by everyone, but it is meant for everyone." He certainly achieved the universal audience he hoped for with his novel, and the musical on which it is based has achieved exactly the same kind of universal acclaim and popularity.

Miss Saigon could not have been a more different musical. Moving away from nineteenth-century France to a contemporary setting in Saigon and Bangkok, Boublil and Schönberg took the opera *Madame Butterfly* and this time expanded the story in their own way. The result was a modern musical tragedy with seriousness and integrity that has a strong topical and political significance as well as heartbreaking emotion. *Miss Saigon* has also achieved a universal audience, and millions of people all over the world have taken it to heart.

Martin Guerre was very different again. The story takes place in a village community against the backdrop of the sixteenth-century religious conflicts in the Basque region of France. Their new musical *The Pirate Queen* is yet again new territory. Although, like *Martin Guerre*, it takes place in the sixteenth century, it is a seafaring adventure set against the turmoil of Ireland under threat of Tudor invasion. Boublil and Schönberg have taken the fascinating yet little known story of Grace O'Malley and created an action-packed narrative with their usual flair for high drama and heartrending emotion.

These musicals have all been developed through a collaborative process with co-lyricists, directors, and producers. In such a collaborative process as musical theatre, many people have been involved that space does not permit me to deal with fully. So, for example, with *Les Misérables*, while acknowledging the excellent work done by James Fenton, I have dealt at length with Herbert Kretzmer as the co-lyricist and adapter of the work. With *Miss Saigon*, some decisions were taken with other directors in mind before Nicholas Hytner came on board, but he was the final choice for director. *Martin Guerre* well justifies the concept that "great musicals are not written, they are rewritten," and here my choice was more difficult because there have been, to date, two major versions, each one having substantial reworkings. The first version was in London at the Prince Edward Theatre with Edward Hardy as co-lyricist and Declan Donnellan as director. It then had a new opening night after some major reworking with Stephen Clark as co-lyricist. The second version opened at the West Yorkshire Playhouse in Leeds with Stephen Clark again as co-lyricist and Conall Morrison as director, and it toured in the UK. It was then reworked in some aspects before opening at the Guthrie Theater in Minneapolis prior to an American tour that finished at the Ahmanson Theatre in Los Angeles. It is, of course, inevitable that some people will favor one or the other version, but, while acknowledging the fantastic work done on the first version, I have chosen to feature the co-lyricist and director of the second Leeds/Minneapolis version because I feel that this version was in so many ways the closer of the two to Boublil and Schönberg's ultimate vision. However, it does seem now that there will never be a definitive version of *Martin Guerre* and that it will always be a show that is constantly evolving.

At present there are plans for a completely new version that will be performed only in Japan; and Boublil and Schönberg are also working on a concert version that will be done in a theatrical way with a big symphonic orchestra. *The Pirate Queen* has been dealt with in a chapter of its own because, at the time of this writing, it is at the point of its "out of town" opening in Chicago.

This book offers a peek behind the closed doors of musical theatre creation. Of course, set design, costume, lighting, choreography, orchestration, and performance are all essential elements to the creative process too, but that is another book entirely. Here you will find comprehensive insights into the writing of the book, music, and lyrics, and into the rationale behind directing and producing, which will provide a greater understanding of the musicals themselves. The final chapter is a Fact File that provides information on the productions in London, New York, and worldwide, with details of the creative teams, the casts, the musical numbers, the reviews, the cities played, the awards, the recordings, the synopses and themes, and some intriguing facts and trivia. All information in the book is current to fall 2006.

In the following pages I would like to introduce you to Alain Boublil and Claude-Michel Schönberg and to their co-lyricists, directors, and producers. This work has been achieved through generously extensive interviews and revised with them all at every stage. Inevitably, there are a few differing perspectives on some points. But it has been my intention to allow them to take center stage and speak at length about their lives and their work without interruption. I have tried to preserve the manner in which they talk and to give the impression that they are speaking directly to the reader.

So if you would like to know how Alain Boublil and Claude-Michel Schönberg move from an idea and a blank piece of paper to a first night performance, then turn the page and enter *The Musical World of Boublil and Schönberg.* ❧

CHAPTER 1

A Question of Identity

A BIOGRAPHICAL PORTRAIT

ALAIN BOUBLIL AND CLAUDE-MICHEL SCHÖNBERG are both intensely private people. Everything that has been written about their personal lives to date would fit on a postcard. So who are these two remarkable men who have written some of the world's best-loved musicals? A good starting point is to look at one of the dominant themes in their musicals, for the musical world of Boublil and Schönberg is pervaded by questions about personal identity.

In Alain and Claude-Michel's work political events often act as a catalyst for change, and personal identity becomes highly significant both as a moral issue and as a question of choice. The idea of choosing who you want to be and consciously directing your own fate is a consistent theme in *Les Misérables* and *Miss Saigon* and it reaches its peak in *Martin Guerre*, where the inherent complexity of identity is explored in depth.

In *Les Misérables* Jean Valjean asks, "Who am I?" while Enjolras tells the students at the ABC Café "It is time for us all/To decide who we are," a choice that decides not only identity but also destiny. In *Miss Saigon* questions of identity are equally significant, especially in terms of national identity and what it means to be American. Chris, looking back at his time in Vietnam, tells Ellen, "I didn't have a clue who I am," while Kim, believing that her son can only have the kind of life she wants for him if he is an American, promises him: "You can be who you want to be." After three years of brainwashing in the rice fields, the Engineer still readily identifies with all things American and defiantly states his true identity: "I'm still what I am…I speak Uncle Ho/And think Uncle Sam." In *Martin Guerre*, the question of identity is the central issue around which the whole drama revolves, and Arnaud finally asks, "Who is this man that I became?" It is then, perhaps, surprising to learn that the issue of personal identity was never intentionally a key theme in their musicals, but seems, rather, to have been worked in subconsciously. It is only now upon reflection of their work, that they can recognize not just the importance of this theme in their musicals, but also its relevance to their own personal lives.

Although Alain and Claude-Michel both consider themselves to be technically French and speak French as their first language, they have no real affinity with or allegiance to France and feel equally at home anywhere in the world. There are many surface differences in their early lives. Alain grew up in Tunisia and Claude-Michel in Brittany; however, there are also many fundamental similarities. They were both born during World War II, their families were Jewish émigrès, and both of their lives, to some degree, have been shaped by political situations. Alain's family had emigrated from Egypt to Tunisia and Claude-Michel's from Hungary to France, so throughout their childhoods there was no sense of old family roots or of being strongly connected to any one place, and both men have a deeply felt sense of rootlessness. Both were very ambitious from an early age, and soon felt restricted by the limitations and smallness of their hometown environments.

Although Alain was born and raised in Tunisia, he has no roots there:

AB: If you are a Frenchman, yet not born in France, you acquire very early a sense of not being dependent on your roots. You don't have the same sense of nationality, the same feeling for the French soil, the French flag. I've never had a sense of nostalgia for Tunisia either, or the need to keep going back there. But I've had a passion for history, and especially French history, since I was 15 years old. The trauma of war in Africa and the discovery of the terrible turmoil in France around the time of World War II, with that dark period of racism and the horrible fate of French Jews, is something that has strongly left its mark.

I was raised in a French culture in Tunisia, and I was very happy living in Paris for twenty-five years. But then Paris became too small for me to do what I had to do. I came to London, and I've never been happier than I am living in London. But I would never want to be limited in my traveling because I love traveling, and the whole world is my oyster. I am a true cosmopolitan. I don't have any strong sense of belonging in one particular place. I'm at ease everywhere. Belonging to a country probably gives you a lot of strength but it also has its limitations creatively. I've never felt these limitations and it has freed my mind.

Claude-Michel doesn't feel attached either to France or Hungary.

CMS: What I feel from my childhood is that I don't feel attached to anywhere. I'm not very attached to France because there is no family home with the traditions of generations and generations. So I could have been born anywhere in the world. It means that I'm O.K. everywhere and I'm not O.K. everywhere. I live in France because my first wife was working in Paris, reporting the news on television, and so we raised our family there. Otherwise, I would probably have lived in London or New York.

This sense of rootlessness means that Alain and Claude-Michel follow in the tradition of many of the most successful creators of musical theatre: émigrè Jews who didn't belong to any one place or nation, and so were free to invent, reinvent, innovate, and create without fear of the subject not being right for their country. It is, of course, true that the most interesting art often does come from people who have been displaced in some way, because art is about imposing order on chaos. Artists can make sense of something that is alien to them and any sense of dislocation as well as contact with a new culture provokes new ideas and stimulates creativity. It was, then, these common elements in their backgrounds that helped to shape and influence their lives, their personalities, and, indeed, their sense of identity.

Alain Boublil was born on March 5, 1941 in Tunis, where his grandparents had settled many years before, having come from Alexandria. The whole family—aunts, uncles, and cousins—lived in Tunisia, which at that time was a French colony. Alain spent his childhood in Tunis, growing up in a predominantly French culture. In many ways he felt it was exactly like living in France. His family was part of the French and Jewish community and lived a very different and separate kind of life from the Tunisian Muslims.

AB: It was like living in any small French capital city. It was not as important as Algiers or Casablanca. It was smaller, but at the same time it had all the pretense of a little capital. We were always trying to be aware of what was happening in the rest of the world, avidly reading newspapers from abroad, mainly Paris, so we could pretend we were in the mainstream of things.

Alain's parents, Henri and Ida, had four children: three boys and a girl, and Alain was the oldest. Henri owned a shoe shop in the busy center of Tunis, and, after school, Alain would enjoy helping out there until closing time, when his father would take him home. Alain went to school at the all boys French Lycée, where his favorite subjects were French literature and history. But he also liked English and Italian literature, and he was an able student who enjoyed going to school. Although he learned English, he did all his lessons in French, with almost exclusively French pupils. He made many good friends.

AB: We all knew we would have to leave Tunisia if we wanted to pursue our studies after school, because at that time there were no

**universities in Tunisia. If you wanted to study after your Baccalau-
réat, you really had to go to France. Then, in 1956, Tunisia became
independent, like the whole of North Africa. In the decolonization
process, more or less everyone of that Jewish colony emigrated
from Tunisia to France at the same time. No one really knew what
was going to happen. It was more than a new political regime, it
was a complete change.**

Alain's parents, however, didn't leave at that time, and there
weren't any major problems as it was a country that stayed quite
peaceful for a very long time. Ida left much later, after Henri died,
so that she could be with her children in France. All Alain's school
friends left at the same time to go to university, and they lived
mostly in Paris. Over the years they have remained good friends,
bonding all the more closely, perhaps, because of their shared background and experience. "They all became doctors or dentists or
lawyers or whatever. I keep in close contact with many of them,
and one of them even became my accountant."

Alain has good memories of a happy, normal childhood and
happy schooldays. His favorite occupation in the school holidays
was putting on plays, and, from the age of ten, this was very much a
part of his life. The plays took the form of little comic book sketch-
es of cowboy stories, which he mostly invented himself. All the
neighbors were invited and paid one franc each to see a play. Alain
enthusiastically got the production together, sorted out the staging
and sets, and organized the local children as performers and really
enjoyed performing himself. At school he took every opportunity
to be involved with drama productions, always wanting to take
the leading role. But as much as he loved performing as a child, he
never wanted to take up acting as a career.

At the age of eighteen, Alain went to Paris, where he studied
for a business degree.

**AB: I enjoyed my life in Tunisia very much until it was time to leave.
I knew even from the age of twelve that one day I would go to Paris**

to study. As I got older my only aim, obviously, was to leave Tunisia because I was getting bored in such a small town, where I certainly wouldn't be able to fulfil all my ambitions or to meet all the interesting people that I wanted to meet. I was not made to live in a small town anyway. That's something I knew from very early on.

When Alain moved to Paris, it opened up a whole new world for him. He became a student at the Institute of Higher Commercial Studies and, after three years, he graduated in Economics. It was, however, a very elitist establishment.

AB: It's the kind of school where people who are going to run the country go. They were mostly the sons of the very wealthy—the people who owned all the factories, the champagne people, even the son of the King of Thailand. I was lost there. I was completely out of their league, and they looked on me with contempt. It didn't really concern me, but I just thought that one day I would top them with something else!

Nevertheless, Alain loved his student years in Paris. He lived in a very cheap, small student house in the fourteenth district, and in his first week he walked Paris completely, discovering every district for himself. So what was his first impression?

AB: I remember thinking that I had never seen as many beautiful girls at the same time, in the same place, on the same day. It took me years to recover from that! That's the main thing about Paris when you are a young boy. It certainly wasn't like that in Tunisia. In Paris we enjoyed the freedom, the café life, the university, and all those different things.

But to start with Alain had no money at all and his parents weren't in a position to help very much. So he took various jobs, including working for Hertz Car Rental at the airport, where he would work right through the weekend. And in this way he earned enough money to have the kind of normal student social life that he felt every young student in Paris should have. "It was an amazing time, and for me it compared to absolutely nothing else."

It was while Alain was studying in Paris that he started to listen intensively to music on the radio. While the other students were working on their balance sheets or comparing the politics of economy during the two world wars, Alain was developing a sound knowledge of contemporary music. He worked on his studies too, of course, and passed all his exams, but he became increasingly preoccupied with the popular music of the sixties.

AB: I was a highbrow student of economics and all that, and yet at the same time I was listening to radio for teenagers, which none of my colleagues ever listened to because they thought it was stupid and childish. But I was very much aware that a musical revolution was going on, and that really interested me.

Alain's interest in music, lyrics, and poetry had been awakened some years before in Tunisia when he was about fourteen. In his teens, Alain listened to classical music very little, and it wasn't until much later that he started going to opera. It was, in fact, Claude-Michel who took him to his first opera, *Parsifal*. But he listened to a lot of jazz, and he loved the great singers, writers, and composers of that time, such as Charles Aznavour and Jacques Brel.

AB: I loved those kinds of songs that were very much based on the text and that had some important message. And that's where I got the feeling, the emotion, and the love for great texts and great stories told through a three-minute song. And that has certainly been an important influence at the back of my mind.

The arrival of the new pop wave in France, while Alain was a student, was nothing short of a musical revolution. There were not only Elvis, the Beatles, and all the great pop music sung in English, but also their French impersonators who adapted the songs into French. A whole new wave of French artists was sweeping away all but the biggest names of the previous era. The new music, rhythm, melodies, and style had a huge impact in France, and suddenly there were new magazines, new TV shows, and new radio shows. It was a fascinating time for Alain, and a decisive one for his career.

AB: When I began my studies, I didn't really know what I wanted to do. It was just a way for me to delay the decision. But I learned a lot there, and that's how today I'm able to manage our business. I enjoy it, and I was trained for a long time to do it. It's a part of me as well as the creative side. But the pop revolution was a new era and I was part of it. I was even the same age as the Beatles. It was something I could really identify with, something that made me think, "This is what I want to do. I want to work in the music world." So that's why when I finished my studies I didn't go into a bank or any other serious institute, but to a radio station called Europe Number One, where all this revolution was really happening.

Alain had made a contact at the radio station who was responsible for music programming, and after talking to Alain for half an hour, he hired him immediately as a pop records programer.

Alain was twenty-one, and he spent a year working for Europe Number One. Part of his job was to decide which records should go on air, and in the course of his work he was in daily contact with publishers and record companies. They gained a high regard for Alain's knowledge and for his point of view on the records and artists they were promoting, and quickly realized that he had an instinctive "nose" for a hit record. He was repeatedly offered work by these record companies and publishers. After a year at the radio station he took a job with Vogue, a small record company, where he worked as head of the publishing department. Publishing was a completely new area for Alain. "But I quickly learned that it meant being at the center of the creative process, bringing together lyric writers, composers, and singers and putting together all the elements of the puzzle in order for the record to be made."

During this time Alain was trying his hand at writing short texts that could be set to music. He had first begun lyric writing in secret as a student, but it was while he was working for the radio that his first song, "La Saison d'Amour," was released. Alain was very happy living and working in Paris and meeting a wide variety of interesting people, but it was directly through his enthusiasm for pop songs that he came to meet Claude-Michel, who had come to Paris to fulfil his ambition of working in the music industry.

Claude-Michel Schönberg was born on July 6, 1944 in Vannes, Brittany, where he grew up. His father, Doli Schönberg, had emigrated from Hungary with his fiancée, Juci, in the mid-nineteen-twenties, and they were married in France.

CMS: My father was a piano tuner, and he had been offered two jobs, one in Tunisia and one in Brittany. Of course, if he had taken the one in Tunisia I would have been born there like Alain. But I think they chose Brittany because it was part of the same continent and, in those days, Tunisia seemed very far away across the Mediterranean Sea. Once they had settled in Brittany they really fell in love with it. We were a Hungarian Jewish family living in a small French community, but as a child I was never aware of any racism.

Living in occupied France, however, meant that Claude-Michel's parents had to tread with caution. They were a religious family, but during the war they had to hide the fact that they were Jewish. All Jewish people were supposed to report to the Local Commandant, but Doli and Juci never did, and there was no way to check their papers of origin because the town hall in Hungary, where they had come from, had been destroyed by a bomb.

CMS: My father would even go to the German barracks to tune their piano and had little conversations with them in German. What they didn't know was that he was part of the French Resistance. As a piano tuner in Brittany he managed to get an *Ausweis*, a German pass for the roads, towns, and villages on the coastline, which in those days had been declared forbidden territories by the Germans. So he was able to bring to those communities orders and weapons for the Resistance. Once he was caught by a platoon, but gave evidence that he was working, fixing a piano for some German officer, and they let him go, not knowing that he had two guns in his satchel. Due to his activities, he and my mother were highly protected by the authorities.

The rest of Claude-Michel's family—aunts, uncles, cousins and grandparents—remained in Hungary, and many of them died during the war. It wasn't until 1958, when Claude-Michel was fourteen, that he was able to visit them. There was still a very tough Communist regime then, two years after the revolution, and entry into Hungary was a big event.

Claude-Michel had a very happy childhood growing up in the small provincial town of Vannes. He was the youngest of three children, with a sister and brother seven and ten years older, respectively.

CMS: But I had a lot of friends and they always enjoyed coming to my house because it was a little bit different. There was a kind of Jewish spirit and a special warmth, and my mother always made a big tea at four o'clock. Jewish and Hungarian mothers always have lots of cakes on the table and a particular kind of generosity and welcoming that isn't really the French way. It was something my friends still remembered years later.

Claude-Michel's parents were not very well off financially, but they were very rich in a cultural sense. Before they settled in Brittany they had lived in Budapest, one of the main cultural centers of Europe, and that was the kind of life Doli and Juci were accustomed to. "They were in love with operas and music, and with books too, and art, because there was a huge cultural life in Budapest." Moving to the small town of Vannes must have been something of a cultural shock, but Doli and Juci took every opportunity to share with their children the kind of cultural life they loved.

CMS: They took us to everything that came around and we had a collection of opera records. We had *Madame Butterfly, Carmen,* and *The Tales of Hoffman,* and we had the Beethoven Symphonies, too. But each opera was a suitcase! There were twenty to thirty records for one opera and each side was only three or four minutes long. But I loved playing them all the way through. When I was six my parents took me to Paris, and the first thing we did was to go to the Opera. We saw *Carmen* and then *Madame Butterfly,* and even now I have a perfect memory of every moment. I can even tell you every detail of the set. I was totally amazed by it. I loved Paris. It was the first time I had been to a big city with thousands of cars and shops, and I thought it was wonderful. It seemed unfair that I had to go back to such a small town afterward. Vannes was three hundred miles away from Paris and it had a population of only 26,000. It was very frozen in its culture and traditions. There were very few cars and no nightlife, and there was no one in the streets after 7 P.M. It would take a whole year before Paris fashions reached our town. Things only started to get better in the '60s with the improvement of communication and the arrival of television.

I had been so impressed with Paris, and I think when you're ambitious you like big cities. I remember my brother winning a competition in which the prize was a year's subscription to *Life* magazine. It was a complete revelation to me, the kind of life that it showed. It was full of gorgeous people with big houses and big American cars, and it showed a high standard of living. It was a dream world. I remember there was an advertisement for cigarettes that showed the Golden Gate Bridge in San Francisco. It looked so beautiful, but I thought I would never be rich enough to go there. Years later, in 1975, when I first went to San Francisco, I hired a car and drove over the bridge straightaway so I could see myself in that picture. In fact I did it three times.

As a child, Claude-Michel had a love of planes. He was totally fascinated by them, cutting out pictures of every different kind of plane and sticking them in a book. "In the late seventies I took flying lessons, and I really enjoyed flying. It's nice to have big toys!" At school Claude-Michel was an average student, his interest in a subject depending mainly on his teachers. "I liked mathematics and physics best. I was quite good at them, although in everything I just did enough to get by." But Claude-Michel's main love was music.

CMS: I can remember one day when I was quite young, young enough to have to hold my mother's hand, she took me to a new department store in our town. It had just opened, and then it seemed so big; it seemed like paradise. They had loudspeakers for music and advertisements. We were going up the stairs, and suddenly I heard this music over the noise of the crowd. I stood, completely paralyzed, listening to this wonderful music. It vibrated through me. I didn't know that anything so incredibly beautiful could exist. It was years later before I heard it again and learned that it was the "Prelude for Strings" in Wagner's *Lohengrin*. I can also remember my mother yelling at me for standing there, because she was worried I'd be lost in the crowd.

Claude-Michel's father had a workshop at home for repairing pianos and harmoniums. "There were always different keyboards around for me to knock on. I could take any piano to bits in half an hour." But could he put it back together again? "Of course!" So Claude-Michel grew up surrounded by pianos and music, and, although he is not directly related to Arnold Schönberg, the twelve tone inventor, they do have common roots in the Ukraine. Claude-Michel took piano lessons for six years, but with some reluctance because he never learned to read music. He couldn't see the point of playing other people's music that had been played millions of times before. He only wanted to play his own music. His music teacher thought she was teaching him to play the piano from printed sheet music.

CMS: But I never told her that I wasn't reading the music. I didn't make the effort to learn to read music, so each week after the lesson I used to come home and redo what she had done. I learned it by heart in an hour, and I could reproduce it exactly. So the next Thursday I would go back with my sheet of music and play, and she never knew I wasn't reading the music. I told her in the end, when I was giving up my lessons, and she was very surprised because each lesson she thought that I had been working hard all week to get the music right.

I was very ambitious when I was young. I knew what I wanted to be and I knew what I wanted to do. I wanted to be an opera composer. I knew there was no other way for me, I just didn't know how. But I knew I wanted a different kind of life. I was always playing for my friends and at parties, and every year I composed a tune for my mother's birthday. It was the best way I could give her something. After my father died when I was fourteen, we were really quite poor because there was no money coming in. I used to help my mother to address envelopes in the evenings to earn some money. And then I started a rock-and-roll group with some friends.

The money Claude-Michel earned from the group enabled him to study at University, and he did a three-year Business Studies Degree at the Ecole Supérieurie de Commerce in Nantes. He rented a room with no hot water for six pounds a week. Nevertheless, it was a time that he enjoyed, and, being so good at mathematics, he found the work easy. "I was very lazy, but in the end I came third out of 160 students, even though I was doing practically nothing but waiting for the weekend so I could play my music." Claude-Michel had formed a pop group called the Vénètes, named after the inhabitants of his hometown Vannes. There were four members of the group, one on the drums, two on guitars, and Claude-Michel playing the piano. He was the leader of the group, arranging all the bookings as well as leading the rehearsals. They played gigs on Friday, Saturday, and Sunday nights and every night during

Schönberg, age 19, with his pop group Les Vénètes outside a restaurant of the same name. (From left:) Alain Vincent-Linder, Claude-Michel Schönberg, Yves Le Nevu, and Hubert Robiou.

the holidays. They were very popular and very much in demand because they were the first rock-and-roll group in the area. They played their own music as well as all the rock-and-roll hits of the sixties that people liked dancing to.

One day Jacques Sclingand, a talent scout from Pathé-Marconi, the European branch of EMI, came to see the group and asked Claude-Michel if he was writing the tunes they were playing.

CMS: I said, "Yes," and he gave me his card and asked me to go and see him in Paris. He told me later that it was watching me lead the rehearsals and the way I worked with a vision of how the music should be that made him realize that I might have a future in producing records. I went to see him in Paris, and the year before I left University I already had a contract to work at Pathé-Marconi as a trainee artistic director, starting as soon as I graduated. I played my last gig on August 31, 1967, and arrived in Paris to start work the next day. I couldn't start any earlier because I had promised my mother that I would finish my degree. Although I had my heart set on a career in music, she didn't think there would be any money in it. In the meantime, we did some recording sessions with Jacques and released a record, but it wasn't a success. However, having EMI as a record label was a big advantage in advertising our gigs.

When Claude-Michel started working in Paris he knew very little about the music business. Jacques Sclingand had also signed up another young man, Michel Berger, and he and Claude-Michel became great friends.

CMS: We were working with Jacques and developing our knowledge of the business—what a recording session is, how to work with musicians, how to make a record, what mixing is, how to use all the equipment, and to understand what a slow process it is. We were writing songs and producing records with Jacques until we were ready to produce records on our own.

Claude-Michel loved the big city life and everything about Paris. "When I arrived in Paris I felt like the king of the world." It was where he wanted to be and it was the beginning of a career in music. It was an exciting time in the mid-Sixties for a young man to be producing records, writing his own pop songs, and meeting a lot of interesting people who were all involved in various ways in the music industry.

When Alain and Claude-Michel met in 1968 it was not, however, through their respective work in the music industry. Their meeting, as much of the story of how their musicals came to be written, was what Claude-Michel describes as "a matter of chance and will." One day Alain was listening to the radio when his attention was caught by a song sung by a young girl. It was called "Tous Les Jours à Quatre Heures" (Everyday at Four O'Clock). "I just loved the song. There was something about the drama in the music that I liked. I called the radio station to find out who had done it because I wanted to publish it, and then I asked him to come and see me." It was, of course, Claude-Michel, and the song was one of the first songs he had ever written. So it was directly Claude-Michel's music that brought them together.

Their meeting was the first of many to come, as the two men found they shared many common interests. They both had a passion for contemporary pop music and for the few musicals of the day that they had seen. It was *West Side Story*, however, that made the most powerful and profound impression on them both. Claude-Michel saw the film version in the early sixties.

CMS: It really fascinated me. I saw it six times in the first two days—three times each day! It was an unbelievable work of art for me—the songs, the story, the drama, the choreography, everything. It was perfection for me then. I was totally upside down with the music.

Alain, however, saw the touring production of the stage musical in 1959 while he was a student in Paris.

AB: Some friends of my parents gave me tickets, and I took a girl with me. It was like an earthquake! I couldn't sleep all night. I didn't get over it for weeks. All I wanted to do was to talk about it: the dramatic situation, the music, everything. But the girl I took didn't understand. She wasn't interested really, no one was. It was a flop in Paris. It was a long time before I met someone who shared my response to it.

By the time they met, Alain was managing a music publishing company and Claude-Michel was working as an A and R (Artistes and Repertoire) manager for Pathé-Marconi. He was the producer for Frank Pourcel, the famous orchestra conductor, and, in addition, he wrote music for him. "I used to enjoy writing for a big orchestra. It was fun for me to write that kind of music, which today I think you would call Muzak." As Alain and Claude-Michel became good friends, Claude-Michel introduced Alain to Frank Pourcel and his daughter Françoise. When Alain and Françoise were married in 1969, there was an even stronger tie between them all.

Alain and Claude-Michel had both written pop songs, but they were keenly aware of the limitations of the three-minute form. Claude-Michel was tired of it.

CMS: The format is always the same—it's intro, one verse, second verse, one chorus, one verse, one chorus, change of key, chorus and fade out. We were totally bored with it. We loved *West Side Story*, but although it had a popular feel to it, the music was technically very sophisticated, and we knew that something like that was beyond us then.

However, on October 12, 1971, along came another of those providential elements of chance. While Alain was staying in New York, some friends gave him a last-minute invitation (a guest was unable to go) to the première of *Jesus Christ Superstar*. Andrew Lloyd Webber and Tim Rice's new musical was a revelation for Alain, an overwhelming experience, for this was a compelling and ground-breaking work. It told, in a uniquely theatrical way, the story of the most significant historical event in the Western world, and yet it was written with the simple chords of rock music.

AB: It was exciting because here was someone young writing pop music with a story about a young historical figure. It was something I could identify with in a way I'd never identified with other musicals before.

But how would Alain find a subject that would match this one in both historical significance and emotional intensity? It was a question he had to answer and to answer that night. With adrenaline running high, he walked the streets of Manhattan for hours, turning over every possibility in his mind, until finally a solution came with the new day. It had to be—the French Revolution.

Back in France, Claude-Michel responded eagerly to Alain's suggestion that they write a concept album outlining the story of the French Revolution.

CMS: We started working straight away in our free time, and we did the basic structure in an afternoon. We instinctively took the main titles of the most important sequences of the French Revolution, but already adding a love story inside, of course, to give it some spice! Eventually there were twenty-four sequences—the Bastille Day, the abduction of the King, the abduction of the Queen, and so on. There's everything in the French Revolution to write twenty-four songs about, adding two or three love songs. They were songs that had the pop sound of the '70s. It wasn't until it was decided that it should be staged that I wrote the linking songs, so it was really a case of putting the cart before the horse. We were totally unconscious of what we were doing as regards the dramatization process, and we were not writing a book as such, as we did with our later musicals.

The French have no tradition of musical theatre, and, as Alain comments:

AB: France is an empty space as far as musical theatre is concerned. Only old-fashioned operettas, but that's about it. Imagine two people living in France, creating something for which no tradition exists. We didn't know exactly what we were doing. In London and New York, there are schools for musical theatre. There are newspapers talking to you everyday about musicals, and there are audiences who are used to going to see these shows. But there is nothing like that in France.

When they were writing, at first they were thinking only in terms of a concept album. After all, *Jesus Christ Superstar* was a very successful concept album before it had ever been considered as a stage show. Frank Pourcel was also involved with the project, and they worked together as a close family group. The concept album *La Revolution Française* was a big success in France, and it was played on the radio all the time. Then they were asked to present an extract on television. Alain recalls:

AB: It was crazy. Everyone was involved. Not only the original singers on the album, but everyone in the office, as well as wives and girlfriends. They were all roped in as extras. We were given a free rein in the costume department, and we put on a six-minute excerpt on a Saturday night. On Monday morning, sales of the album rocketed.

Indeed, it quickly went Gold, selling 350,000 double albums. One of the songs, "Chouans en avant!," became a number-one hit. It told the story of people in the west of France resisting the French Revolution. A strange subject for a hit song!

It was then suggested that they turn their work into a stage musical. There were no suitable theatres at the time, but there had been a cancelation at the Palais des Sports, which is a huge arena like Wembley. It was a forty-five day slot, and they took it. Working on the show was an exciting new experience that Claude-Michel remembers well.

The program cover for *La Révolution Française.*

CMS: While we were writing the album, Alain worked with

Jean-Max Rivière on the lyrics and I worked with Raymond Jeannot on the music. But when we had to turn the songs into a stage show, they didn't understand how to do it. Alain and I were the only ones who knew instinctively how to work on the construction of a show.

It opened on October 2, 1973, and it was an enormous success, with people lining up around the block for tickets. *La Revolution Française* became the first-ever French rock opera, and although France is a country that has never responded well to musical theatre, this kind of historical pageant proved immensely popular. Set against the background of a momentous political and historical situation was an intimate story about the love of a poor man for an aristocratic young lady. There were no sets, but the show was full of exciting dramatic action, and Claude-Michel, who is considered to have a fine voice, took on the role of Louis XVI. "I enjoyed the rehearsals and the first three nights, but after that I got bored."

During the period after *La Revolution Française*, Claude-Michel was busy writing songs. He wanted to make a living from his writing alone. By 1974, he had a collection of new songs waiting to be recorded. He had written both the music and the lyrics, but despite the success of *La Revolution Française*, nobody wanted to sing them. So Alain suggested that Claude-Michel should sing them himself. Although he had always shied away from a career as a singer, he recorded an album that became a huge success in France; in fact, one of the songs, "Le Premier Pas," was number one for sixteen weeks. "After that everyone wanted me to be a pop singer, but I didn't want to be. I turned everything down."

When Alain and Claude-Michel found a new subject that captured their imagination, it not only changed their lives, it changed the face of musical theatre. In 1978 they started working on a musical adaptation of *Les Misérables* in French. In 1980, they released a concept album. The white front cover showed the full motif of the Emile Bayard lithograph of the little waif Cosette with her broom, and the album sold 260,000 copies. In September of that year, the great French director Robert Hossein staged their work as a show, which was a mix of musical theatre and dramatic musical tableaux. Staged again at the 4,500-seat Palais des Sports in Paris, it was a triumphant success for such a new genre in France, and it was seen by half a million people in three months.

Two years later Cameron Mackintosh arrived at Alain's office in Paris to discuss an English production.

AB: We took Cameron out to lunch at a fashionable Paris restaurant and all the time Claude-Michel was pretending that he couldn't speak English because he wanted to size him up! So I had to do all the talking, but it didn't take long to realize that here was someone who really knew what he was doing. Cameron first convinced us that we were the ones who were able to conduct the reshaping of our work in order to adapt it to a show for audiences who would not know the story as well as a French audience. He was clever and generous enough to understand immediately that what we had written was the bulk of the musical, and to convince us at the same time that it needed some improvement in order to be made into the show that it is now. We may have written a great musical but Cameron has turned it into a miracle. All the way he brought his artistic knowledge to it as well as his financial clout and managerial knowledge and he helped us to understand what he thought should be done. He brought on board the best artistic team to the enterprise and still knew that Claude-Michel and I were the basic team, having control

Cameron Mackintosh on the set of *Les Misérables.*

over whatever changes or improvements were to be done. The project was probably too patrimonially French for anyone else to have done it in a way that would be what the show is today, which is really a perfect mix of what we all had to bring to it. I don't believe in coincidences too much; I believe that it was meant to be Cameron who heard that first recording and who then produced our first three major hits. We've always had a good relationship with Cameron. It's an extraordinary relationship but it's been a working relationship rather than a personal one, and we've never fallen out. We have disagreed over things and sometimes we've even pretended to disagree! But Claude-Michel and I have always stuck up for ourselves and I think that's important in any working relationship, especially a long-term one like this.

At that time Claude-Michel did speak English, but not fluently.

CMS: I remember the first meetings we used to have with Cameron, Trevor Nunn, and John Caird. I was always having to ask Alain

Photo by Herbert Kretzmer

Schönberg and Mackintosh take a coffee break during the writing of *Martin Guerre* at Schönberg's house in Ramatuelle, France.

or Cameron what something meant. But even at two o'clock in the morning they used to speak to us as if we were born in Brighton. They didn't care about the fact that we were French, we just had to follow. Eventually, one day I realized that I was talking and listening to people without translating into French and that's when I really knew that I understood.

So what has the success of their work meant to them? Apart from the obvious financial aspects, Alain believes, "it's the freedom to be a full-time artist. To choose what I want to do and when best to do it." Among other things, Alain has written a prize-winning French novel, *les dessous de soi, Le Journal d'Adam et Eve*, a play that is based on two short stories by Mark Twain, and a new theatrical adaptation of Jacques Demy's French movie musical *Les Demoiselles de Rochefort* , with music by Michel Legrand, which played in Paris in 2003. Indeed his first collaboration with Cameron was not *Les Misérables*, but the fairytale musical *Abbacadabra*.

AB: It was ABBA songs turned into a musical. So really it was the blueprint for *Mamma Mia!*, but for children. It was a kind of fairy tale, and it was a big success in France as a record and a TV series. Then, at the end of 1983, Cameron produced it at the Lyric Theatre in Hammersmith, where Elaine Paige was a brilliant witch along with many other famous people in the company. I was the French publisher of ABBA, with whom I had been working for years, so we were long-time friends and that's how and why they allowed me to use the music of their biggest hits with new lyrics of mine fitting the story of the play.

Although Alain revels in the international aspects of his career, he loves to return to his home in Knightsbridge, where he lives with his second wife Marie Zamora. Marie played Cosette in the Paris production of *Les Misérables* and still continues her successful career as a singer and actress. Alain has two young sons now, Adrien and Maxime, as well as two grown sons, Stephane and Sebastien, from his first marriage, who now live and work in New York. He is very proud of his family, and protects their privacy fiercely. There is no doubt that his family is the most important thing in his life.

Claude-Michel is equally family-oriented. He lived for many years with his first wife Beatrice on the outskirts of Paris.

CMS: We have a son Thomas who is 24 and a daughter Margot who is 12. After our son was born, my wife continued her career as a journalist, and, later, when we wanted another child, she wasn't able to have one. We wanted to adopt a baby, but not a Caucasian child, so there would be no confusion with neighbors, friends, or the child about the parentage. Through our work with *Miss Saigon*, I had so many good friends in the Philippines, including the President, so we decided to go there. We had all the papers done in France and the Philippines. One day they rang to say they had a baby girl, and I wanted a daughter. She was six months old when I saw her, but it was another month before we could bring her home, and our friends in the Philippines looked after her for that time. She's the best thing in my life I ever did. But then I felt that we had taken one baby for ourselves but what about all the others? So I opened an orphanage in Manila, and our friend's wife ran it. It's called the Sun and Moon, Home for Children, and we can take eleven babies at a time. We take the most severely malnourished babies and we specialize in that. But when they have good food, the best medical care, and doctors, as well as toys and warmth and love, then in a couple of months they are healthy babies. We have a license to keep the children until they are three, but within a year or eighteen months at the most they are adopted through an international agency. I go out there about twice a year. It's a very happy place and they have a lot of love.

The orphanage is a place Claude-Michel loves to visit, and in a way it is an extension of his family and it is something that has been enabled by his successful career. There is, however, a note of sadness when Claude-Michel looks back on his life.

CMS: It is a personal tragedy for me that I lost both my parents before the worldwide success of *Les Misérables*. My father died in 1958 and my mother in 1981. My mother, in particular, was always very worried about the financial instability of my life as a composer, and I'm very sad that they couldn't see what has become of me, perhaps all the more because there was a strong possibility that I might not have been born at all. When my mother was pregnant with me in 1944, she was 42 years old and she was afraid that she was too old to have an unexpected baby. At that time it was considered that there was a high risk for older mothers of having a baby with Down's syndrome. So she wanted to have an abortion for medical reasons, but my father, as a man of principle, wouldn't hear of it and completely rejected the idea. At the end of the day, I couldn't show him he was right.

As with Alain, Claude-Michel's success has also meant artistic freedom and choice. In addition to working on the many worldwide productions of their musicals, he has also composed the music for the ballet of *Wuthering Heights* for Northern Ballet Theatre, which premièred at the Alhambra Theatre in Bradford, England on September 21, 2002. The ballet was originally commissioned by Derek Deane, artistic director of the English National Ballet, but when he left ENB they were no longer able to do it. Claude-Michel remembers:

CMS: It was Angela Rippon, who was chairman of ENB who then contacted Northern Ballet, knowing it was the kind of work they did and they were very interested. Writing a ballet was a kind of experiment for me; it was new territory to be writing music without words. I found the experience very interesting, and I managed to understand a lot about dance and choreography.

I read a lot about Emily Brontë and I visited her home in Haworth, Yorkshire. I went through the novel and wrote a scene-by-scene scenario for the ballet. What you can express through ballet and choreography must be very simple so I had to transform the story In very precise and simple sequences. The Brontë sisters used their writing as an escape from reality, and if you want to portray escape from reality then the format of the ballet is working very well. When an audience is watching a musical they can at least make believe it's reality, whereas with ballet that's totally impossible, it's so obviously a fantasy world. So the story fitted very well with the format. I was left very much on my own to write the score. I didn't want to be innovative, but to tell the story through the music and to be true to the period and to the characters of Cathy and Heathcliff. I thought that the most natural sound for the score of a nineteenth-century story was the very classical, traditional sound of all the ballets I love. I didn't want to be contemporary. I wanted to give the audience the feel that we are in the nineteenth century. I don't write in an intellectual way, but from an instinctive point of view. I try to imagine what's happening on stage and to think what I want to hear. The wind and the moors are very important in the story and they were the starting point for my inspiration. So my first impulse was to describe with music a storm on the moors. I wanted it to be very clear what was happening on stage so that you didn't need to take the program to find out what was going on. Writing in this way was a fascinating process.

Claude-Michel's involvement with *Wuthering Heights* had an unexpected impact on his personal life, as it was how he met Charlotte Talbot, an English ballerina who played the leading role of Cathy. They married in November 2003, and in 2005, they became the proud parents of a beautiful baby daughter, Lily.

Alain and Claude-Michel's relationship is a very close one and so solid that each is perfectly happy for the other to work alone or with someone else. Alain describes it as "a kind of brotherliness, an intimacy—like family, but we're even closer than my own brothers." Having known them and watched them working over a long time, John Caird summarizes this closeness with a novel yet fitting image:

JC: What makes them such a good partnership is that they fit together like one of those Chinese puzzles—they're a couple of nails locked together, and you just can't tell how they were put together or how you get them apart. They're so strong you could use them as links in a chain, but you could also untangle them and say, "Look, they're two completely different pieces of the same puzzle." Their partnership is a lovely mixture of political savvy and strong human feeling. This is at the heart of their gift as writers. They both have a sophisticated view of the world politically and socially, but to pull the two nails apart for a moment, Alain is a great businessman as well as being a very fine lyricist and writer and above all thinker—he's an inspiring mongrel, an entrepreneur-philosopher. Claude-Michel is just as savvy, but his mix is a rather different one. There's the clever, mischievous, puckish Claude-Michel, never happier than when he's mocking himself or others, and there's the ethereal, romantic Claude-Michel that nobody, least of all himself, can explain. This is the side of him that expresses itself in those soaring, heartbreaking melodies, but they are just the outward sign of his own natural sweetness. He's a little bit embarrassed by this talent at times, but he also knows that it's his lifeblood. In the end, Alain's analytical shrewdness and Claude-Michel's fine mockery of all things serious are both covers. What they conceal is yet another mixture—on the one hand a burning artistic ambition and on the other a passion for social justice and a preoccupation with the have-nots of this world—especially those whose lives have been made tragic by circumstance. The whole of *Miss Saigon* was based on an overwhelming emotional response to a piece of photojournalism, the picture of a woman parting with her child. It's remarkable how that little mustard seed of meaning could grow into such a mighty piece of work."

A picture, then, emerges of two highly talented, successful artists happy with their own strong individual identities who are bonded together by creative endeavor. Alain and Claude-Michel are, indeed, like two sides of a coin, and they have a close partnership based on mutual respect for each other's strengths. ❧

CHAPTER 2

Do You Hear the People Sing?

WRITING THE MUSICALS

Boublil and Schönberg at the piano.

WITH THEIR FIRST MUSICAL SUCCESS *La Révolution Française* under their belts, Alain and Claude-Michel began working on ideas for their next project. Between 1973 and 1978, there were several ideas. One of these was a musical based on an old French legend about a submerged forgotten city. But this concept and all the others were eventually discarded because they failed to inspire Alain and Claude-Michel sufficiently, or they failed the one essential test—what was it about this subject that called for it to be sung about on stage? So, despite the success of *La Révolution Française* and the excitement it had generated in their lives, they both realized that it could have been a one-time occurrence. However, inspiration sometimes strikes when least expected. So it was one evening in 1978 when Alain went to see a production of *Oliver!* in London. It was Cameron Mackintosh's latest revival, although his was a name that meant nothing to Alain at the time. But he clearly remembers:

AB: When the Artful Dodger came on singing "Consider Yourself," the image of Gavroche came immediately into my mind. All of a sudden I could see how it would be on stage—not only Gavroche, but Valjean, Javert, Fantine, Cosette, Marius, Eponine—all the characters from *Les Misérables* up there singing and living through all the emotions, all the joys and sorrows that defined their lives.

When I returned to France I went through Hugo's book and wrote a first draft. It didn't seem difficult at all and it was so obvious to me as I went through the book that this chapter would make a good section of the story, this one was a song and so on. And straight away I wrote in the book "J'Avais Rêvé D'Une Autre Vie," which became "I Dreamed a Dream," above the chapter on Fantine. (See *Les Misérables* photo insert 1.) I already knew this was the way I wanted to treat Fantine's descent into hell. It all came so quickly and so easily that very soon I had the scheme of what the backbone to the book of the show would be. I did this first stage on my own as I was not sure if it was a good idea or even if I was going to show it to Claude-Michel. But he loved the idea and we immediately gave up our jobs to work full-time on the project. From our very first discussions about it all the decisions were made quickly and instinctively and there was no suffering in it. It was obvious to us that the Thénardiers would be turned into comic characters, or that after a sad song like "I Dreamed a Dream" we would have to change the mood, not with something funny because Fantine was going to die in the next ten minutes, but with some exciting musical moment, which became "Lovely Ladies." (See *Les Misérables* photo insert 2.) So the whole novel quickly developed itself in our minds like a natural opera.

Alain and Claude-Michel are essentially musical dramatists; that is to say that everything that they write is motivated by the story. When they start working on a project together there is no division initially between lyric writer and composer, for they are both "book" writers. They spend several months telling and retelling each other the story visually, and not until they are completely satisfied do they write a word of the lyrics or a note of the music. It is through this process that the subject is allowed to grow and develop with a single vision. The whole creative process and the working methods they employ in writing their musicals are best told in their own words.

THE BOOK

CMS: It's always difficult for us to choose a subject for a show. I don't have any particular criteria but I must be moved or have a sparkle and it must be a wonderful story. Of course I have to deal with emotion, passion, and real people's lives, not in an intellectual way but with all the deep fibers of human feeling. I know I will never write a show about a painting; I don't know what to do with that kind of subject. It's very important to Alain and me that we do something different each time that is not a straight repetition of what we have been doing before. We're trying each time to be heading to another territory of music or style, and even if that's not true of the final result we have to believe that's what we are doing. You have to be able to surprise and excite yourself with something new every time. It would have been so easy and obvious after *Les Misérables* to start writing a show about the Count of Monte Cristo or Napoleon but for us that would be the worst thing that could happen, to have the feeling that you are doing the same thing

Photo by Michael Le Poer Trench

Schönberg and Boublil, April 1989: five months before *Miss Saigon* opened.

twice. Each time the subject must be challenging, dangerous, rIsky. We enjoy working on the edge without safety measures because I think it is not safe to try to create safety. That's partly why we enjoyed writing *Miss Saigon* so much. Cameron realized very quickly that it was a very risky thing for two Frenchmen to be writing an American story about Vietnam. It's also much more of a challenge to make people sing and dance on stage in a contemporary show. When the characters are in the costume of the nineteenth century it's much easier because there is a convention for the audience to admit that the characters are singing. When they are wearing jeans and shirts, when they are dressed exactly like you, then it's much more difficult to understand why they are singing.

We were trying to have a kind of popular opera approach to the theatre and we wanted to escape all the recipes for tap dancing and happy songs and a happy ending. We wanted to be totally free to tell the story we wanted to tell, even not being afraid to have death on the stage. *Les Misérables* expanded the vision and the scale of what the public can watch, going to see a musical. It's another way to entertain an audience because what the public wants is to have fun or to have emotions. We're giving them emotions—tears and love. When *Miss Saigon* opened I saw people who needed two days to recover because they were so shocked and moved by what they saw. I still have the news photograph showing a Vietnamese woman parting with her child at Tan Son Nhut Airport so that child could have a better life with her G.I. father in the United States. I had been having a coffee break one autumn afternoon in Paris when this photograph in a magazine caught my eye, but there was no way I could have predicted the impact it would have on me. The woman stunned by her grief and the child's tears were the final condemnation of all wars, which shatter people who love each other. It was the most moving, the most staggering example of the ultimate sacrifice just as you have in *Madame Butterfly* with Cio-Cio-San giving her life for her child. But *Miss Saigon* is not a history of the Vietnam War. It's a story of two people lost in the middle of the war.

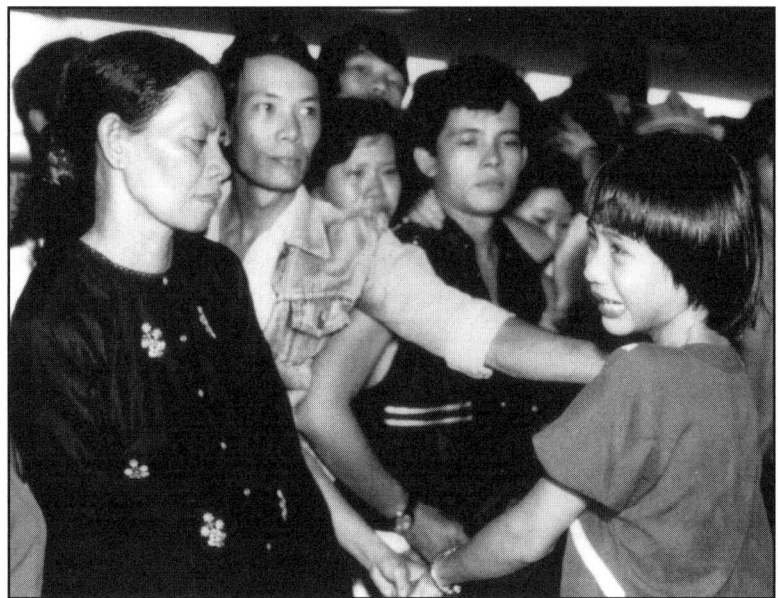

The photograph that inspired *Miss Saigon*.

With each musical I was trying to go one step forward to an operatic structure. It's the dramatic situation and the fact that it's all sung-through that give you an operatic feeling. *Miss Saigon* is more operatic than *Les Misérables*, despite the fact that a lot of people think the opposite, and *Martin Guerre* is even another step further. That's the one work that could easily be adapted for opera voices and orchestra. But now, with *The Pirate Queen* we wanted to go in a totally different direction so as not to repeat ourselves. All our shows have had a tragic ending and it has always seemed more difficult to find a good happy story. *The Pirate Queen* has all the drama of our previous shows but it's wonderful at last to be able to write a happy ending. I would like to write a funny subject one day but I don't know if I can write the relevant music for that kind of show. I think Verdi was 80 before he wrote a funny work!

Before Alain and I start working, first of all we have to agree on the subject and it takes us a long time. Once we agree we have to talk all around the subject, all the stupidities, everything. It's like entering a rain forest, trying to find our way through. You have to clear the way through the story to find where you are coming and where you are going. So that always takes us a long time too and once we are sure what kind of story we want to tell through the subject we start writing.

The main research we do is to make sure that the facts are right from a historical point of view in order to make the show credible, because it's happening in reality. With *Les Misérables* we had Victor Hugo's book, the only and perfect reference, as Hugo did all the research for us. It's easier to work with a fixed text because you have a strong reference for the story which gives you how the show starts, how it's going to finish and roughly what happens in the middle. With *Miss Saigon* we had Puccini's opera so it's practically the same process. We wanted to respect the story of *Madame Butterfly* but we had to be sure that the story could have actually happened in Vietnam the way we were telling it. We didn't go to Vietnam but we read a lot of books for the historical and political background. There is a big Vietnamese community in France and so we spoke to witnesses, including an old teacher who saw that kind of story actually happening. So we knew how some American soldiers were still in Vietnam, how the tension increased the nearer the North Vietnamese soldiers got, what was happening in the bars, the way mothers of American mixed-blood boys were treated, how the evacuation of the Embassy took place. We learned about the uniforms, the flags, the habits, and the colloquial expressions, and we did all this ourselves quite easily.

With *Martin Guerre* we had to do a lot more research on the original book by Judge Coras. We went to Lyon first, to the National Library to see one of the three original books, which is in old French. We got a lot of information too from Natalie Zemon Davies, who is the expert in this period in France, and that helped us understand the religious differences between the Protestants and the Catholics and how people were living then and how they could be in the center of a Catholic community and be hiding the fact that they were Protestant. We recognized very soon that the story itself was not enough to justify that people are singing and dancing on stage. So we had to invent a lot of situations and characters and we had to understand what the payoff for this story was at the end. In the original story Arnaud is tried and executed and Bertrande has to go back to her husband, so we had to find a way to twist the story just to give you some light or hope or human feeling bigger than life at the end.

Our shows are always more action driven than character driven. We took a simple rule—where you can show something through the action you show it; we don't want our characters just to be telling you what's happening. You have to have a logic in each character and you have to understand them to justify why they are doing something. If you have a bad character—the logic is that nobody is a villain for free, there is always a reason why. The most villainous people are the most unhappy, generally speaking, and there is always a reason why they are unhappy. There's a logic in Thénardier because he's a caricature of a crook, but he's so crooked he's sincere. He's a caricature of an innkeeper and of a miser. A lot of comedy is based on telling what people are really thinking but can't say. We don't try to be intellectual and we want to tell the story in

Photo by Herbert Kretzmer

Boublil and Schönberg in "thinking mode" during the writing of *Martin Guerre* at Schönberg's house in Ramatuelle, France.

a very naturalistic way; it's about very basic human reactions, gut reactions. We are telling the stories of very simple people whose lives are shattered by the background they live in. If there is one common point between the three shows then maybe it's redemption. You have a kind of redemption with Valjean dying and atoning for his sins. In the same way you have a kind of redemption for Kim committing suicide so her child can have a new life with his father and she's trying to erase her faults. There's a kind of redemption too in the death of Arnaud. It's always redemption by death.

When we are writing a first draft we don't think about technique or structure. It's practically like throwing up, we just have to get it all out and then we can think whether it's good or it's wrong. Later a little drop of technique must be involved in the writing because you have to be sure that you have time for a change of set or a change of costume and you can't have a scene with thirty people on stage and the next scene is thirty people on stage in different costumes. And you can't have two or three ballads one after the other. So you must think in terms of technique, balance of the show, how it's going to start and how it's going to finish.

AB: After several drafts we end up with a script that is somewhere between the book of a musical and a movie script. It tells the story in detail and we describe every scene exactly, working out everything dramatically. We know where the main songs will be and what the emotions are, and even when a song will be reprised. We know where a reprise will be even before the song is written because the situation demands it. So we have a kind of synopsis to start with of how the musical will eventually be. But you can imagine the first version of that is very naked. It's very different from what it will be at the end. We enrich it and we add to it every day, every week, so every idea finds its way through the script until we have a story in seven or eight pages that we can read and be pleased with. In the case of the first version of *Martin Guerre* we were unsatisfied with the "signposts" that help us structure the story, and we had the impression that they were not in the right place. However, one thing we have always rejected was the idea of suspense, of whether or not Bertrande and the audience would know if Arnaud was the real Martin Guerre. The films based on the story relied heavily on this but Claude-Michel and I thought that kind of suspense is the worst thing you could do in a musical. Because once you know it, then, would you tell your friends to go and see it? Are you going to keep the secret? Or, if you think of *Les Misérables*, which people have seen several times, would you go back and see it again? Dramatic structure is really important, and Claude-Michel and I have a kind of obsession with detail, that makes us tick or not tick the same way. When we see a movie and one detail betrays a lack of attention from the people who are doing it, we lose belief in what we are seeing.

People talk about the difference between a book musical and a sung-through musical, but a sung-through musical has a book too, only instead of dialogue there is recitative, where the words are sung. The sung-through musical is a different convention from the dialogue/song musical. It's not necessarily more difficult because it needs a genuine talent to bring a song out of a dialogue, but it's another art form. What I don't like at all is when you don't know why they've started singing or why they've started talking. The change from one to the other can make you too aware of the form, and so make it less believable. The magic of the sung-through form is that it allows you to treat a very serious story. There has to be a good reason why people are singing on stage. But it has to seem so natural that you almost forget that they are singing. That's the ultimate scope of what we are doing, and at the same time if there is a good song you will remember it forever. That's the double challenge, but obviously the first one is to forget that it's sung. We don't have a storyteller or narrator either because these kinds of characters break the convention. James Fenton designed the Prologue for *Les Misérables* and it tells a lot of the story without the need for a narrator. The Prologue works wonderfully well and I just can't imagine the show without it anymore. Whatever you do, right at the beginning, if it's going to be a serious story or a funny one, the audience wlll accept it, but the convention has to work from the beginning.

We started working on *Miss Saigon* the day after *Les Misérables* transferred to the Palace Theatre. One day in a secondhand bookshop in Charing Cross Road I found, quite by chance, a copy of Pierre Loti's autobiographical book *Madame Chrysanthemum*, which was about the short-term contract marriage between a French Naval Officer and a Geisha girl in Nagasaki. It was that very story that *Madame Butterfly* had been based on. So in a curious way the story had been returned to us. It freed us from Puccini and, at the same time, freed us to write a story that began in Saigon in 1975. After all, Vietnam was a French colony and a French mistake before it was an American one. We saw it as our own story retaining the basic *Butterfly* plot of a misunderstanding between two individuals of highly different cultures, but projecting it into a tragic period of modern history—and at a time when that basic misunderstanding between two people could reflect the deeper misunderstanding between their respective countries.

When we are writing the book we always have a strong sense of parallels, of necessary similarity between the way characters must progress, whether it's in the same direction or the opposite direction. There is a kind of cyclic organization, because we like the kind of storytelling where there are strong reminders of what the characters have said in Act One, which comes in Act Two. We need them to be in the original storyline, and that is why we spend so much time on the book, because we need to have all that already written. So that is certainly part of what we call our way or craft. But in a way it is very similar to what Italian opera composers were doing all the time.

THE MUSIC

CMS: When the first draft of the story is done I can start thinking about the music and the sound of the music. Quite simply what

I want to do with the music is storytelling. In the choice of the subject and even sometimes in the title you have a sense already of what kind of color the music will be. For *Miss Saigon* I knew I wanted in the very beginning of this score to hear a clash between two cultures. In the first ten bars we must understand that we are East but at the same time there is some Western influence. I wanted to have a very conventional Western philharmonic orchestra, but mixed with plenty of little gamelan instruments, so we could have violins and brass facing gamelans, percussion, and gongs. The story drives you to a style of music. It's very important that you have the sound of the music that you're going to write. If a subject doesn't bring you any idea of the music or any sounds of music then you can't start. Sometimes we have a few words coming and we try to interpolate them and work together but generally 90 percent of the music is written before the lyrics.

I try to start writing the music chronologically from the beginning of the show to the end. Sometimes I have in advance one theme or one melody I have already imagined for the show and I will base a whole sequence on this theme. When I begin I know the story I want to tell and what I want to say but I don't know how. I know the emotion or the feeling this section must bring to you but I don't know how it's going to be, I just know how I want it to be at the end of the sequence. I try to imagine what's going to happen on stage—the set, the lights, what the characters are singing and I have a vision of the shape of the music. I have a concrete perception of the music through my hands, like touching something, it must be the hands of my soul, I don't know. But it's very concrete, it's like a sculpture and if an angle is not the right angle I can correct it. When I achieve a score I can travel inside it. I am the only one to know the score from the inside. If you can imagine a wonderful castle, I'm the only one with the key. I can go from room to room and change the decoration and everyone else has to look from the outside. How it's coming to my mind, why sometimes it's easy and sometimes it's difficult I can't tell you at all. When I'm writing I want the music alone to tell you the story we are describing and what the character is telling you without the need for words. My main goal is to express through the music itself the emotions and feelings, the mood of the character and his state of mind and practically what he's going to say, so it's describing a little bit of his soul.

I write specifically for the story and I can't take any song from *Les Misérables* and put it in *Martin Guerre* or *Miss Saigon*. I don't have any songs I keep in a drawer like some composers. I don't have that system for working and the songs are more integrated into the score so it's much more difficult to take one song out to stand alone. I'm always writing from the start and there is always a difference in the music of the shows because there is a difference in the period of time and the story. *Les Misérables* is high spiritually and set in the nineteenth century. In *Saigon* it's something very risky, very dangerous, always dancing above a volcano because there's a war on. *Martin Guerre* is a rooted, rough and primitive kind of work. So the music is following all that. Every composer has his own style, his own tricks to write. Why do you recognize any Puccini music even not knowing the work? It's because he has his own way to articulate the harmonies, the chords, and to change keys. We all have habits that make a style. So of course the style of the music in our shows is the same but the motivation, the sound, and the soul of the music is totally different. The only thing I know is that when I'm not a very good composer, 90 percent of the time it's because the story is wrong. When we have a strong book Alain and I both work well.

I believe some people can have the lyrics and straightaway write the music in three minutes. But I have to think a lot and it takes me a long, long time. I have to be at the piano and think and play and then walk about and come back to it. I have to chew it over; it's like a process of digestion. You have to work every day to try to get it right and it's always very difficult for me to give birth to a piece of music. I know a lot of people imagine that you're at a piano and there's a moon and you have inspiration. But it's not like that at all; it's only work, work, work. I can spend a week on three or four minutes of music and generally I play it thousands and thousands of times until the moment I think it's good and I can tape it. When I was writing the finale of Act One for *Les Misérables* it took me months and months. It was a huge traffic jam in my head because I had to put together all the characters of the show in only one song. The scene of the return of Martin Guerre was also a nightmare and what I hate when I have to face a sequence like that is the lack of unity. It was really a very difficult task because practically on the same music people had to speak, to shout, to have dialogue and finish by a dance. Once I tape something then it goes very quickly. If I had learned to write music, to notate, it could have opened a lot of doors to me technically, to give me a greater level of sophistication. But I have been told that if I could write music then I could never have composed the kind of music that I do because it's totally against all the rules.

I work in sequences of about twenty minutes and then Alain and I have to decide if it's right or if it's wrong. If it's good then I give it to Alain to write the lyrics and I do another sequence. Alain and I understand each other very well and he knows how to do it. Sometimes I have to expand it or make it shorter because it's too long. Once we have finished all the lyrics and the music we make a recording of it, where I'm singing all the parts, and it's at this stage of the project that we approach our producer. If it's O.K. then I write down the piano score with somebody.

My only work after I've finished writing is to fight in order to get the music as close as I can to my original vision. I have the sound of the orchestration already in my mind. When you are composing something it's always the most beautiful melody on earth, played by the Berlin Philharmonic orchestra and sung by Barbra Streisand. It's always perfect in your imagination, but it's the first and last time that you hear it like that, afterwards it's only a process of destruction. That's why I used to say I'm not working *with* people but *against* them because it's true for the guy who's writing down the piano score, for the orchestrator, the musical director, the musicians and the singers, for everyone. When I get 70 or 75 percent of my imagination then I'm already very happy. However, if I'm convinced a criticism is justified I'll have no hesitation in making a U-turn. I have no sense of proprietal ego about my music because I'm not working for myself, I'm working for the show. It's the show that counts. I like working with Bill Brohn as an orchestrator because he understands my vision so well and sometimes he can even improve it. He gives me what I want and even some more too. And it is always very rewarding for me working with the cast as, many times, when they are very talented they have a beautiful and shining personality too.

The way I'm writing, whether it's recitative or even songs, I'm always trying to write in the rhythm of spoken language. The lyric will be delivered with the music at the same speed, the same phrasing and the same structure as if it were spoken. So if the audience forgets very quickly that people are singing on stage it's because we did a good job; it's what we aim for. The music follows the patterns of speech in temper and mood of the situation. It's not exactly French or English rhythms. If you are nervous you speak more quickly, when you are relaxed or when you want to be tender you speak in another way. To say it's a Gallic score is rubbish; it's more to do with the mood and atmosphere of the situation.

If the script is well-written it always sounds natural where the songs will be. You don't learn how to do it, you must have an instinct for it and you must understand why there is the right moment to do a song. In the old days the justification for a song was a happy situation. It was natural for people to sing when they are happy, not when they were sad. But for us it's very important that the song keeps the story going. If you have a musical where you have a song and it stops the action and you are only telling through the music what you have already been telling through the spoken language then that's awful. So we are very cautious about where the songs are and there has to be a subtle link between the recitative and the song. What we call recitative is everything that could be transferred to spoken dialogue. When you get to the aria or the song you enter a different universe. In *Les Misérables* if you take the ABC café scene from the very beginning you could have spoken lines until you get to "Red and Black" and then in the song it's not possible at all to have spoken dialogue. You have recitative in the confrontation between Javert and Valjean at the hospital. They're starting in a different mood and Valjean is singing one way and Javert is singing another way but when they start to fight they're both so furious and so angry that they're singing practically the same rhythms and melody. Through the writing there is alternate foregrounding with one singing more present melody and one underscoring with low notes what the other one is singing in high notes. It's totally forbidden to the guy controlling the sound to push one voice up. I tell them that it's already in the score so don't touch it.

Sometimes there is a right moment for a song but you don't have one. In *Les Misérables* after "Stars," when Eponine sings, "Cosette, now I remember," there you could have a song but it was too close to "Stars" so instead you just have a citation of the music she was singing when she first met Marius. Eponine is always introduced by the same instruments. It's a way of using leitmotif, which you can attach to a character or a situation. So once it's done the reprise is just a subliminal way to tell the story, to express what the vision and the words can't say. If you have a character being very sad because of the death of somebody and you have a leitmotif there, then half an hour later you can have the character just sitting on stage with the same melody coming and you understand immediately his state of mind and what he's thinking about. It's a shortcut to tell you a situation that would take two or three minutes to explain on stage and you can express it all in fifteen seconds of music. Music is very flexible. For instance in *Saigon* you sometimes have a citation of the "Dju vui vay" music just to express the fact that Kim is still true to Chris and her memory is going back to the day they had that little ceremony together. You can express all her feelings with only three bars of music and you don't have to explain everything. So the music is pure storytelling.

What I would like to do one day is to use the capacity of the music more so that it is telling something different from what the singer Is singing. So the most interesting sound is coming from inside the orchestration and the orchestra is expressing all the unconscious of the character on stage. Because sometimes you can speak and your unconscious is telling you something totally different. That's what underscoring through the orchestration can express, something different from the voice, but it's a very difficult thing to achieve.

Sometimes you can use the music in a reprise in different ways because you can take it in different keys, different modes. *Les Misérables*' "Do You Hear the People Sing" is used in many, many ways in majors and minors. It's in the Finale of Act I, in "Turning," and in the music for the prostitutes. You can take it as a challenge, the way you use a reprise. For example, in *Saigon* I used the theme of "You Will Not Touch Him" in many ways. I was playing around with this little line of music so I could hold the tension of the scene and the attention of the public. I used the same line over and over changing keys, changing the link each time. It's a kind of game, it's fun to find ways to explore the melody. Also in *Saigon* in the scene of the evacuation of the Embassy with the helicopter, of course there is the music of the Embassy but at the same time there is underscoring with a lot of citation of "I Still Believe" and "Why God Why?" in a different key, in a different mode. But I'm turning around all those things together to express the relationship of two people and to bind them together. It's the story I'm telling and I'm using the subconscious of the audience, because they don't realize it, but they are feeling something at a subliminal level.

A reprise must be driven by the story. It's very rare that you can do a straight reprise of a song with two different characters. But I decided to do it for Javert's suicide and Valjean's conversion when he tears up his ticket of leave. It's exactly the same situation, the turning point in a man's life, and it was a perfect symmetry for me. (See *Les Misérables* photo inserts 8 and 9.) If a reprise is well justified like that then you have no problem with it. The reprise must come naturally because the story must drive everything, then it will give you good impulsion, good motivation, good writing. The reprise of "Bring Him Home" at the end of the show links that moment on the barricade when it's sung for the first time and it's part of the big arc of the show, the big unity of the construction of the show. But often it's more a question of craft than inspiration; for example, the ending has to bring together all the ingredients of the show and it has to be uplifting because after three hours of something so long and heavy you must have something that makes the people want to stand up and sing. It is reassuring to see Valjean reunited with Fantine and Eponine at his death and although I'm not sure it's going to really happen like that it's nice to imagine it. We have had a lot of people writing to us to say that this show has changed their lives. But it is so successful because of the story, which is Victor Hugo's. It's about tolerance and compassion and it's the genius of the story that you have a description of the whole scale of human nature. Each character gives you one aspect of the human soul and joined together they give you a vision of all humanity. It helps you to know a little bit more about yourself.

It probably takes about a year to write the first draft of a musical if the story is right and you don't have to do anything else. It was different with the ballet *Wuthering Heights*. It took me eight months and it went very quickly. It's not the same kind of work and it doesn't monopolize my mind in the same way. There were no restrictions and no rewrites, whereas with a musical you have all that. It takes several years to bring a musical to the stage and a lot of other people must be involved too.

When we started working on *Les Misérables* in London, Trevor Nunn and John Caird were very helpful in shaping the show and James Fenton too. We worked on some new songs, and while "On My Own" had the existing music "La Misère," I wrote new music for "Stars," "Bring Him Home," "Dog Eat Dog," and "Empty Chairs at Empty Tables." In fact, "Bring Him Home" was specially written for Colm Wilkinson as he has an outstanding falsetto voice, and I thought it was a shame to miss it. We all felt that a song for Valjean in Act II was a necessity.

Working on the show in London, we were surrounded by professional theatre people. It was the first time it was happening in our life and we were so thrilled to be working in London for an opening with the Royal Shakespeare Company. That's something we never imagined in the most foolish dream of our life. We learned a lot from working on *Les Misérables* in London. We learned how to craft a musical other than just by the story, and that has influenced our other work.

THE WORDS

AB: In all our musicals it is the dramatic situation that is the most important thing. The music and the lyrics have to tell the story right the whole way through. Sometimes you have to compromise because the best words will not always be the best words for a musical. The kind of verse that James Fenton wrote for *Les Misérables* was totally amazing. He wrote some versions of some of the songs that were absolutely extraordinary. But we all agreed that it just didn't sing as a musical should. It was not because it wasn't good enough but maybe because it wasn't musical enough. The words have to sing naturally. You may have a critic talking about the lyrics, saying this is banal or trite or whatever, but that's fine because what they don't realize is that if it were T. S. Eliot all the time then, in a dramatic narrative, it wouldn't work because it probably wouldn't tell the story so well. *Cats* is a very different kind of show and of course it works so well because it has been devised to fit entirely around the poetry rather than the story being the driving force. So in the end what really matters is that the lyrics tell the story the way you want it to be told dramatically and with all the emotions you want to see on stage. Of course we find out a lot during the rehearsal process and sometimes the lyrics are changed accordingly because it's then that you see what the show is becoming. But we work into emotions and maybe people say that we have our hearts on our sleeve but that's what it is, putting our heart on the stage, and that's what people seem to like.

As my first language is French I need to work with a collaborator on the English lyrics, but no experience has been the same as the previous one; it is always different, always new. When we started in London with *Les Misérables*, I was not even thinking that I could ever write in English, so there was absolutely no frustration at that stage. *Les Misérables* had already been a huge hit in France so it was a French import which had to be revised a lot in order to be put on the English stage. In the French version the dramaturgy was not as tight but the French show was 70 percent of the final show, although sometimes in a different order. It was our first experience in England and I had complete control on everything and collaborated with Herbert Kretzmer on the new songs that were written, just by suggestion, not by writing, because he wrote all by himself.

It's only when I wrote *Miss Saigon* that the problem started. I have been through an unusual experience with this musical as I have written it twice in two different languages. I wrote it all in French first and I could feel that it was so close to what the final show would be, it was 85 percent there. I knew that this time I would feel very frustrated if I had to sit down on the aisle, while an English or American translator would tell me—this works, this doesn't work, and all that. Cameron and Claude-Michel thought my command of English was good enough for me to collaborate on the lyrics; so I knew that this time I had to take the risk. And so I worked together with Richard Maltby. Richard was very bold and generous in agreeing to work with me. He accepted my linguistic flaws at the time as much as he respected my intrinsic knowledge of the piece. I had an exact idea of what English word I wanted or didn't want and he made sure that what I meant was what we wrote together in English, with a lot of his own additional creative input. So that's how for the first time I found myself writing in English, and I must say that if it hadn't happened that way I would certainly not only have been frustrated, but I think *Saigon* probably may not have been possible. To write in English at that time was indispensable.

For *Martin Guerre* I started writing it in French, which was the usual way. I tried working with Herbert Kretzmer first, on the English adaptation, but it didn't seem to work out and I was a bit reluctant trying it again with someone else. That's when Edward Hardy came into the picture at the instigation of Cameron Mackintosh. Edward is not really a collaborator because he is a gifted loner who usually writes both music and lyrics; someone who I think will always work on his own. He is that kind of writer and at that stage I was prepared to step aside. So in the end it was really his English text based on my French text that was presented at the Prince Edward when the show opened in June 1996. When we started to make corrections to the show, Edward was doing other things and suggested that I continue the work with Stephen Clark. Stephen, with my cooperation, did some rewriting while the show was still playing at the Prince Edward in London.

After *Martin Guerre* closed at the Prince Edward eighteen months later, having garnered an Olivier Award for Best Musical, we were

Richard Maltby, Alain Boublil, and Claude-Michel Schönberg work on the score for *Miss Saigon* in Boston: December 1987, the day after *Les Misérables* opened there.

still not happy in our heart of hearts with our own work. It was just not the show that Claude-Michel and I had conceived at the beginning. It was a show by which I was not moved at all; I was sometimes thrilled but I was never moved. And many people felt like that. I even agreed with some of the negative comments in the reviews. But it doesn't mean I didn't like the production; there were many aspects that I loved. Declan Donnellan is a very innovative and unexpected person, who not only directs a show but every time reconceives and reinvents the theatre. It was an extraordinary intellectual and artistic experience to be able to spend several months of our lives with someone of such intelligence and originality. The work done on the show by Declan and the choreographer, Bob Avian, was absolutely fantastic. But instead of doing the kind of small show that Declan is known for, everyone was trying to please us, to turn a little, intimate and crazy love story into an epic that it is not and never will be. The music seemed to us all to be calling for a bigger show, and ultimately there was probably a contradiction between the soaring, operatic music and the story. It was really a small story between a man and a woman and I wanted to feel that the passion that they felt was so incredible that they couldn't stop what they were doing. That sometimes things go beyond reason and they just couldn't help it. And none of that, I thought, was the focus of the show. It was not the central point anymore; it was going in too many directions.

But we couldn't get it out of our system and we couldn't move on to anything else as we knew deep down that even after six years working on it that the writing of the show was not yet finished. So we had to go back to its roots, to what we call the original impulse, which was a show of limited size, to be played by a cast of about twenty with a medium sized orchestra combining sounds of the Middle Ages with contemporary synthesizers in the pit of a medium-sized theatre. From the beginning we had wanted to do something different from a big show like *Les Misérables* or *Miss Saigon*. We had been looking to the future to do, not the third of the same breed, but something of a new nature. So we felt the urgent need to repossess and complete our own work and we know by experience these impulses cannot be stopped until they have been fulfilled. Then I tried, just for fun, to write an English version of one of the first songs that was written for the show when it was in French. And that's how I came to write "How Many Tears." It was the first song that I had ever written in English on my own without a French text or draft and it was soon followed by "Live with Somebody You Love." (See *Martin Guerre* photo insert 2.)

Working on those songs helped me to make the decision that I should write directly in English a fully revised version of the show but that I couldn't do it on my own, and Stephen Clark was the obvious person I wanted to collaborate with. He is a born collaborator because he really respects what you do. Cameron has been very supportive and he never wanted this show to be finished the day it closed at the Prince Edward. He is always very involved with our shows at every stage from the moment we show him what we're working on. He knew that *Martin Guerre* would have another life, and Jude Kelly invited us to present a new version of the show at her theatre in Leeds. The show that opened at the West Yorkshire Playhouse in December 1998 was the first show that I had co-written in English from the beginning. I may never be brave enough to write in English on my own. I'm not sure if I will. Maybe I will one day.

However, I like to start working on new material in French so that I can find all the psychological dimensions of the characters and all the implications of the historical period in which our shows are set. It's easier for me to do that in French because then I can let my mind wander into that kind of intellectual, studious mode which draws on everything I have been reading over the years which has made my culture, which is basically French. So I don't have to worry about anything other than what I want to say or the way I want the characters to behave. That has become a very intimate process that I can only go through in French. It's just more natural for me. I know I could do it in English but I would unconsciously be framed by a kind of different behavior that comes to you naturally when you think or speak in English, and it probably wouldn't give me all the elements that I want to introduce from the beginning in the characters in the play.

Starting to write in French is also important for the sound. In the English language there are many more imperatives regarding rhyme and how you construct a rhymed scene with music and it is as different as a French song is from an English one. A French song is all about the emotion and the flow and although it obviously rhymes it is in a much freer manner. Because the rules in English are so much stricter I'd rather let the emotions flow in French. But more and more often when I'm writing in French there is a much greater involvement with English and I put on the side the English equivalent, if there is one, the English title sometimes or two or three lines which are already rhymed in English. This makes my work later with my English co-lyricist very different now than when I started. However, it's not simply a preference for writing in French because when I get into the English phase of writing I enjoy it completely; but the first step is a very important part of the process. Sometimes when we're working on the English version there may be one or two songs or one or two moments in the show which we redo from scratch because there is a better idea that has come from the original idea that takes us in a completely different direction. It doesn't happen very often but when it does then I love writing or co-writing in English directly.

It is difficult sometimes to keep the same sense within the different cultural boundaries because it's not like translating a novel when you have to be as faithful as you can to the original. The emotions, and especially the romantic emotions, have to be translated from French in a way that not only respects the English equivalent of words but also makes that same emotion palatable in English without being too French but without losing its Frenchness. That is partly why I admire so much the work that Herbert Kretzmer did in *Les Misérables*. After writing a French version we have to keep close to the so-called sacred original impulse of what the work is going to be forever, if it survives, and at the same time to find in every language things that could never have been there If It had been written in these other languages first. But a musical should not belong to one culture. Our shows don't spring from one particular culture but they survive because they convey with music and lyrics the kind of emotions that could be a part of any culture. It's not that we do it on purpose, it's just that that's the kind of subject we work on, and, for that reason, it's a difficult thing to do.

My original French draft has all the impulses but many things are missing which are then found during the first English adaptation. Now that I am part of the adapting process myself I have to create all these original elements and then protect the original impulse as well as open it to the new influence that will give it its definitive shape in English. So it's a difficult and thin line between these two notions in order to make a show which will be an English language musical but which will keep everything of its original flavor. If I ever have any problems with the English translation or I feel disappointed that I can't say in English what I was trying to say in French I just keep working at it with my co-lyricist until we get it. There is always a way to say exactly what you wanted to say in another language; you just have to dig deep enough to understand what makes it work. If it's difficult it doesn't mean the emotion is wrong but maybe it just needed an approach from a different dramatic angle.

In French lyrics the rhyme process is much easier—it's really quite lax—and it is the opposite in English. Sometimes we try to keep the same rhyme schemes but it can be quite difficult. Generally we are led to the rhymes by the music because in the kind of theatrical music that Claude-Michel writes you can hear where the rhymes are the first time you hear the music. If you're writing a dramatic lyric then you stick to very classic rhyme schemes like *abba* or *abab,* but if you are trying to write a funny lyric in English the rhyme will have to come at the place where the joke is, so that the rhyme adds to the joke. Generally there is less need to rhyme in the recitatives and sometimes I make a point not to rhyme them at all. That doesn't make the recitatives easier; in fact they can be much more difficult than the songs. I never fix a rhyme before the rest of the line in French although I might occasionally do that in English. If I find the constraints of rhyme are limiting the choices of what I want to say then I destroy the construct of rhymes and go back for new choices.

There is an element of French speech rhythms in the music Claude-Michel writes but it is also much more than that. It's extremely theatrical and it's written in a very Italian operatic manner and also has a very Hungarian-Jewish kind of emotional feel. When you are writing the lyrics they have to be totally satisfactory aurally and if they are not we get rid of them and you will never hear them on the stage. There are various things that determine whether a line sings well, for example, where the open vowel sounds come in a line or if you have people in the cast who are classically trained, then you certainly want to give them the best possible sounds. We do bear in mind each singer's voice when we are writing and we try to respect it.

I usually fix a melody in my mind very quickly and if I don't then usually that melody disappears from the show. When you start writing you often find the lyric is already there in the melody and I may have a note or two about what the lyric needs to say, although it may be written on a piece of tube ticket or a parking ticket! Soliloquies come naturally and they are a fundamental part of the writing for me because that's how I can understand where the show is at and where I can find the proper balance of the show. A soliloquy not only expresses the innermost feelings of a character but it allows me to go into my own mind to really ask myself who I think the character is and I need these moments or I start writing just songs.

Writing the lyrics is certainly made easier because we spend so much time working on the storytelling in the first place. If we do get any problems, then Claude-Michel and I spend another afternoon discussing that point of the storytelling. Some musical scenes, of course, are more difficult than others; for example, the Finale of Act I of *Les Misérables*, "One Day More," when so many people sing about the same subject matter on different melodies that are interwoven with each other (see *Les Misérables* photo insert 4), and the court case in *Martin Guerre*. A court case is a very difficult thing to do in a sung-through musical, and it's something that would certainly be easier with spoken dialogue. You have to find a device that would make it worth musicalizing, and although you have to include the full story, it mustn't be too long or it would be boring. In the end I think it works well enough and you forget it's sung, but it was a very challenging thing to do.

Sometimes it's possible to distill the essence of the entire plot into a single song. We managed to do that at the end of Act I in *Miss Saigon*. It took a long time to come up with the idea for a solo there but the idea of saying: "I'd give my life for you" was the moment that suddenly I realized that the purpose of the show could be encapsulated into one song. It becomes a kind of pledge to Kim's son and it's one of the most moving moments in the show. Once I had the idea it was one of the easiest songs to write. I wrote it in French at first as usual, and "Je donnerai ma vie pour toi," translates exactly word for word as "I'd Give My Life For You." As the father of young children these lyrics were emotionally very personal to me, and I was totally happy with them. I had finished writing the song one winter evening in Deauville in France and then I went for a walk on the beach. There was a stranger walking toward me from the other side of the beach and in my highly-charged emotional state of mind I found this very threatening. After all who would be walking on the beach at one o'clock in the morning in the middle of winter unless he had bad intentions? But I thought that if this guy really was a murderer then the last thing I would have done finally in my life was to have written "I'd Give My Life For You" and I felt quite O.K. with that! But we walked past each other and nothing happened. Of course, maybe he had just written a song he was very pleased with, too!

Although all our musicals have been set against a background of historical crisis—the student insurrection in Paris, the American withdrawal from Vietnam, and the religious wars in sixteenth-century France—we were never politically motivated, never fighting for a good cause. But it seems as if we cannot choose a subject that doesn't have a political background to it or a kind of social background. We only try to find very good stories to achieve our goal of writing musical theatre, to take the art form further and enjoy ourselves in the first place. It's only now we realize that we have been doing things that all relate to each other, but it was not conscious. In the same way many of our themes reoccur and yes, it looks like a question of identity is very central to all the subjects that we care about. I also strongly believe in a sense of fate, and obviously this has to do with the fact that I was born in Tunisia and had a kind of oriental upbringing. But what I hate is when people think that because of that you should sit down and relax and wait for events to happen. I believe the opposite. Kim thinks that the gods control her life, but she tries to do everything she can to make sure that she gets what she wants for her son. It's not because there are limits that you do nothing, it's the opposite. Because there are limits you have to explore every avenue.

The images of sun and moon, which represent Chris and Kim, also symbolise the opposition between East and West. They are signs, which are linked to the sky and the planets, and they show the religion, mysticism, and a permanent sense of fate. The sun represents the male and the moon the female. So when we talk about the sun meeting the moon in the sky it symbolizes the union of Chris and Kim. The blessing of Kim's room takes place on the feast of the full moon. That doesn't just mean a romantic evening, it means the day is blessed, and that's very important.

Some writers say they have a love/hate relationship with writing but I enjoy it fully. In fact I love it. When our work is brought to life on stage I feel reborn. When the shows are being translated into other languages I have control over everything that is written and sometimes I have a direct input too. But I am always sent the script in every language by the producer's office with a literal translation so I can check the translation from the retranslation and that's how I work. The only country where I did direct work with the translator was Japan. I worked on *Les Misérables* with a Japanese translator, Tokiko Iwatani, who is a very respected and wonderful old lady. In Japanese you have to say things in a completely different way and also it either doesn't rhyme at all or it rhymes in a completely different way. So she and I had to get into all that process with an interpreter and a musical assistant or pianist, and it was an amazingly slow and rewarding experience.

Claude-Michel and I work through the script chronologically and once we have something on tape and on paper we can work on it together. We have a permanent and friendly relationship that has lasted for over thirty-five years now. It's like we're one divided in two which complete each other. If one of us goes off course then the other one pulls him back and it never lasts long. We have a permanent interactive influence on each other. If Claude-Michel violently dislikes anything I've written, however strongly I might feel about this part of the text, it is almost always discarded. He is equally responsive to what I have to say about the music. Claude-Michel and I have always had an operatic vision of what a musical should be and in America our musicals are often called operatic musicals. We are taking it one step further with each musical but we have the strong belief that our audience is going one step further with us every time, and we have the impression that they are totally ready for what they are getting. ❧

CHAPTER 3

Words on the Page

THE CO-LYRICISTS

C O-WRITING THE LYRICS FOR A MUSICAL is a very different process from writing alone. Although it has the advantage that you can bounce ideas off someone else and perhaps be inspired by new thoughts, ultimately there has to be a unified vision of the piece and a very special working relationship which is egoless on both sides. Alain is considered to be a very fine lyricist in French—when *Les Misérables* opened in Paris he was highly commended by the hypercritical French press as being Victor Hugo's lyrical counterpart. But although Alain is now completely fluent in English, because he is not a native speaker and because he writes the script in French first, the choice of the best co-lyricist for each show is of the utmost significance. Alain believes:

AB: It is very difficult to find a good lyricist because if he has written his own shows then why would he bother to sit in a room with me and work as my co-lyricist? If his ego is too big then he won't accept that. I need someone who has respect for the original piece I've written in French and at the same time someone who knows that I completely respect what he is bringing to the piece and understands that I'm not trying to make him less than he is. Every time I'm writing now the first version is more and more complete and already full of hints of what the English version is going to be.

As Alain's English has increasingly improved, his needs have changed. In addition, each musical has required a different kind of co-lyricist. James Fenton was the first co-lyricist *on Les Misérables*, and he designed the Prologue and had the idea for the Café song that later became "Empty Chairs at Empty Tables." He had been working on the lyrics for eighteen months but the progress had been very slow; the planned autumn 1984 opening had already been delayed by a year. Eventually Herbert Kretzmer was called in to take over with a breathtakingly short time to write the new lyrics before the 1985 opening. For *Miss Saigon* it was important to have an American co-lyricist with a deep understanding of what the Vietnam War meant to the American people and who would have American idioms at his fingertips. This time it had to be someone who was prepared to sit and co-write with Alain. Richard Maltby was the only and perfect fit for the job.

For the English script of *Martin Guerre*, Alain first started writing the lyrics with the show's director Declan Donnellan, who has a good knowledge of French and some songwriting experience; however, Cameron Mackintosh found the first draft too poetic. As Martin Guerre was a French period piece like *Les Misérables*, Alain then started working with Herbert Kretzmer, but after they had been writing for eighteen months to complete the English draft it was eventually rejected as not having the right tone for the show. There had been some differences of opinion about the use of period syntax—Herbert believed that a medieval story should at least have some semblance of period syntax while Alain felt that it was imperative that a contemporary musical should have modern language in order to reach a modern audience. Mackintosh knew Edward Hardy from the Sondheim Masterclasses that he had set up at Oxford University, so Edward was asked to take on the job and he wrote mostly on his own. When it was decided to rework the show at the Prince Edward Theatre Stephen Clark, also from the Masterclasses, took over. He worked again with Alain on the new version.

Finding the most suitable co-lyricist is obviously a process fraught with difficulty. Each show has had completely different requirements. However, the three co-lyricists whose personal accounts of the writing process follow, could not have been better choices.

HERBERT KRETZMER

Herbert Kretzmer began work on *Les Misérables* after long and successful twin careers in journalism and lyric writing. He was born in South Africa in 1925. He grew up there and as a student began writing words and music for university shows. He came to Europe after World War II and for a while lived in Paris, playing piano in a bar in St.-Germain-des-Prés. He rubbed shoulders with Jean-Paul Sartre and eventually became a friend of one of France's greatest singer-songwriters, Charles Aznavour, with whom he formed a musical partnership. Herbie has lived in London since 1954, working as a feature writer and a drama critic for the *Daily Express* for eighteen years, followed by eight years as the television critic for the *Daily Mail*, during which time he won two national press awards. On being asked to write the lyrics for *Les Misérables* he gave up his job with the *Daily Mail* and set to work in his Basil Street flat. With only a few months to go before rehearsals began, he and Claude-Michel worked long hours together, getting

Photo by John Nathan

Herbert Kretzmer

through copious amounts of smoked salmon obtained from Harrods Food Hall around the corner.

Herbie considers journalism and lyric writing to be compatible professions. "For one thing, they share the element of compression; they deal with words written under constraint and restriction." His extraordinary talent for satire and his ready wit ensured an impressive career as a lyric writer, which has been marked by the award-winning songs "Goodness Gracious Me," sung by Peter Sellers and Sophia Loren; and two songs "Yesterday When I Was Young" and the chart-topping "She," written with—and for—Aznavour. "She" was more recently recorded by Elvis Costello as the title theme of the film *Notting Hill*. Herbie regularly wrote some of the brilliantly satirical, topical lyrics for the popular weekly BBC television show *That Was The Week That Was*. He also supplied the lyrics for the Anthony Newley film *Can Heironymous Merkin Ever Forget Mercy Humppe And Find True Happiness?*

Herbie's connection with the West End began when he wrote the book and lyrics for *Our Man Crichton*, starring Kenneth More and Millicent Martin, and the lyrics for the Drury Lane comedy *The Four Musketeers*, starring Harry Secombe as D'Artagnan. He is currently collaborating with Benny Andersson and Bjorn Ulvaeus of ABBA on a musical about Swedish emigrants to Minnesota circa 1850.

HK: I began working on *Les Misérables* on March 1, 1985 with only five months to go before rehearsals started on August 1, at which time my work was by no means completed. This meant working fast and under pressure, but speed is, of necessity, a journalist's forte. The materials I had to work from were an expurgated English translation of Hugo's novel (there was no time for the huge, uncut original), Claude-Michel's music on tape, a literal English translation of Alain's French lyrics, and a very detailed, scene-by-scene synopsis of the new extended plot adaptation made by Trevor Nunn and John Caird. This was a meticulous blueprint of the reorganized shape and structure of the piece, breaking every sequence down to its most minute fragments. It was not my task, thank heavens, to find new dramatic pathways through the complex story; that had already been done by Alain and Claude-Michel, Trevor and John. The shape of the musical had also been influenced by my predecessor James Fenton, whose contribution, though considerable, is not to be found so much in any surviving words and rhymes as in the general architecture, shape, and structure of the whole. However, I saved or adapted quite a few of his lines; only a fool would walk away from the fine work he left behind him.

The work I was engaged in was of a varied nature. About a third of it consisted of adapting or transforming the original French words and passages, turning them into singable English lyrics. A third was a much looser adaptation, with new words and new themes written to existing music; at least another third of it involved writing entirely new songs. The original French production in 1980 opened with the scene at the factory gates ("At The End Of The Day") and the whole show had a running time of a little under two hours, whereas our final, definitive British production told much more of Victor Hugo's story and ran at least one hour longer. A third of the show as it now stands had no counterpart in the original Paris production.

It was not a question of translation. I don't like the word translator. I don't acknowledge the term. I don't speak French, for a start. Transforming a song or a musical is not like translating a textbook or a novel, where absolute fidelity to the original is required. With a song you are reinventing an idea, a phantom, a fiction made up of words and images which have a particular resonance within a specific culture, to whose members you are appealing. Every culture has its own tribal assumptions, its own linguistic nuances. Lyric writing is not about stating the obvious. It seeks to set in motion a certain trail of wonder and imagination, to hint at something lurking beneath the surface. Poetry digs deeper yet, but I'm talking here about a more accessible level of appeal to the imagination.

When I started work on *Les Misérables*, I worked, not chronologically, but by choosing first the songs I most wanted to do. There were some easier—or so it seemed—bits of the musical that called you to do them first, and then there were those other more daunting, almost impossible passages which you just wanted to push aside, to do later or, like, never! I think "Master Of The House" was the first one I went for, because it sounded like the most fun, though fun is not really a word that I use much when talking generally about lyric writing. A lyricist may enjoy brief flashes of satisfaction when two lines or six lines eventually fall into place and seem to work. As with most writers of every kind, you have good days and lousy days; there is always pain, and on the days when there's less pain—those are the good days. But generally, nothing is fun until it's done. The songs that came most easily, like "Castle On A Cloud," are those where you know right away where you are going, where the song is going, and what the character is feeling. But even the tricky difficult songs like "Bring Him Home" or "On My Own" must not sound like hard work in the end. The best lines have to sound like they fell out of your head; they must seem a moment's thought. That's the trick. That's what we try for, and we don't always get it right.

The process of writing appropriate lyrics for a major musical with a large number of characters is not the same as writing lyrics for a one-shot song. The words one chooses to put into Cosette's mouth are not the words one would write for Eponine, a child of the streets. It's not just a question of contrasting the language of the gutter with that of the convent school. The words must seek to reveal individual character as well as social background. In a sung-through musical, remember, the lyricist is also a playwright. Cosette grew up in a closed, repressed, religious environment. She is a protected child, unaware of the brutishness and crudity of street life that Eponine has always known. A world of difference divides them, and the lyrics must reflect that. It's a secret world, a secret between the lyricist, the work, and the characters he seeks to create. You have to slip in and out of gear, to identify with, to feel at one with one particular person at one particular moment. Then the right words may come. It's a secret process, and a solitary one.

When you write a show, you have to start working on each song with a clear awareness of its direction and function. Is the song there to advance the plot, or to emphasize a dramatic situation? Is it there to provide information, or to describe the character? Many of the songs in *Les Misérables* take the form of soliloquy, where characters directly express what is going on in their heads. This is one of the things that is wonderful about musical theatre. You can move with dazzling speed through a narrative process, which, in a straight play, might take half an hour of exposition and action to cover. A song is the ultimate dramatic compression; nothing is more compressed than a song. In a musical you can have characters at the start of a song feeling one thing quite strongly, and three and a half minutes later they may have gone through several psychological or moral hoops, resolved their difficulties, and decided on a course of action. You can't do that in a straight play. Not that quickly anyway.

It goes without saying that the lyrics in a musical must be accessible, must be instantly understood. There is no time for the audience to dwell on obscurities. The words you select should, of course, set in motion a certain resonating process that can continue while the new words are being absorbed in the minds of the audience. But the lyrics must not draw undue attention to themselves and so get in the way of the storytelling that is going on. Accessibility is vital and that is one reason, I guess, why most poets do not make successful lyric writers, and vice versa.

In *Les Misérables* I always strove to find proper rhymes. All lyric writers are showoffs and wish to be noted for surprising and ingenious rhymes. But I was careful not to be too clever when I was working on *Les Misérables* because, it's a very strong story requiring plain words, as plain as I could make them. The story is the most important thing; what will always undermine and subvert the story are lyrics that are too smart, too attention-seeking. Any lyric that is self-regarding, by definition, is going to distract attention away from the narrative and from the character. The moment one thinks "what a clever rhyme" you have distracted the audience, you have let the story down. The innkeeper, Thénardier, is an exception because he is always congratulating himself on his own cleverness and so inventive rhymes can be used in his songs. (See *Les Misérables* photo insert 3.) In his boastful song "Master of the House," "Jesus" is rhymed with a succession of unexpected words. The word "Jesus" was not used at all in my first draft, but Trevor felt that the combination of notes at the culmination of each chorus required what he called a kicker, a verbal trick that would launch the singer into the last line with extra snap and vigor to announce the end of the stanza. I came up first with "But lock up your valises/Jesus! Won't I skin you to the bone." Then I thought, if I could do it once it might be a wheeze to use "Jesus" throughout the song, so I started making a list of possible "Jesus" rhymes down one side of the paper. Some are slightly harder rhymes because they don't all have the soft, buzzing *z* of "Jesus," but I felt a little push from the soft *z* to the harder *s* would be O.K. for the song. This series of rhymes gives a flamboyant signoff to each verse, and is in keeping with Thénardier's outrageous character.

With little Cosette in "Castle On A Cloud," it was deemed wiser to avoid the more obvious rhyming patterns. My first draft contained the expected rhyme of "toys" with "boys," but, again on Trevor's suggestion, it was decided to frustrate expectation; so instead of the predictable rhyme we had, "There is a room that's full of toys/There are a hundred boys and girls." The very employment of rhyme implies and suggests that the singer possesses a mind that is organized and ordered in some formal way. But the child Cosette is a badly treated little girl, with no pattern to her life, no schooling or education, so you try to avoid the expected rhyme, which would indicate too advanced and orderly a mental development in one so young. Instead, you substitute something deliberately askew, off-center and adrift.

The choice of an individual rhyme scheme, of course, is strictly governed by the constraints of the music. You cannot negotiate with a bar of music. It is non-negotiable. You can't say, "Stretch a little, give me another syllable," just because you've got a wizard rhyme that will be remembered forever. You've got to find your freedom, as I have said, quite literally within the bars. In songwriting less must always try to be more.

Another constraint to be considered is the singability of a line. Some words sing easily and attractively and some do not, and you'd better know which words, or combinations of words, trip off the tongue more smoothly than others. An awareness of these things is, or should be, part of the basic equipment of a lyric writer's mind, for he is as much concerned with sound as he is with making sense. If you take a word like "marriage," for example, you cannot extend the second syllable beyond its natural articulation; the syllable is over and done with as soon as it's said. There are also certain sounds that you should not too often ask a singer to sustain on a high note, like "me," or "shriek" or "scream," because the *ee* sound closes and tightens the singer's throat. Again, a line containing too many *ss*'s can just become an incomprehensible shower of sibilants, especially if sung by a large chorus.

When I was writing the lyrics for *Les Misérables* there were additional technical problems having to do with the very cadences of the French language. Although music is an international language, it is, when linked to words, shaped to reflect the flows and flurries of a particular national tongue, and so it comes to possess its own codes, which are not easily broken. The French language is full of emphatic consonants, staccato tricks of rhythm, and fading double syllables at the ends of sentences, which have no ready equivalents in the English language. Claude-Michel's score for *Les Misérables* was unmistakably Gallic. I was helped here because of my experience over thirty years writing lyrics for Charles Aznavour, so I'm used to their little French ways. But even so there are certain phrases that you never really conquer. I had hellish difficulties with the lyrics of "On My Own," because of those little double-syllable formations at the ends of lines, which are termed feminine endings, like "finding" and "binding," where the last syllable is weak and unstressed. You can use such rhymes once or twice in a song, but it's tiresome when they keep coming at you over and over again. "On My Own" was a hard code to crack. It was like a little dark cloud hovering over me during the five to six months of writing. We discussed it endlessly and everyone, including Trevor and John, contributed to it, but I can't say that I'm really happy with the result.

Sometimes in a musical the mood created by the music is really stronger than the words. One of the strengths of Claude-Michel's score is the way certain melodies are cunningly reprised. *Les Misérables* uses repetition a lot, often in unexpected ways. It is an essential part of the structure of the musical and one of the things that defines it. With Claude-Michel the theme may be repeated, in different and surprising ways; it can be slowed down or speeded up, or put into somebody else's mouth entirely. Of course, it is important that it should first oblige the demands of its original use. Take, for instance, the song "Come To Me," which Fantine sings early on, when she is dying. That's the first established use of the melody, and must be absolutely true to its dramatic situation. Much later the melody, with a different theme and lyric, is sung by Eponine, but now it's called "On My Own." So the reverberations set in motion in the mind of the audience are that they are combining the melodic cadences of that tune, into a mental, almost semiremembered dream landscape, which they couldn't put a memory to, but something inside their recent memory is telling them that they've heard that song before. The use of musical motifs like these is as old as composition itself, but I cannot recall a popular opera or a musical that has made use of the idea so comprehensively and so well. You might call it spinal music, music that runs through the show like a backbone. There are always good reasons for these duplications of melody. The way Alain and Claude-Michel employ reprises in *Les Misérables* is, I believe, one of the many reasons for the show's hold over audiences.

In our preparation of the 1985 British production, several songs from the original Paris production were changed, or substantially redirected, sometimes because of the expansion of the story, and sometimes for other reasons. But I tried to ensure that the spirit of those songs was sustained. "On My Own," for instance, in the Paris original was "L'Air De La Misère," a song about the hunger and misery of the poor. We gave the song to a different character entirely and made it a lament about unrequited love sung by a tough little dreamer. Similarly, I changed the basic nature of the whores' chorus "Lovely Ladies," which in Paris had been "La Nuit," a somewhat gentler idea altogether. (See *Les Misérables* photo insert 2.) Another lyric that underwent a radical change of theme was little Cosette's "Castle On A Cloud," originally "Mon Prince Est En Chemin," which concerned itself with a prince coming to rescue the abandoned little girl from her pitiable plight. Cosette is a baffled child suffering rejection and isolation; and I felt she would not be thinking of princes, but much more likely be dreaming of acceptance and friends, and comfort, of a loving mother figure—"a lady all in white." This is Cosette's dream world, her castle in the clouds.

Among the half-dozen or so brand new songs that we invented for our British production in 1985 are "Empty Chairs At Empty Tables," "Stars," and "Bring Him Home." I still think of "Empty Chairs At Empty Table" as "The Café Song," which I guess is a tribute to the strength of the original idea of the song, which was James Fenton's. He felt that the structure of the narrative needed, at that juncture, a scene in which Marius, the sole survivor of the barricade, would be seen deep in a kind of mourning meditation, which would also be part of his healing process and the exorcism of his guilt. Marius asks himself, "Why should I have been spared, I alone and not the others?" (See *Les Misérables* photo insert 10.) So the core idea of this song was already in place before I started looking for the words to express it.

With "Stars," I was required to write a lyric that would state Inspector Javert's basic credo. Javert's role needed expansion, more beef, and more muscle. It was necessary to give Jean Valjean a truly worthy opponent. *Les Misérables* works because it displays in conflict two morally incorruptible protagonists, or antagonists, each of who could, if they chose, claim the moral high ground of the story; there is no real evil in either of them. The theme and the title came to me at some ungodly hour of the night, when I was looking at the night sky and I chanced upon the idea of the heavenly stars as sentinels of the night and the symbols of unchanging order. The song describes and celebrates the unquestionable ideal in Javert's life, which is the moral constancy of the world, expressed as discipline and law. "Stars" is, in one way, unlike any other song in the show because it was the only time I wrote the lyrics first, and the music was written afterward.

It was altogether different with "Bring Him Home." This was written during rehearsals and first performed, I think, only seventeen days before the paying public came in. Originally we had all convinced ourselves that this was going to be another kind of song entirely, one that we code-named "Night Thoughts." You must remember that Jean Valjean was a normal French male, after all, and thus the song was originally intended to show his struggle to control his jealousy at the prospect of losing his delightful adopted companion, Cosette, who thought of herself as his daughter. Valjean's sexual and psychological torment at this point was certainly something that Victor Hugo had not shied away from. Before I wrote the lyric, I had naturally anticipated from Claude-Michel a melody that would be appropriately agitated, and busy. There would have to be lots of words, lots of thoughts rapidly expressed—so, I was naturally looking for a tune with plenty of notes in it. When Claude-Michel eventually presented his tune I really didn't know what to say. I could see the charm and allure of the melody, but I was appalled that I was required to find so many words for so very few notes! The tune of "Bring Him Home" is largely built on a stately progression of three-note phrases separated by lengthy pauses, which meant that you could not run on the words beyond a line; you couldn't have a long pause and then continue the same sentence after the pause. Each line would have to be more or less self-contained, without being dependent on the next, or previous lines. To convey Valjean's agitation and anguish in so few notes was, of course, an impossible assignment for any lyric writer alive. After about a week of my own agitation and complaint, we were all together at my Basil Street flat late one night. We were talking about this song, and John spoke six words that opened the door: "Sounds like a prayer to me." The light just flooded into what was darkness, and there it was—a prayer. It meant a total change of plan. You ignore the sexual jealousy, you ignore the torment, you cut straight to Valjean the Christian altruist, who wants Marius saved for his beloved Cosette's sake. "Let me die/Let him live"—that is one hell of a leap from our original ideas. (See *Les Misérables* photo insert 7.) This song had begun to strike me as the most difficult and intractable of the numbers waiting to be done, an Everest that I would eventually have to climb. But in the end I wrote almost the whole lyric overnight.

"One Day More" did not pose me the same kind of problems at all. The real work had gone into the preparation and planning, the design of the scene, long before I got to it. Claude-Michel had somehow been able to make it all work musically and he planned it like a military operation. The idea of bringing the entire cast on stage at the same moment, on various levels of consciousness and dramatic purpose, was an astonishing one. The sequence tells us what all the characters in the musical are feeling, what is likely to happen from now on, for each of them, how their individual worlds will change, or how they hope they will change. I think it's a scene of huge musical ingenuity, and it is undoubtedly one of the high water marks of twentieth century musical theatre. (See *Les Misérables* photo insert 4.) As for me, once the blueprint was firmly in place, I just had to go in there and find the words that expressed the themes common to all of them—tomorrow—one day more—the future. We all had a hand in the making of this extraordinary moment in the show. *Les Misérables* is truly a collaborative musical in every sense.

RICHARD MALTBY, JR.

Richard Maltby, Jr., son of the well-known orchestra leader and a graduate of Yale University, is a highly experienced American lyricist who has also directed and conceived many successful shows: *Ain't Misbehavin'*, an anthology celebrating the work of jazz musician Fats Waller, not only won the Tony, New York Drama Critics Circle, Outer Critics Circle and Drama Desk Awards for Best Musical of 1978, but also gained Richard the Tony Award for Best Director of a Musical; *Fosse*, which he directed and co-conceived with Ann Reinking and Chet Walker, won the 1998 Tony Award for Best Musical as well as the Outer Critics Circle and Drama Desk Awards.

Richard's association with Cameron Mackintosh began with the Broadway production of Andrew Lloyd Webber's *Song and Dance* in 1985, which he directed and adapted with lyricist Don Black. The show won a Tony Award for its star, Bernadette Peters.

Photo by Margaret Vermette

Richard Maltby, Jr.

In collaboration with composer David Shire, Richard directed and wrote the lyrics for other award-winning musicals: *Starting Here, Starting Now* in 1977, which received a Grammy nomination, *Baby* in 1983 with librettist Sybille Pearson, which was nominated for seven Tony Awards, and *Closer Than Ever* in 1989, which won two Outer Critics Circle Awards: Best Off-Broadway Musical and Best Score. He also wrote *Nick & Nora* in 1991 and *Big* in 1996 with librettist John Weidman, which received a Tony nomination for Best Score. Most recently he directed *Ring of Fire*, a new musical of his own creation using Johnny Cash songs, which opened on Broadway in March 2006.

Richard has a long association with the Manhattan Theatre Club, where he directed five musicals including the original production of *Ain't Misbehavin'*. Maltby's pleasure in playing with words is further evident from the devilishly cryptic crossword puzzles he supplies for *Harper's* magazine. He is married to Janet Brenner and has five children: Nicholas, David, Jordan, Emily, and Charlotte.

RM: My work on *Miss Saigon* had something of a delayed start because when Cameron Mackintosh first approached me about it I turned it down! What Cameron gave me was a rough translation and a tape of the first act. I went home and listened to it. Claude-Michel was playing all this thumping music and singing all the parts, in the same voice, in French, which I don't understand. If you don't know what Boublil and Schönberg are doing, all you hear are the recitatives. I hadn't seen *Les Misérables* and I didn't understand what they were up to. At that time, 1986, Vietnam was still a taboo subject in America. Every dramatization of it had died at the box office. I was working on a show with David Shire and I have to say I was not unhappy to turn Cameron down. I thought that he was vaguely mad, and that Boublil and Schönberg, who I'd never met, must be crazy, setting the *Madame Butterfly* story in the context of Vietnam.

Then over the next six months, while the story and the songs were running through my head, three things happened. The project I was working on with David came to an end. The movie *Platoon* opened, and finally it seemed America could look at Vietnam again. Ten years had gone by, and finally Americans felt enough distance to look at what had happened there. And *Les Misérables* came to the United States. I went to see it in its pre-Broadway run in Washington D.C. and I was astonished. I thought, "*I get what they're doing. This is a completely new way of writing a show.*" I finally understood their use of recitative and I could see the passion and the power in the writing. So I went back to play the *Saigon* tape. Before, it had sounded incomprehensible to me, as it would to anyone who was accustomed to the set conventions of American musicals, where a song is a song and then there's dialogue and then you have another song. Andrew Lloyd Webber and Tim Rice had, of course, broken some of the conventions, but this went further. This was a new kind of musical storytelling, and I loved it. So with some embarrassment I called up Cameron to see if the job was still available and Cameron said, "I knew you'd come around. I haven't talked to anyone else and they've just finished the second act." I loved him for that.

Cameron had an instinct that *Miss Saigon* needed an American mind, an American sensibility for the subject. He was wiser than he knew. I don't think Europeans really understood what Vietnam meant to America. The English and the French had lost colonies for years. They didn't understand the investment America had in it. Indeed few Americans understood it either. In America, we had a mythology of moral superiority, a smug image that we were the guardians of freedom and democracy. In our hearts we thought we were always the good guys, always on the side of the right. But in Vietnam we were the bad guys, and even worse—we lost. We had never lost a war before, ever. Even as Saigon was falling we still expected John Wayne to come over the hill and save the day. Losing this war had a devastating effect on the American spirit. It was something that Alain and Claude-Michel, and even Cameron, hadn't really understood, at least not enough to make it the essence of the piece. Cameron's instincts were right that they needed an American co-writer. When *Miss Saigon* opened in New York there was a great sense of pain. It's the kind of show American musicals became great on, a popular entertainment on the major American event of contemporary history. We should have looked at ourselves this way and in the end it's a great sadness because this is the show that we should have written.

Cameron arranged for me to meet Alain and Claude-Michel at

a restaurant in New York. They wanted to "check me out" to see if we could work together. Subsequently I wrote a couple of pieces as a sort of test. Then they gave me the original novel, *Madame Chrysanthemum*, on which David Belasco's play and Puccini's opera were based. They also gave me James Fenton's book *All the Wrong Places, Adrift in the Politics of Asia*, which covered the fall of Saigon in detail. It was Fenton's book that cemented my attachment to the project. His description of the fall of Saigon was astonishing. Few events in history have ever been such a perfect metaphor. Alain and I started working. Our method was to sit in a room together and hammer it out. It was never a case of me simply translating what Alain had written. We sat down together and wrote a play in English. Alain and Claude-Michel had already laid out the piece and its design, and they already had the truly brilliant structural ideas, like delaying the fall of Saigon to the second act. But the scenes were diagrammatic; the intricacies of the drama in the scenes were not fully worked out.

We worked on *Saigon* for about two years altogether, and it was really the best working circumstances I've ever experienced. We worked on it in a way that was unlike anything I've ever done before. I'm accustomed to a show being in your consciousness all day, every day. But we worked in blocks, starting chronologically and taking one section of the story at a time. We'd work for a week or two in Provence, or a hotel in New York or Brittany or some other, usually beautiful, place. We'd work all day and then have a wonderful dinner. When a block was finished I would type it, we'd hand it in and then I'd put it away. I would forget about it totally and do other things until we started on the next block.

Claude-Michel always writes the music first. In this sense he is a true opera composer since the primary dramatization is his. The music shapes the scenes dramatically. Alain and I would always stick to the written music, because there was always something right in it. Luckily I'm accustomed to working that way, as David Shire always writes the melodies first. Working with Alain was remarkable because, while all writers are egotists to some extent, when we sat down to work there was no ego at all, nothing but a concern for how the work could be more truthful, more honorable, and more accurate. The collaboration was a definite two-way street, because I was being taught by people who had done a lot less than I had done. What Alain brought to the work was a sense of raw passion, which is something I need to be led to. I've made my career on witty, cerebral characters, people who hide their emotions behind verbal trickery. But it soon became clear that this show did not want any of my skills in writing witty lyrics. There are no cerebral characters in the story. Instead, the task was to bring some kind of richness to the simple language of ordinary, unschooled people.

Alain has an amazing ear for idiomatic English. He understands American idiomatic phrases that mean something else, and he understands the double-edged nature of American English. We Americans get by all the time on the assumption of what things mean. We don't necessarily say what we mean. It always astonished me that Alain would instantly understand all the nuances of a phrase like, "The heat is on in Saigon." We were working on the opening number and I brought in a page of about twenty different settings of the opening line of music. Somewhere down around twelve or thirteen was "The heat is on in Saigon," and Alain knew straight away that was the line that fitted the situation. The heat is on because it's a hot night and because of the girls, but also because the city's days are numbered and there was a time pressure to escape. Then, of course, there are the police detective connotations of the phrase. (See *Miss Saigon* photo insert 1.) I found it amazing for a non-native speaker to pick up all that. Strangely and humorously, Alain's ear for rhyme was less precise, perhaps because in French everything rhymes!

At some point in the writing there was going to be a concept album and a certain amount of time was spent on this. We were going to get pop singers to do various songs and we wrote pop versions of most of them. We had actually started to make the album and spent a lot of money on it when Cameron pulled the plug on it. He decided a pop album would somehow demean the show. By now he saw the show as an important, maybe even historic, theatrical event, and wanted to protect it. So the songs have never had a life outside the show. They are so closely woven into the fabric of the show that no one has been able to separate them from it.

Alain and Claude-Michel's idea of setting the *Madame Butterfly* story in Vietnam was a brilliant one for many reasons. It allowed us to develop the plot and in particular the character of Chris. He is no longer an unsympathetic Pinkerton who uses the girl, deserts her, and comes back to take her baby. In *Miss Saigon*, Chris could really be in love with Kim, because when the city fell, the country closed down completely. There was no possibility that Chris could come back to get Kim, and so he goes on with his life and remarries. And this leads to the one thing that I think makes the show so successful. It is that it's a tragedy without villains. It's a genuine love story, a powerful story of forces beyond the control of the individual. The story is driven by history. Everyone tries to do the right thing, and it leads to a devastating conclusion. At the end of the day, what pleases me most is that *Miss Saigon* is no longer simply an adaptation of *Madame Butterfly*; in fact there are very few correlates to the opera left in it. It is its own story. And Chris is now truly an American. He's not smart, he's not political, but he's good-hearted and he wants to do the right thing. In that sense he can be seen as a metaphor for America. His story becomes something much bigger, because on a human level his attempt to come in and save the girl leads to tragedy, and it's exactly the same story as America's involvement in Vietnam. It is an epic story but it's also an intimate play. In fact I think one reason why the story works is because it's a series of two and three character scenes. It is all extremely intense in terms of what's going on between them. And yet around them are these crowds of people on stage giving the story its wider canvas.

When we were writing the script it was difficult to imagine what all these people would be doing. But when Nick Hytner came in he gave it physical life all the time. In the Sixties, I was always off in a small hotel room writing the lyrics, while everybody else was in rehearsal having all the fun. I felt powerless. I would write something one way, and then it would go on stage and be different. Then I realized the director had not understood the song; he didn't make it happen and so it died. So I started to direct myself. However, although I'm a director, when I'm writing I don't get deeply involved with how the play will look. I like to think that being a director affects the way I write, but actually it doesn't. I'm very schizophrenic on this subject. When I start directing my own work, I look at the material as if I'd never seen it before. Early on, in writing *Miss Saigon* I'd often get sidetracked by trying to figure how a scenic transition would happen on stage. But Alain would say, "Don't worry about that. That's a director's problem." When he first said it, I was appalled. It seemed irresponsible not to address those problems in the script. But slowly I reversed myself. Alain was right! We *didn't* have to solve everything. We could write scenes as tightly as we wanted and leave the details to the director. In a short time I came to find this exhilarating, liberating. What a great concept! It's the director's problem. So I found myself happily writing, "The Marines enter the Embassy and barricade the doors, moving up floor to floor until they reach the roof where the helicopters land." How could this impossible action happen on stage? Not my problem! It's the director's problem. And when I saw how simply and brilliantly and cinematically Nick Hytner solved the problem with John Napier and Bob Avian, I was thrilled I hadn't wasted my time. (See *Miss Saigon* photo insert 8.)

From the beginning it was clear to us that we couldn't just tell the story. In order to make the characters live and breathe, for us as well as for the audience, we had to construct a backstory for each character. We had to work out what events in their lives had led them to this point and what had made them the people they are. Then we had to find the right places to put the back stories into the narrative so the audience could really understand these characters. We had to figure out how the audience could learn all this and not feel they've just been given chunks of exposition. How do you do this? There are moments when people are introspective, when they check back to their past in order to understand what's going on now. So with Chris we have, "I went back and re-upped/Sure, Saigon is corrupt/It felt better to be here driving for the Embassy"; with Kim, "Do you want one more tale of a Vietnam girl?" and the Engineer, "My father was a tattoo artist in Haiphong." These are all moments when the characters are trying to make sense of themselves and their lives, and they bring their past into the present.

The characters make the story, and Alain and I spent endless amounts of time talking about the characters and what sort of people they were, especially Chris. He was the center of our discussions because he was the character furthest away from Alain and Claude-Michel's sensibility. In their early draft he was the same callous American that Pinkerton was. In order to build up the backstory we started asking ourselves questions like, "Where was he from and why was he in Vietnam?" Well, we decided he was probably from the South, not well-educated, but not dumb; he was probably drafted, probably a redneck, yet his best friend was probably black, because in the war odd things happen. In the South a redneck would not talk to a black guy, but in the war they could well become buddies. He probably served in Vietnam and went home after the war. But veterans were not welcomed back. He had nothing going for him at home—no trade, no experience—so he re-upped. All the Americans in Vietnam in 1975 were there by choice. In the army he would have been well paid, better than in the United States. The work was relatively minimal; he probably drove a car for somebody in the Embassy, and he was in the pleasure pit of the world. So we worked out the facts of what it meant to be an American in Saigon at that time, in order to place Chris in context. He ceased to be a Pinkerton. While not intellectual, Chris gets what's happening in Vietnam. He understands that there's something wrong in still going out to the bars, with the drinking, the drugs, and the bargirls, when the city is about to fall. He doesn't want to do it anymore. In his non-intellectual way he understands the big issues. Basing Chris in reality allowed us to write the breakdown scene in Act II. I'm more proud of that than anything else, because in this scene Chris admits to all sorts of unspeakable things. It's not just the breakdown of a man who fell in love and couldn't help the girl. It reflects the nervous breakdown of America's involvement in Vietnam and it has big reverberations. Chris admits that he never really understood Kim or her country, and at the end fled back to the safety of a woman from his own world. Chris is the most interesting character to me and funnily enough he turned out to be the centerpiece of the casting of the show. When the show had a strong Chris, as it did when we opened in London with Simon Bowman, then it really works, but if it had a weak Chris then the story lost focus. (See *Miss Saigon* photo insert 6.)

Kim was a more straightforward character. We just talked about why she came to the city and what she was doing there. She wasn't an experienced bargirl, so she had to be someone who had just come to the club, and had probably just come to the city itself. Her family had probably been killed and she had no money. We talked about her mysticism and the sense of the gods coming in and protecting you. She tells her story to Chris at the moment he's leaving her. So the back story also serves a purpose dramatically because it brings Chris back to her. We provided a back story for the other characters as well: for Thuy, an arranged marriage and his going over to the side of the Viet Cong; for John, a sensitivity that would set up his involvement with the movement about orphaned Bui-Doi children. As each individual story was worked out the overall plot got tighter and tighter. The Engineer was a brilliant invention of Alain and Claude-Michel's and their vision of the character remained pretty much intact. The character exists in *Madame Butterfly* but in a very different form. We don't hear his back story until late in the show: "My mother sold her body, high on betel nuts/My job was bringing red-faced monsieurs to our huts." In the present we see a man whose life is in danger. He is now selling girls to Americans. As such, if the city falls he'll be branded a traitor. He has to make enough money to leave Vietnam fast. This desperation leads him to bring Kim into the club because he'll make more money with a new, virginal girl. Everything that happens is now part of a design. It all came together.

Ellen was a lot more difficult. Chris's wife is not a character the audience has an investment in. Ellen is a simple American girl. She is in over her head, but she wants to do the right thing and convinces herself that she can—until she *sees* Kim—young, beautiful, passionate, and exotic. In an instant Ellen sees everything. She sees that Chris lied to her about how much he loved Kim, and even worse, Ellen understands why. The emotional terror of a good-hearted American girl learning of her husband's love for an exotic woman she suddenly fears she can never compete with is part of the design of the plot. Ellen is so American, and we have to see that while she is willing to accept Chris's oriental child into her house, she is emotionally unable to extend that generosity to allow Kim even to come to America. She is terrified of having Kim around. She makes Chris choose between her and Kim, and in doing so personally sets the stage for the tragic ending. Ellen's song in the hotel room was the hardest song to write. We wrote three completely different songs for that spot, and changed the lyrics to each one many times. They were good songs, some of the best and most commercial in the show. But just being good songs wasn't enough. We figured the audience would only tolerate a song from this character if it were pure raw emotion. Claude-Michel wrote the final melody late in rehearsal. It was originally built round the choosing motif, "It's Her Or Me Now," and that's the one that got recorded. But we were not happy with it, me especially. The phrase seemed cold and selfish. Worse, its rhythm wasn't an exact match with the syncopation of the melody. I kept running phrases over in my head. The phrase "Now that I've seen her" kept recurring. It sat on the melody exactly—and it was emotionally the truest thought. So after the show opened we rewrote the lyric, to arrive at the one that is now in the show.

About six months into the run we reconceived the opening ten minutes. We hadn't directed the attention of the audience to the central characters clearly enough, and when *Saigon* opened in London the audience weren't engaged for the first ten or fifteen minutes. There's a sound an audience makes when it's engaged, it's a sort of rapt attention, and it didn't happen. You have to remember that when the curtain goes up all information on stage is neutral to an audience. The main characters, minor characters, scenery, mood, song—all that is of equal importance to an audience. It is up to the show to tell them who to look at and what to pay attention to. In some shows you use a follow spot, it says—look at this person over here. However, we didn't use follow spots and we had a lot going on in that opening scene with the bargirls and the soldiers to give it texture. The audience didn't know who was who. So when we made some revisions we specifically focused the audience's attention on Kim and Chris and John, through both words and staging, so that it became clear which characters matter. The changes were not subtle, but, do you know—instantly that sound changed—the audience was engaged. This was, for me, an important lesson in stagecraft. But working in theatre is a constant process of relearning the oldest and truest principles.

There is an overall theatrical rhythm that must be fulfilled when you're writing a musical. Generally it's a case of ballad followed by action, followed by dance movement; comedy at regular intervals; a flow from solos and duets to chorus numbers. Musicals have roots in vaudeville as well as opera, and the play of popular entertainment requires variety. There are inner rules, which can never be ignored, although they change and are reinvented with every show. With *Miss Saigon*, the structure was laid out very early on by Alain and Claude-Michel. It was their decision to delay the fall of the city to the second act, which is theatrically shrewd. If you do it in sequence you're into the *Gone With The Wind* problem. All the big action would be in the first forty-five minutes, and the second act would be all small events. However this means that there is a big leap of time in the first act. What an act of faith in the audience! We can go from "The Last Night Of The World" straight to the reunification scene. Three years have passed. Yet I've never talked to anybody who was confused. Audiences are just wonderful; collectively they are unbelievably smart. It's the wonder of the theatre how engaged they are and how you can count on their intelligence.

You can trust completely that the audience is listening. When the Engineer says, "Three years of school was nice," they make the leap right away. In this scene the Engineer jokes, "I speak Uncle Ho/And think Uncle Sam." The best way to insert exposition is through a joke. If the audience laughs they don't realize that they've been given information.

Alain and Claude-Michel's overall design of the show was brilliant. If you think of the plot in terms of diagrams, then you know the show is on course when these diagrams begin to shape themselves into a beautiful design. Part of the design is in the big themes. Alain and I talked endlessly about the idea of the American Dream, what it means, what it meant to Alain growing up in Tunisia. We talked about America's vision of freedom, America's constitution, the Bill of Rights, the Declaration of Independence. The myth of America is universal; it hovers over people of any education anywhere in the world. The American Dream was a fundamental theme of the show right from the start, but it gave us one lyric problem. "Le Rêve American" was the original French title for the song that became "The Movie In My Mind." The French title fitted this melody perfectly but "The American Dream" didn't. I wanted to keep the French title because, after all, Gigi—who sings it—is French. But Alain felt strongly that it absolutely had to be in English. The line, "The movie in my mind" was a line in the second half of the song in an early version I wrote to audition for the job. The American Dream is, after all, transmitted around the world by American movies. Cameron said, "That's the fresh thought," so we focused the song on that phrase. But now the actual phrase, "The American Dream" didn't appear anywhere in the script. The production number near the end of the show was originally quite different; it lacked a lyric and a concept, and we wanted to rewrite it—but we couldn't find a good title! Then one day Alain realized that *that* melody exactly fitted the words "The American Dream." It had just been sitting there. We'd missed it, and it's the perfect setting. We were thrilled, though I will admit that, as an American, I always felt *I* should have been the one to come up with the idea!

So The American Dream at last became the kind of central image in the lyrics of the show that we wanted it to be. Of course, it is also linked to the theme of identity, Chris's identity and America's identity itself.

It wasn't until we had sorted out a lot of issues that Alain and I could start working together on the lyrics. Lyric writing is about the technical use of language. You have to be very dogged because lyrics aren't so much written as they evolve. By changing a word or a phrase the line leads somewhere new. It's always a challenge, but for someone like me, a verbal game player, it can be fun. But it's also painful. It is interminable. I have a love/hate relationship with it. It can be so difficult and the payoff is so small. You can work so hard to get a precise phrase or fresh rhyme and if it really does work, it's so graceful and inevitable that nobody even notices it. They only notice when you get it wrong! *Miss Saigon* presented a challenge for me because I had never written for unschooled people before. The characters in *Miss Saigon* are not cerebral. Often to start with I would come up with cerebral language. I didn't think it was cerebral, I thought I was writing simply. But Alain would yell at me and drive me to go for the most naked, bold, raw emotion. Now, naked, bold, raw thoughts tend to have simple, obvious and often clichéd language, so it was very hard to keep the language simple, yet rich enough to hold interest. With these kinds of characters there can be very little verbal cleverness, therefore very little rhyme. To have an interesting sense of rhyme you have to have an interesting sense of language, therefore you have to be educated. Kim and Chris are not well-educated people but they are good people. They needed to have simple language and simple rhymes. What we had to avoid was crossing the dangerous line between simple and simple-minded. In *Miss Saigon* the only character who has clever rhymes is the Engineer because he is sharp and devious. I normally like puns, but in all of *Miss Saigon*, there is only one and it's from the Engineer: "My father was a tattoo artist in Haiphong/But his designs on mother didn't last too long."

Recitatives give more opportunity for rhyme, because they are factually specific, and facts often allow for unexpected language. For example, "Selling your mom is a wrench/Perfume can cover a stench/That's what I learned from the French." The facts of Kim's story provided images, such as the village burning, that enrich her language. But generally it was a battle of how to get language of any richness from characters who do not have any verbal skills. We didn't have too much of a problem with Kim because she also has a spiritual side to her—sun, moon, weather, a sense of atmosphere, texture, place, sense, smell. Chris was harder because we couldn't give him poetry. But he has a poetic soul, and I think we managed to express it in lines like, "Why does Saigon never sleep at night?/ Why does this girl smell of orange trees?/How can I feel good when nothing's right?/Why is she cool when there is no breeze?/Vietnam/You don't give answers do you friend?/Just questions that don't ever end." This language is rich and still consistent with a non-cerebral character because the vocabulary is coming out of very specific things, exotic things that someone like Chris has never encountered before.

When you start working on a new lyric you write down on a page all the things the audience needs to know, everything that has to be put across in the lyric. We ask what the moment is about, what is happening, what is the emotional center of the moment. It's these thoughts that come first, even before the song titles, and they usually coalesce around a thought or phrase that is a natural expression of the musical emotion. For the song titles we sometimes used a translation of Alain's thoughts, "You Are Sunlight And I Moon," but sometimes we found new phrases. For example Alain's French original lyric for "The American Dream" roughly translates, "I sell what they want and they buy what I sell," while "If You Want To Die In Bed" is a rather close approximation of Alain's French vernacular phrase, "If you want to make old bones."

Once the thought is in place I listen to a tape of the music and I set the rhythms and melody lines in my head. Sometimes I write a dummy lyric just to get something down so I can figure out what language rhythm is *in* the music. I count syllables. Imagine you had a thought that you needed to express, but you had exactly ten syllables, accented on the third and seventh, *and* you'd like to end on a last syllable that isn't another *o*, an *a* or an *e* rhyme. Occasionally you might spot a rhyme first. For instance, "re-upped" is the correct term used if you re-enlisted, and it rhymes with "corrupt," which is fresh to the ear and accurate for Saigon. An unusual rhyme like that usually comes very quickly. But sometimes I'll go through and say, "This line could end with 'page.' We haven't had an '-age' rhyme in a while and it opens the door to a lot of fresh, interesting possibilities—"stage, gage, cage, wage, engage." Then the rhyming thought has to be found.

In my other work, I use triple and quadruple rhymes. I like them because everybody expects the first line to have its matching second line. But the third takes you by surprise and the fourth can thrill you, but only if it's completely graceful and you don't feel the writer's effort. There are very few triple rhymes in *Miss Saigon*. In "The American Dream" we have "wrench, stench, French," and "banks, thanks, Yanks," among others. "The American Dream" is also a feast of "-air" rhymes, which we can only get away with because of the syncopated inner rhyme, "What's that I smell in the air?/The American dream." (See *Miss Saigon* photo insert 10.) "Air" rhymes with the "mer" sound in "American" and that gives you a little extra bounce that emphasizes the inner rhythm of the music. That inner rhyme really holds. It freed us to use endless "-air" rhymes: "Bel-air, pair, hair, Times Square, spare, there" and "Fred Astaire" and never get tired of them. Luckily there are lots of "-air" rhymes. I had at least another fifty of them that we didn't use. We had so many different versions that we kept juggling them around. But there was one elusive line, the last one in the song. We had, "There I will crown/Miss Chinatown." But I could not get the next line and neither could Alain. It had to be a topper thought, have seven syllables ending with an "oun" rhyme—and climax the song. I must have written two hundred lines for that spot, but they were all a little weak. As a climactic line, they'd all disappoint. Then the phrase "10 percent down" came to mind—a good American phrase for getting something cheaply in a capitalist society. "All yours for 10 percent down" is a perfect final thought and I was thrilled to find it. (See *Miss Saigon* photo insert 11.) It took weeks and weeks. But, being effortless, it goes by without anyone noticing it! That's the tragedy of lyric writing. You kill yourself for a phrase and if you find it, it simply seems as if you couldn't have said anything else.

It isn't difficult to determine which bits of the story become songs and which recitative. Emotional outbursts and private expressions of feeling become songs, and actions become recitative. Mostly, of course, a good song usually has an inner action too. None of the songs were easy to write. The ballads took a great deal of time, and were constantly picked over and altered. Working on the rhymes in lyrics, you are constantly trying to defeat expectations. You have to avoid predictability because you don't want the audience to guess what the second rhyme is going to be as soon as they hear the first one. We could seldom keep the rhyme scheme of the French lyrics. French rhymes are so fortuitous. Everything rhymes. If we used the same patterns in the English version it would be leaden and you'd just hear the same sounds over and over again. You'd be so bored. So we constantly broke up the French patterns. We also broke up the lines, sometimes splitting lines between characters to enrich the sense of dialogue being played.

With Claude-Michel the music and the narrative are inseparable because he is a brilliant and natural musical dramatist. It always amazed me how Alain and Claude-Michel would talk about a scene together and then Claude-Michel would go off and dramatize it musically. He wrote the music and the recitatives, the whole thing as a musical scene, shaped to the rhythms of the dialogue, but without dialogue. Then Alain and I would write scenes that would parallel or express the drama that was already in the music. It's absolutely true that we felt the right words for the song were inherent in the melody. The lyric is already in the music, you just have to dig it out. Yet to do this we sometimes had to go against Claude-Michel's expectations of what the words would do, in order to make the drama happen. We would sometimes put more dramatic action into four lines of music than he expected. Very occasionally we would go back and say, "We don't need this much time. We can get from here to there—do you really need these last eight bars?" Or conversely we might say, "We need four more lines to fit this thought in. In the design of this scene it would be wonderful if this extra thought happened as well." Claude-Michel would often find a way to put the lines in, or make the cut. But often he'd argue for leaving the music alone. In these cases, if we found we had more narrative to cover than the music he gave us, we worked to find a way to compress the thought. By compressing it to fit the music, the thought usually came out better. For example, there is a very short section that comes between Kim telling Chris how her family were killed, and the song "Sun and Moon." In this section there are very few notes of music, very few syllables, yet in that time Chris has to decide to stay, and ask Kim to live with him. In fact, he falls in love with her. I must say we worked on that section at great length because it seemed like we needed more time. We could have asked for more. But it also seemed like the right amount of music, the right emotional transition. Alain is deeply respectful of Claude-Michel. He exactly understands Claude-Michel's genius. So we decided it was up to us to do the transition elliptically in precisely the number of syllables we had, and I think it works better for it.

The difference in working with a French composer is that French is an uninflected language, so therefore any beat can be important. But in English only certain beats can be important. French music tends not to have accented beats in the middle of sentences. An American composer might write something that's more jagged. But it was essential to give the American GIs American rhythms. So we had to find phrases that were American-sounding in an uninflected sentence. For example, the music of the line, "The heat is on in Saigon," has no inflection but we used the inner rhyme of "on" and "Saigon" to emphasize those two beats, so you suddenly had an American syncopation within the uninflected line. There is a slight difference to the ear. We suddenly have an American rhythm superimposed on a French rhythm. The recitatives tended to have flattish, not very complex melodies so we also had to write against the predictability of the musical patterns. In that way the uninflected French forms became the opportunity for playfulness; we could play off our language against the flatness of the melody. We could add little inner and elegant beats, "The tension is high/Not to mention the smell." Such little word plays were jokes but also added a rhythm on top of a rhythm. It's the inner rhymes and the inner rhythms that add textual complexity and elevate a simple thought to a more sophisticated piece of writing. This we found we could do without making the characters cerebral.

A lyricist has to find words that are graceful on the music. You have to have an ear for how the words sit on the music. For example, the phrase, "The American Dream" has long sounds on the long notes, which makes it sing well, which wouldn't have happened if the phrase were "The Mexican Dream." Lyricists have to understand singing and how singers sing. Sometimes you are presented with odd, quirky musical choices. I love that because it can lead you to the fresh, quirky expression of language. And when you've finished you'd absolutely swear that the language came first and the music set it perfectly.

STEPHEN CLARK

Stephen Clark has written extensively for the theatre, and his work includes a wide range of both plays and musicals. He worked on the relaunched London version of *Martin Guerre*, which won an Olivier Award, before co-writing with Alain Boublil the completely new version, which opened at the West Yorkshire Playhouse in Leeds in November 1998. Stephen graduated from England's Dartington College of Arts in 1984, with a B.A. (Honors) in Theatre. In the final two years of the four-year course he specialised in writing for the theatre. On leaving, he began a successful career as a playwright, and his plays include: *A Twitch on the Thread, Rock, Takeaway,* and *Making Waves.*

Stephen's musical credits include the book for *Yusupov,* at the in-

vitation of Andrew Lloyd Webber at the Sydmonton Festival,
which was later retitled *Killing
Rasputin* at the Bridewell Theatre in the West End; book
and lyrics for *My Father's Son,
Sing to the Dawn, Watermark,
Cordelia, Forbidden City,* and,
most recently, the West End
production of *The Far Pavilions.*
Stephen also wrote the book for
The Challenge, a collaboration
with twenty-eight other writers, and the short film *Dance
to Your Daddy,* starring Helen
Lederer.

Stephen Clark

Stephen's most recent play,
Stripped, won a Jefferson Award
for Best New Play at the Circle Theatre in Chicago in 2003. He is
currently writing a musical theatre adaptation of *The Mahabharata*
with Nita Sahwney, and the lyrics for *Zorro* in collaboration with
Helen Edmundson and The Gipsy Kings. He also translated *La
Traviata* for the English National Opera in 2006, and has just been
commissioned to write *Love Story,* a new musical, in collaboration
with Howard Goodall. Stephen lives very happily in Brighton with
Debra Stych.

SC: My involvement in musical theatre had never initially been part
of the plan in my career as a playwright. But I played the guitar
from the age of eleven and started writing songs as a teenager,
which were mostly angry political songs or love songs. Then the
course at Dartington had been very much an experimental one that
led me to try my hand at many different kinds of writing, and one
of my plays, *Icarus,* had some songs in it. It wasn't a musical, but it
had songs in the way Brecht uses songs. It was put on in Baltimore

and it was recorded live. Then in 1991, when they were looking for people to take part in a six-month series of Masterclasses with Stephen Sondheim at Oxford University, the composer I had worked with sent off the tape, unbeknownst to me. The first I knew was a letter inviting me to join the Masterclasses in two weeks' time!

To be honest, I didn't know a lot about musicals so I had to rush out and buy a few videos. I didn't know Sondheim or Cameron Mackintosh, who was involved with the project, while everyone else was completely steeped in musicals. But Sondheim was a wonderful, wonderful teacher and I learned a lot. We had to write a show in teams so he could critique it and help us with it. I wrote a show called *Eyam*, about a small village in Derbyshire that got the plague, and Cameron invited us to showcase it at the Old Fire Station in Oxford. It was a time when everyone was suddenly realizing that the book was really important and Cameron was going around saying: "There are three important things about a musical: the book, the book, and the book." There had recently been a lot of serious flops, like *Mutiny on the Bounty*, *Children of Eden*, and *Leonardo*, and it was nearly always because you didn't care about the people. Everyone was realizing that it doesn't matter how great the choreography, the lighting, or the music; if you don't actually buy the characters and care what they're going through, the rest goes for nothing.

I was first asked to work on *Martin Guerre* about a month into its London run. Cameron, Alain and Claude-Michel had decided that some changes needed to be made, but Edward Hardy, who had been working intensively on the show for over a year, felt he couldn't take it any further and he suggested me as a replacement. I knew both Ed and Cameron from the Sondheim Masterclasses. Cameron called me and arranged a meeting with Alain, to suggest what changes could be made. He got me a ticket so I could see the show again and I sat up all night thinking it through before we met the following day. My ideas were pretty much in keeping with what they had in mind already and we started work very quickly. We went to a health farm in Quiberon, where Alain and Claude-Michel like to go when they need to really focus.

It was, in many ways, a fascinating time, but it was also very frustrating. We had an extremely committed cast at the Prince Edward, but there was only a limited amount we could do, even though in some ways it was quite drastic, because the show was taken off for a week to put in the big changes. We were putting in other changes over a three-week period and the cast were exhausted. It was also right in the middle of the highlights album being recorded. So I would be sitting in the control booth at the recording studio, rewriting a lyric, in appalling handwriting, and handing it to actors, who were then going down to sing the new lyric for the first time, although it was to a tune they obviously knew very well. It was crazy, and there is tremendous pressure in writing that fast. Alain and Cameron were standing over me, literally watching the words appear. Fortunately, I write very quickly and I think deadlines are a good thing, even if they are terrifyingly abrupt—like fifteen minutes! In that particular batch of rewrites Alain and I would talk about what we felt the new song needed to say, for example, "Working On The Land," which was the new opening, and then because of the need for speed, I tended to write the new lyric so that Alain could critique it and we could work on the changes together.

When it came off at the Prince Edward and Alain and Claude-Michel decided to rewrite the author's version, to bring it back to what they felt was their original vision, then it became a much closer collaboration. When Alain asked me if I would like to work with him again he had already written a version of Act 1. He was now writing from the start in English for the first time, and it made it a lot easier for me to see what he was trying to get at. Alain's English is remarkably good, but there are always going to be some things that will be more difficult for a non-native speaker. And also, because I'm a playwright by trade, my skills are mainly about things like character development and plot structure. I was really pleased to be starting from scratch. I could do a lot more research than for the London rewrite because there was more time. The director Conall Morrison encouraged the cast and everyone involved to do a lot of research, too: on medieval magic, the politics of the time, superstition and folklore, and so on. Conall was already on board before we started writing and I went to Dublin for a meeting with him about how he saw the piece. He liked all the sorcery and folklore that Alain and I had already been thinking about—the fact that when it rains it's not just rain but a sign from above. Cameron also was very anxious that it should capture more of the flavor of a peasant community that had a closer relationship with the planets and with nature, and the peasants themselves were more individually characterized too. So I think it helped the texture of the piece and the veracity of that period of time.

When Alain and I started writing it was a very concentrated process. I lived at his house for three weeks, and we worked from 9:30 a.m. to 9:30 p.m. every day—and then went out and grabbed a pizza. We worked chronologically, and it was very intense, but it meant we were lost in the piece and that's the way I prefer to work as the continuity makes it easier. Alain's version of Act I was a good starting point because it was very clear what he wanted. It's always more fun writing with someone else because if it's a good collaboration you've got someone to throw ideas around with and to respond to what you're writing. We completed a first draft of Act I so that Cameron and Conall could give us some feedback. Then I went to Tuscany, which was nice, and spent a few weeks there with Alain. I didn't see much of Tuscany though, as we spent the whole time writing Act II. We'd always sit in the same room together, working, reworking and developing the material. Alain is particularly good at critiquing and pushing it until it becomes what we want it to be.

In some ways it's quite a difficult process because Alain and Claude-Michel work by consensus. Both of them, Cameron and myself need to feel absolutely happy with it. Inevitably when there's a process of consensus it can become clumsier, and there are times when the three of us think something is terrific and the fourth one doesn't. So you end up writing something again that you were actually happy with in the first place, which isn't easy when you think you've already said it. But strangely enough, when you *have* done it and the four of you agree, you realize that they did have a point and it really has turned out better. But the same goes for the music, the design, the lighting, and the orchestrations—it requires everybody to be happy. That's a demanding way of working. But maybe that's why their shows, when they are right, work on so many levels.

One of the biggest problems with *Martin Guerre* has always been to get the Protestant and Catholic backdrop to tie in with the love story. What is fascinating about the piece is that Martin Guerre is whoever the village needs him to be at a given moment. So when they want Arnaud to be Martin Guerre, then he is Martin Guerre. When they discover he is a Protestant and no longer want him to be Martin Guerre, then they go for the fact that he isn't. When Martin comes back they need a Martin Guerre so they decide that he is. But the sense of a community defining the identity of an individual is what the piece should be about, and anything that intrudes on that actually forces apart the love story and the religious background. Originally they only operated in parallel, but now, hopefully, they collide a bit more. And there's more at stake for the protagonists in terms of what the machinations are, and of where the Catholics and Protestants are. But that's the hardest thing to try and get right.

It was never a problem to decide that Bertrande knew from the start that Arnaud is not Martin. But that is one of the things that people complained about most, because it's not like the film, and they think that the suspense is the only interesting thing. But obviously nobody knows for sure in the original true story to what extent she knew and to what extent she connived, so the story can be told in lots of different ways. Alain, Claude-Michel, Cameron, and I all believe that Bertrande is a far more interesting character if she does know that he is not Martin; otherwise, especially in a theatrical context, she would seem rather stupid and it would weaken her character fatally. But to have her make this extraordinary choice and then to see how they sustain the myth that he is Martin—that's far more interesting dramatically.

The story in *Martin Guerre* is very much driven by the characters and the conflict between them. And because very little is actually known about any of the historical characters it gave us a lot of freedom to take the story our own way. But we had to invent things which felt true. The key thing is to work out what is at stake for each character. If you keep aware of that they begin to respond to you and you get to know them. Sometimes when the writing is going well the characters seem to take over. They develop a kind of autonomy and the writing becomes like reading. Then the characters might surprise you with a joke or an action that you didn't expect. It's really the words that define the characters. You build up a life for each of them, what their trade is and what kind of metaphor they'd be likely to use. It's a privilege to be writing in English because it's such a rich language with a mixture of Anglo-Saxon and Latin-based words so that you can choose which language to write in within the language. For a peasant you will draw more on Anglo-Saxon–based words and without anyone consciously realizing why, the character will have a more down to earth, prosaic quality. But if you use more Latin-based words then the character will seem more sophisticated.

The actors help to flesh out a character and they invent a lot of details for themselves which enable them to play a role with conviction. So what is already written feels truer because of the work they do. Conall was a defining energy for the production. His passion about small warring communities is huge, which is largely why Cameron thought he would be the right director. His background and the part of the world he comes from give him a deeply felt understanding of personal and political reactions in troubled times, which he expresses wonderfully articulately in that kind of big, bearlike gush of energy that he gives the group. That was a huge contribution to developing what was there.

Getting characters that you really care about is essential. One of the problems with the London show was that Arnaud didn't come on stage until quite a way into the show. His first appearance was a brilliant piece of staging and it built up the mystery of the man but I don't think it was finally helping us get into the character. To see Arnaud and Martin together on stage right at the beginning, with their lives in danger and sharing confidences, is a much better way of getting into both characters. For the Leeds version and the British tour, "Live With Somebody You Love" was the opening song and it was reprised at the end giving a bookend effect. From a writing point of view it's very satisfying to bookend a show and it's done a lot. (See *Martin Guerre* photo inserts 2 and 12.) When we were working on the American tour we lost that effect and it was a shame, but we made a much greater gain dramatically, by opening the show with "Without You as a Friend," and moving "Live with Somebody You Love" to the point later on where it really fits in with Arnaud trying to persuade Martin to return to Bertrande. It was Cameron's suggestion and it made so much sense to swap the position of these two songs that it's hard to see how we had missed it. And now the opening song really introduces the themes of friendship and trust and we start to take a real interest in both the characters straightaway.

The first ten minutes of a musical are the hardest to write and the beginning is always the most rewritten part. A lot of your storytelling happens in Act I, whereas in Act II it's the consequences of what you have already set up in Act I. You've got some momentum, you've done all your exposition, so it's then about following things through and tying up loose ends. The hardest thing about exposition is to get all the information across without the audience having any sense of being told. Chekhov is the master of that, and it certainly helps if you can put things across through action rather than dialogue, as when Martin proves his friendship for Arnaud by risking his life for him.

The main themes in the musical are about friendship and trust, honesty and personal identity. It focuses on the conflict between the individual striving to be who they are versus the community attempting to define who that individual is. I think it's the same for all of us, that clash of perceptions. The central philosophy is simply about living with someone you love. The idea of impossible love is one of the things that Alain and Claude-Michel are especially interested in. It's the first thing they look for in a story and it's their starting point. It's in all their shows, people who love each other but their love can never come to fruition; it's cheated. There is something about the tragic form that is irresistibly appealing, and tragic flaws are something we can all recognize and identify with.

The new version probably worked better for being in a smaller theatre space and with simpler sets. *Martin Guerre* is not a cinematic piece like *Les Misérables* or *Miss Saigon*; it's an intimate psychological drama in many ways. There were many times at the Prince Edward when I watched the rehearsal of a new or adapted lyric and it would be so moving in the rehearsal room, and then I'd see it that night in that huge barn of a theatre and somehow it never got past the footlights. Whereas in the West Yorkshire Playhouse you could sit anywhere in the auditorium and still feel connected to the show. And then John Napier gave us a phenomenally simple set so we weren't distracted by the intrigue of technology. It was a joy to work with because it served to tell the story. You have to be classy and brave to be that simple. But it had always been Alain and Claude-Michel's original vision to have a much smaller show and not one that would compete with the kind of thing they'd done in *Les Misérables* and *Miss Saigon*.

The music is also closer to their original vision as there is a much smaller orchestra. Because the music comes before the lyrics, Claude-Michel actually composes the emotional structure of the show and we write in response to it. We work from tapes on which Claude-Michel plays the piano and sings quite emotionally, and sometimes the song never gets as good as it is with him just "de-de-da-ing" along to the music. When he used to de-da along with "Live With Somebody You Love," he'd give it that old French wobble and it was just great. But from that you really know what the emotional sensation of the song needs to be when it finally reaches the audience's ears, and the lyric you then write is so informed by the dramatic needs of the music. In a dramatic sequence,

like the drought or the deluge, Claude-Michel will record it, playing the piano and de-da-ing the tune, and then he'll also say who
he thinks should be singing each bit—Madame de Rols, this bit;
Guillaume, that bit; and so on. So the music will then characterize
each person.

There aren't many composers that understand dramatic structure as well as Claude-Michel does. And that is why their musicals
are sometimes referred to as musical operas. A lot of musical theatre composers can write terrific tunes but they don't always fully
understand the need of a dramatic impetus or momentum. Claude-
Michel is as much a book-writer as a composer, and that's rare, but
it means that the music always has a dramatic reason, rather than
just being a great tune. The fact that they are also great tunes is
wonderful, but you are getting both, and I think that's what makes
his work so special. Sometimes the mood and the emotions created
by the music are stronger than the words, and then lyrically you've
just got to stay out of the way and not spoil it. Claude-Michel writes
so much from the heart and it's so instinctive that he won't even
learn to read music properly because he's frightened of all that
getting in the way. His relationship with music is just himself and
the piano. He writes in such an emotional manner that the music
inevitably sets the agenda for the show.

Another thing which makes Claude-Michel's work very special
is the way he uses reprises both on an overt and a subliminal level.
He will set up a melody in a particular moment to have a particular
emotional effect so that maybe half an hour later you only need
a tiny moment of that melody to trigger the learned response to
the first time that melody was stated. It's not a short cut but it's a
very direct route into reawakening the emotional state that was,
hopefully, awakened in the first place. But reprises can also be used
ironically, for a different set of emotions, and that often makes the
reprise all the more poignant. For example, when Martin visits Arnaud in jail, his previous lines: "Where would I be/Without you as a
friend," are reprised poignantly as: "I'll live my life/Without you as
a friend." If Act II was written without any reprises it would halve

the emotional impact and you'd lose that resonance. Sometimes a reprise will include the same or similar lyrics, perhaps with a twist, or it can be just a reprise of the music but with different lyrics. Or it might be in a different key or at half the speed, for example, "Don't" is a much slower musical reprise of "Martin Guerre." A good reprise often works as much on a subliminal level where you have little hints of a tune like, "How Many Tears," at other moments. You may not be consciously aware of it but it's very clever and it does subliminally give the score cohesion.

The orchestrations also make a huge difference in dramatizing the piece. Bill Brohn likes to sit in rehearsals and really see what the director is doing, and the questions that the actors are asking, and the discussions that are going on, and get fed by all that. Some of the time he had a table in the rehearsal room and was orchestrating a number as it was actually being rehearsed, so that his orchestrations became infused with the ideas that were in the rehearsal room—rather than doing it in abstract and second guessing what it might be.

Claude-Michel's score does pose some extra challenges for an English writer, because the rhythms he writes the music in do lend themselves to the French language. He has French rhythms in his head, and you get a lot of lines with feminine endings and fading syllables, so sometimes you just have to be extra inventive about it in order to find a solution. And also, Claude-Michel doesn't believe in pickup notes, so that the accent is on the first beat, for example, "WORKing ON the LAND." Whereas with English lyrics there is often a pick-up note, as in, "We're OFF to SEE the WIZard," where the stress is on the second syllable. But he would never have something like, "We're WORKing ON the LAND," as for him that would lack impact. So that sort of thing is a constant issue and just requires a lot of extra thinking to make it sound like decent English. Sometimes I'll even write a dummy lyric like, "I need a pint now/And some crisps too," just to get the shape of the line and the rhythm of the words into my head before I work out what the line really needs to say.

It's also important to make sure that the words sit well on the music, and that can be difficult sometimes. For example with "If You Still Love Me," which was originally "Here Comes The Morning," the notes are so drawn out that, although it's a great tune, it's hard to find words that will last that long. And they must also add up at the end of the sentence to a big enough idea to deserve the hugeness of the melody. It's also about the stresses of the words fitting exactly on the stresses of the music so the actor doesn't have to cheat a weak syllable, and about there not being ugly consonant clashes or "s" sounds together, which blur. And the vowel sounds, especially on top notes, must be good strong vowel sounds for the singer.

With sung-through musicals the book has to develop in tandem with the music. Any use of dialogue suddenly becomes huge, because to suddenly speak when you've only heard singing for twenty minutes has a major impact, and what is said becomes very important. So in the new version of *Martin Guerre* that intimate moment during the washing, when Arnaud wonders if they should tell the village the truth and Bertrande says, "No, they would kill us." That is spoken instead of sung, and so it really stands out. (See *Martin Guerre* photo insert 7.)

Writing a sung-through musical is a completely different challenge to writing a musical with dialogue and songs. I don't think one is innately better than the other, but there's a definite trend now toward the sung-through musical. But it's a case of horses for courses, and I think there are some subjects that lend themselves to it. If you have an epic subject like *Martin Guerre* or *Les Misérables*, which can deal with the life of the characters in a consistently heightened way, then a sung-through musical allows you to do that and you're in that hugely emotionally charged world all the time. But if the story is more prosaic or humorous, then it's not going to work. There are some things that are best said, and as Sondheim says, "You can't sing about putting out the garbage."

In musicals with dialogue there is certainly more freedom and it's probably easier to write than recitative. Recitative is there to provide information and to move the story along. There's less focus on it than on the songs and it doesn't have to be a lovely poetic line. In fact if you write a gorgeous line in recitative it will sound out of place. It's always harder to write the big songs because you know they are going to be judged as big songs. "The Day Has Come," which in America became "Alone," was the most difficult song, and we must have written about fifteen sets of lyrics for it. It was partly because we kept changing our minds what it should be about, and we were always worried that it would be too much like "One Day More" from *Les Misérables*. But it wasn't easy to get it right as a love song, that was a private declaration of love yet stated in public, and it had to be a fitting climax to end Act I.

In *Martin Guerre* there tends to be less rhyme in the recitative than the songs, and rhyme helps to mark out the songs as songs. I think that rhyme is primarily about catching or exciting the ear and drawing attention to a particular thought. If you really want to make an idea land in the audience's mind, then you put it in the line that rhymes, because there is something so satisfying and resolved about it that it will stay in the mind longer than the unrhymed lines. In the title song, the line "Martin Guerre is my name," is a key thought and it rhymes with "They all look for someone to blame." (See *Martin Guerre* photo insert 5.) If there was no rhyme there there'd be no resolution, the idea wouldn't land, and you'd be filled with an unsatisfied feeling. Sometimes you might write the end of a song first if it's a key line and then work backward. On the other hand, sometimes, if you're using a lot of rhyme, you might deliberately not rhyme a key thought, and then the impact is in the non-rhyme.

Rhyme, or even the repetition of a word, binds a lyric together. It's like an egg white, and I think that's especially true of internal rhymes. When Alain wrote, "How many tears through the years can I cry/How many prayers to the Lord must I try," I thought the internal binding of the rhyme was gorgeous. In the song "Don't" we used repetition: "Each step we take/Takes us too far"; "We'd start to lose/Lose who we are"; and internal rhymes: "Never let me come near you/Or I fear you will regret"; "That I let myself hold you/When I told you all I feel." The "hold you/told you" echoes the "near you/fear you," as the "lose/lose" echoes the "take/takes," and they hold the whole thing together. (See *Martin Guerre* photo insert 8.) There's something very intimate about a lyric with internal rhymes, as they bind the characters as well as the lyric. When the characters come together in duet form, they're overlapping slightly and it increases the sense of their intimacy. Because the lyric is binding itself so closely it helps to bind them together as well.

When you're writing music first you are, fortunately, forced out of defaulting to an *abcb* rhyme scheme because the music doesn't ask for that, and Claude-Michel, especially, never writes in straight quatrains. He just doesn't do it, partly because he's musically more interesting than that and partly because he's writing in French rhythms. The music often dictates where the rhymes will be. For example, "Don't let it start/Know in your heart;" those two melodic phrases are so similar they're just asking to be rhymed. But there are endless times when you've got a really good line and you can't keep it because it needs to be a rhyme and it simply won't rhyme with anything that adds to the sense. At all costs you have to avoid writing rhyme-led lyrics, where you're not actually quite saying what you wanted to say, but you're saying something because it rhymes well. You have to be careful not to over-rhyme because otherwise it can become too much like a nursery rhyme. You have to retain a sense of unpredictability. Likewise you have to avoid reusing the same rhymes. If you find a really unusual rhyme then you can't use it twice anyway, but more ordinary rhymes tend to come up again. Certainly in *Martin Guerre* the "name, blame, shame, same" rhymes crop up a fair bit, rather more than I'd like, but then it *is* a show about a name.

Sometimes we've chosen to rhyme lines and then later unrhymed them because we realized it sounded a bit too trite. Because of the period it's set in you have a limited vocabulary, as there is an extraordinary wide world of contemporary reference that is immediately ruled out. Also, you can't get too tricksy in a historical show or the characters sound too smart and it just sounds like the writer's words, not the characters' words. These are uneducated characters with plain language and sometimes you just have to write very simply because that's how these characters talk.

Writing for musical theatre is intensely challenging and people are becoming more and more demanding of the form. But I love writing and I can't imagine doing anything else. From the moment I left college and started work on my first play I've loved it and I always enjoy writing to the edge rather than staying safe. I like the intensely private solitude of the writing process that results in such a social, collaborative, crazy period of time when everyone else arrives. I need both sorts of moments and there are very few jobs where you can get sustained periods of both. Working on *Martin Guerre* was a great experience. When we had achieved the final version the audiences were clearly moved, they were laughing and responding and there were those proper silences, which show a real communal focus and let you know that the piece is working as theatre should. It was something I felt very proud to be involved with. ✿

CHAPTER 4

From Page to Stage

THE DIRECTORS

ONE OF THE MOST IMPORTANT MEMBERS of the collaborative team is the director, for he has the task of bringing alive the words on the page to a full visual and dramatic staging. Cameron Mackintosh's experience and skill in producing musicals has always instinctively led him to propose the most appropriate directors, although the final choice is always a joint decision reached after much discussion with and the approval of Alain and Claude-Michel.

As with the co-lyricists each show has had different requirements for a director. In the case of *Les Misérables* the work was not only that of direction but also of adaptation—too big a job for one person. Peter Farago, the young Hungarian director who had brought the French recording of *Les Misérables* to Cameron's attention, had wanted to direct it, but Mackintosh felt that Farago didn't have the experience for such a huge project. Trevor Nunn had already shown his flair for directing a musical with Mackintosh's production of *Cats*, and Trevor, together with John Caird, had gained considerable storytelling experience in adapting and directing a lengthy classic novel with many characters and subplots through their work on *Nicholas Nickleby*. Although Trevor had been inundated with other offers, he and John took on the work, while insisting that it would be done under the banner of the Royal

Shakespeare Company. This meant that the show would be produced first at the Barbican Theatre so that it could be developed using the artistic resources and extended rehearsal period of the RSC.

When Cameron was putting together the creative team for *Miss Saigon* it was initially assumed by Alain and Claude-Michel and by Trevor himself that he would be offered the job of directing it. However, a producer is often faced with making difficult choices and Cameron instinctively felt that Trevor was not the perfect director for *Miss Saigon*. Although he had done such a remarkable job with *Les Misérables* in directing and adapting from a classic novel, *Miss Saigon* was a contemporary piece, an original creation and also much more complete than *Les Misérables* had been when they'd started on it. There was some concern that Trevor might impose too strong a personal imprint on the show that would not fit the vision of its creators. Trevor had also believed he could direct both *Miss Saigon* and *Aspects of Love* in the same year, an undertaking which Mackintosh felt was too much for any one person, even someone with Nunn's extraordinary commitment and energy.

Another major factor was that Mackintosh had intended to premiere *Miss Saigon* in New York and therefore felt that an American director would be more appropriate; he eventually decided on Jerry Zaks. However, when the time came there were no large theatres available in New York, whereas in London the Theatre Royal Drury Lane became available when *42nd Street* closed. This was the theatre Cameron wanted most in all the world for the show. Jerry Zaks was unable to spend the required amount of time in London, and so Cameron finally decided on the British director Nicholas Hytner. Nick came on board months after the rest of the creative team had been assembled, a team which included the American co-lyricist Richard Maltby, the American choreographer Bob Avian and the British designer John Napier. Although it is unusual for a creative team to be assembled without the consultation of the director, Nick readily accepted the team and immediately set to work. John Napier had already done some work on the sets with Jerry Zaks but their work was ditched in favor of Nick's more poetic, diaphanous and impressionistic vision of the show, although the helicopter remained as an essential element. However, the uncertainty and misunderstandings with Trevor over the choice of director, which Cameron admits full responsibility for, lasted for months and resulted in a falling out between the two men that continued for many years.

During the writing of *Martin Guerre* there had been a period when Alain and Claude-Michel were facing some problems and they received much encouragement and moral support from Nick Hytner. When it came to choosing a director for the show, Nick felt he was not the right person to direct it, and he recommended Declan Donnellan as "the only really serious director in the world who could do peasants." Declan did indeed have much experience in directing Irish, Spanish, Norwegian and English peasants from his work with his innovative *Cheek by Jowl* touring company, which he had formed together with his partner the designer Nick Ormerod. As they always work together Cameron was saved the trouble of finding a designer. Before long the choreographer Bob Avian (*A Chorus Line*) took on the task of finding the relevant language of dance for the production, while Declan began his work of recreating the tensions in a divided village community and bringing to life a spectacular production.

When it was decided to do a completely new version of *Martin Guerre*, Cameron, Alain, and Claude-Michel flew to Dublin to visit the Abbey Theatre where Conall Morrison was an Associate Director. There they saw the award-winning *Tarry Flynn*, which Conall had adapted and directed. It was a very physical, free-wheeling portrait of rural Irish life and convinced them that Conall was the right director to bring their new version to life, together with his regular colleague the choreographer David Bolger.

Producing a musical is an extraordinarily complicated process because it is so dependent on a collaborative team. Therefore the right choice of collaborators and especially of director is crucial to its success. A producer must have the single focus of who is best for each show regardless of personal feelings or loyalties. Having the right director for each particular show is imperative as the director is the pivotal cornerstone around which the rest of the creative team functions. A good director can, on occasion, also help the writing team to write better. Once on board the director has absolute authority; so it is essential that he respects and shares the ultimate vision that Alain and Claude-Michel have for the finished piece.

TREVOR NUNN

Trevor Nunn is a multi-award-winning director of international renown. He has had an illustrious career as a director of musicals, opera, television, film and every kind of drama on stage and

 his list of credits is phenomenal. He was appointed a CBE (Commander of the British Empire) in 1978 and knighted in the 2002 Queen's Birthday Honors List. It was during his time as Artistic Director of the Royal Shakespeare Company that, together with John Caird, he directed and adapted *Les Misérables* in London and on Broadway, where it won eight Tony Awards.

He was born in 1940 in Ipswich, England and he was just five years old when he decided

Trevor Nunn he wanted to become an actor,

much to the surprise and amusement of his parents. There was no family background of theatre or acting and he had never seen a live performance. He came from an area where few children even considered the possibility of higher education or a professional career. At the age of thirteen he won his first role when a local company needed a child actor. However, when he was sixteen his plans for acting as a career were quickly revised when he realized there was such a job as directing. He had been given the job of directing the school revue, initially because he had the loudest voice! And the rest, as they say, is history.

After winning a scholarship to attend Downing College at Cambridge University, Trevor took an English degree. While there he became a member of the prestigious Marlowe Society, the Amateur Dramatic Club, and the Footlights Club and was also President of the University Actors. In 1962 he won a Director's Scholarship to the Belgrade Theatre, Coventry, where as resident director his productions included *The Caucasian Chalk Circle*, *Peer Gynt*, and a musical version of *Around the World in Eighty Days*. After two years his old Cambridge acquaintance Peter Hall came and saw one of his performances. Peter asked him to join him at the RSC. They worked together for four years and Nunn was made an Associate Director in 1965. In 1968 he became the company's youngest ever Artistic Director. He was responsible for running the RSC until he retired from his post in 1986. His productions included *The Revenger's Tragedy*, *The Relapse*, *The Alchemist*, *Henry V*, *The Taming of the Shrew*, *King Lear*, *Much Ado About Nothing*, *The Winter's Tale*, *Henry VIII*, *Hamlet*, *Macbeth*, *Antony and Cleopatra*, *Coriolanus*, *Julius Caesar*, *Titus Andronicus*, *Romeo and Juliet*, *The Comedy of Errors*, *As You Like It*, *All's Well That Ends Well*, *Once in a Lifetime*, *The Three Sisters*, *Juno and the Paycock*, *Othello*, *The Blue Angel*, and *Measure for Measure*. In 1979 he made theatrical history with an eight-and-a-half-hour stage adaptation of Charles Dickens' *The Life and Adventures of Nicholas Nickleby*, which he co-directed with John Caird and which won five Tony Awards. He also co-directed J. M. Barrie's *Peter Pan* with John Caird. He created The Other Place in Stratford-upon-Avon and the Donmar Warehouse in London. In 1982 he opened the RSC's new London home, The Barbican Theatre, with his production of Shakespeare's *Henry IV, Parts I and II*. 1986 saw the opening of the Swan Theatre in Stratford-upon-Avon, which he conceived and for which he directed one of the first productions, *The Fair Maid of the West*.

Working with Andrew Lloyd Webber, Trevor has directed the musicals *Cats*, for which he wrote the lyrics for "Memory," *Starlight Express, Aspects of Love, Sunset Boulevard*, and *The Woman in White*. He also directed the Tim Rice, Bjorn Ulvaeus, Benny Andersson musical *Chess*. Other work includes *The Baker's Wife, Timon of Athens, Heartbreak House, Skellig, The Lady from the Sea, Hamlet, Acorn Antiques*, and *Richard II*.

Trevor was the Director of London's National Theatre from 1997 to 2003. While there his production of *Oklahoma!* won Evening Standard and Olivier Awards for Best Musical Production. With the National Theatre Ensemble, he has won an Olivier Award for Best Director for *Troilus and Cressida, Summerfolk* and *The Merchant of Venice*, and a Critics' Circle Award and Evening Standard Award for *The Merchant of Venice* and *Summerfolk; Summerfolk* also won the South Bank Show Award for Theatre. His other productions at the National are *Arcadia, An Enemy of the People, Mutabilitie, Not About Nightingales, Betrayal, Albert Speer, The Cherry Orchard, My Fair Lady, The Relapse, South Pacific, The Coast of Utopia, A Streetcar Named Desire, Anything Goes*, and *Love's Labour's Lost*.

At Glyndebourne he has directed the operas *Idomeneo, Porgy and Bess, Così Fan Tutte* and *Peter Grimes*. At the Royal Opera House he has directed *Porgy and Bess, Katya Kabanova* and *Sophie's Choice*. Many of his most famous stage productions have been restaged for television: *Cats, Les Misérables*, and Emmy Award winners *Nicholas Nickleby, Oklahoma!* and *Porgy and Bess*. His other television work includes *Antony and Cleopatra*, (BAFTA Award),

The Comedy of Errors, Macbeth, The Three Sisters, Word of Mouth, Othello and *The Merchant of Venice*. He has directed three films, *Hedda, Lady Jane* and *Twelfth Night*.

TN: I remember very clearly my first impressions of *Les Misérables*. Cameron Mackintosh had given me a tape of the original French version and I first listened to it on a car journey with John Napier. The tape almost began with a song called "La Misère" and I thought it was the most extraordinary melody. There were other similar sounding melodies and a glorious "to the barricades"–sounding song that was very brief and underworked and I wondered quite why something with that potential hadn't been developed more. Then there was a lot of very staccato music, some of which has been retained in the show, but en masse I thought it was slightly alienating. But by the end of the car journey, having listened to this tape, I thought that these people had found an idiom for this piece of work. It sounded contemporary and yet it sounded entirely believably something of a previous century. It sounded classical and yet there were obvious connections for a contemporary audience.

However, I have to confess that 95 percent of the lyrics were completely closed to me because the people were singing in French very fast. After a number of brief talks with Cameron I asked to see the French text. It was only then that I came to realize that what I had been listening to hadn't dealt with the complete narrative of *Les Misérables*. It was described as a "nine tableaux epic" and although it included major incidents from the novel there was a lot that had been left out and certainly the conclusion was undealt with. It finished on the barricade, and that's where Javert's suicide was fitted in. Later on Alain and Claude-Michel told me that in Paris there was absolutely no need to tell the whole story of *Les Misérables* because everybody in France knew it so well; they were brought up with it and it would have been insulting to tell it all. But here that is not the case. Everybody knows the title but not necessarily what lies behind it and therefore we would have to tell the story in very great detail. I then asked for a literal translation and frequently put on the tape and listened to the first few songs. These included "I Dreamed a Dream" and "La Misère," which was to give us considerable problems later on. But by this time it was clear that I was hooked on the potential of the piece.

I made it clear to Cameron that it was something I was very keen to develop and I told him that I could only be involved if it was an RSC project, with John Caird as my co-director. We had worked together on the RSC production of *Nicholas Nickleby* and I knew that I would be using all of the techniques, rehearsal methods, staging devices and so on that we had devised for *Nickleby* in order to develop *Les Misérables* and make a fully-staged narrative work out of it. So I sensed that it would be inappropriate and almost a form of stealing if it was not done under the RSC banner and with the presence of my co-director, and Cameron agreed.

John Caird and I then started seriously reading the Hugo novel and listing and charting all the things that we felt were absolutely vital to be included. Then we began thinking how some original musical material could be pressed into service and how it might be restructured. All the time we were working with Alain and Claude-Michel about what story we were going to tell and how best to tell that story. John and I had an enormous creative involvement, I think to an unprecedented degree, with the possible exception of *Nickleby*. The eventual version was the production and the production was the version. How you tell the story was not only a writing job but a conceptual job and a staging job and they were all linked together. It's very thrilling to be involved in that kind of work.

James Fenton was brought on board early in the process and we had some very good initial conversations with him. James is a great poet, he's an extraordinary voice, and it was wonderful to be around him for his political insight. He also has a lot of political experience because he was a journalist. He'd worked in Japan and Korea where there were protests and he'd witnessed extreme danger and violence and the kind of amplified warnings to give up arms that we were able to incorporate in the barricade scene. But when it came down to lyric detail James wrote poems and, sadly, they just would not "sing." We tried and tried to adapt phrases and get vowels in better places and consonants in unexposed places and so on but it just didn't happen. So we urged that James should collaborate with the lyricist Herbie Kretzmer. We had a brilliant first meeting together and Herbie was very happy at the thought of collaborating with James. So we tried to do that but it was impossible for James to relinquish things that he'd written or to trust in somebody from a different discipline.

Herbie then took on the task alone and he was able to render Alain's ideas and concepts into an English that perfectly found the idiom. So the show, and the possibility of the show, was utterly transformed. Alain, Claude-Michel, John, and I worked together to achieve a number of connections in terms of incident, in terms of where things happened, who uttered what and when, but detailed lyric solution was Herbie's achievement. It was all the more remarkable because there was a relatively short space of time yet he found the idiom almost immediately and then it was torrential; it was very, very extraordinary. That's not to say that nothing was ever challenged; we sent lots of things back and sometimes required him to find different solutions. But even so we made amazing progress with all of us working together. It was during that time that so many of the structural things really paid off with musical and lyric ideas in a truly organic process.

There had been, however, a certain point when I felt that there were so many suggestions around, so many ways to go, that I needed to cut the "Gordian knot," because it was ultimately my task to say "This is the story we must tell." So I wrote a detailed synopsis, part one and part two, which thereafter Alain and Claude-Michel referred to as "the bible." When we talked about adaptational change Alain and Claude-Michel were very generous spirited, very open and very willing to take the piece another stage further. They were very willing to listen and very "unprickly." They were much more interested in how John and I thought it should go, so there was never a "hands-off" opposition to be overcome. I think things changed for Alain when the synopsis was completed, so although he often referred to it jokingly he was also serious and most of the contents of the synopsis were eventually carried out in full.

One of my proposals was that Valjean needed to sing something that was the fulcrum song for his character at the barricade. I didn't think that it was possible to have the leading figure of the work at the barricade and yet not utter a word. That song became "Bring Him Home," which was the most wonderful commissioned song one could ever imagine! (See *Les Misérables* photo insert 7.) And quite clearly the song, both musically and lyrically, took the whole piece to another level, another emotional level, an operatic level and a new level of character complexity.

I also felt that Fantine had too many utterances early on, especially as Fantine was going to depart the show and Eponine didn't really have a major musical opportunity. She was part of other people's material but there wasn't a great Eponine song. I was very keen that Eponine should emerge as a potent character and I felt that the triangle that Claude-Michel had emphasized between Marius, Cosette, and Eponine was something that needed to figure with great prominence and that we, the audience, really did need to understand the extent of Eponine's sacrifice. Eventually we identified "La Misère" as the melody that we should use for Eponine's situation, her sacrifice.

It was also clear that we wanted to keep a connection of sacrifice between Eponine and Fantine, and so Claude-Michel suggested that the scene at Fantine's bedside should be built around the first statement of the melody we know as "On My Own." This has a very emotional impact, but it's a narrative impact not an aria impact and therefore I always think it's theatrically powerful that when Eponine begins her song, the image of Fantine comes into our minds. With Eponine you have the suffering of unrequited or unrequitable love and the sacrifice she's prepared to make for it, which then connects to Fantine's story. So when Fantine and Eponine emerge at the end and they sing "Come With Me," the connection is complete and we understand that they have both sacrificed and we understand that in so many ways the work is about human love being stronger than all other influences on our behavior.

However, setting lyrics for Eponine to the melody of "La Misère" posed enormous problems. Herbie had several goes at the song and couldn't make it work. He even went to Claude-Michel and asked him to rewrite the tune. That was an occasion when Claude-Michel did go somewhat berserk and discovered he could swear in English! He absolutely refused to rewrite the music as it was *the* first thing he had written in the score and it was *the* central theme of his communication of Hugo and, so not one jot of music on the manuscript paper was going to be changed. So there was an impasse. Frances Ruffelle was patiently waiting for a lyric to sing. She knew she'd got a wonderful tune to sing but she didn't know what the words were going to be. So I thought I'd better do something about it. It had happened to me once before in *Cats* when I wrote the words of the song "Memory" in rather similar circumstances, and so I had a go at this song. Then John, Herbie and I were sitting outside a café, somewhere near Soho Square, and I read my proposed lyric to them. Herbie changed one line "The trees are full of starlight" because it was more prosaic in my version and John adapted a line in the last verse about "pretending" and so on until we finally agreed that we had arrived at the lyric that should go forward. Alain and Claude-Michel accepted it and it went into the show and I'm bound to say that I think it works very well. What we were all fascinated by in the character of Eponine was this notion of her living in her imagination. Hugo shows us that she lived in a dream world only to wake up to the squalor around her. So it was picking up on that idea that she lived only at night and that she would wander through the streets of Paris, when it would become a completely different place. The fantasy about Marius is very strong in the book so the idea of a love affair conducted in your imagination and which has nothing to do with reality is very fitting.

One thing that we had to keep reminding ourselves was that Javert is not a villain, because otherwise the argument of the work becomes much more simplistic and much less satisfying. The point is that Javert is a religious obsessive, he's a fundamentalist. His passionate belief in God having created all things instructs him to also believe that those people God has created criminals will always be criminals and cannot be redeemed and therefore he represents "God on Earth" in terms of punishing and even removing those elements from the rest of healthy society. So that when he confronts the idea that somebody, who he insists is bestial and criminal, behaves as a redeeming angel, he can't cope with it. He can't cope with it because his life has been devoted to something he could no longer believe in. That's fascinating, because the point is Javert is not entirely wrong. Valjean is, indeed, exceptional because of the effect of his meeting with the Bishop of Digne. Valjean's acts of goodness in saving Fantine, in finding and bringing up Cosette and in saving Marius stem from this meeting and, therefore, Hugo insists that an individual act of good is capable of reversing what the fates appear to have planned for the innate criminal. Dickens and Hugo are very similar in that respect. Hugo was much more politically active than Dickens but even so both of them believed that if everybody could find it in themselves at some moment in their lives to be good in a self-sacrificial way the world would be transformed into something closer to the utopia we dream of.

Political idealism and religious zeal are both very important thematically in *Les Misérables* but Hugo seems to be saying that it is possible still to believe in God and still to believe in the future through the operation of human love. The last line, before the final chorus, is "To love another person is to see the face of God" and when that line came from Herbie we knew that we'd got absolutely to the center of the work and had said something that Hugo would be moved by and acknowledge the truth of. But the final chorus goes beyond that perception because, as I have always explained to the performing company, all those who have sacrificed, all the dead re-emerging and joining the living are actually asking a direct question of the audience: "Is this not what you want? Don't you want a better world or a world to be made new?" The chorus line ends with the phrase "Tomorrow comes" and it's partly a repeat of the larger phrase "When tomorrow comes." But that very final repeat "Tomorrow comes" is not just a repetition of two words for emphasis; it is an affirmation of the question that Hugo asks at the beginning of the book: "We may be tempted to ask: Will the future ever arrive?" The show finally declaring "Tomorrow comes" is the most felicitous bit of writing in summarizing Hugo's theme, both in terms of the lyric vocabulary of the show and its meaning for an audience. And I like to think that an audience stands up at the end of *Les Misérables*, as they so invariably do, not only in the traditional way of expressing their admiration of the performers but also to bear witness to this message. That may be pure sentiment on my part but I have felt that surge so potently on many occasions to the point where I do believe a yearning and an idealism is aroused which, at least for a while, displaces our pervading cynicism.

The themes of *Les Misérables* are revealed by the musical structure as well as the lyrics. We were always aware of the parallels and contrasts, as I have explained, between Fantine and Eponine, and, relatively late in the writing process, Claude-Michel had the wonderful idea of using the same music for Javert's crisis as he had used to climax the Prologue of Valjean's story with the soliloquy. When a composer works through the possibilities of leitmotif and of melody attached to a particular character or a particular theme it is very exciting because you're working in what is essentially an operatic way. You're not working in the traditional style of musical theatre that collects numbers together; you're working in a more integrated way where music has a thematic significance. I always felt, from that very first encounter with the tape recording, that the melody "La Misère" was *the* triumphant melody of the show and it needed to become central to the show.

In the same way that the work on the adaptation was influenced by our production of *Nickleby*, that was also my starting point as a director. It was essentially the same kind of creative work with an ensemble, and even though we didn't have a collective narrator, as we did in *Nickleby*, and there was no proposal that we should, nevertheless it was quite clear to me that there had to be a sense that the work was being created by a company, quite tangibly and recognizably a company, who would play many changing roles because they were providing the audience with this piece of story theatre. So the Prologue section was very important in that respect, where the audience sees change after change and the performers recycling themselves into different characters to make deft, swift story theatre strokes. In the sequence at the factory those who are outside the gates then change to become those inside the gates, and on the quayside all the men recycle themselves into a host of different customers as the girls play prostitutes. It was very important that the ensemble was the presenter of all that and therefore the rehearsal method of achieving it was to begin with improvisational work. It was a thrilling time.

We took sections of the novel, as we had done in *Nickleby*, and we challenged groups of the company to improvise a specific page, having built up to it with a lot of exercises, company building work, sensitivity work, and the work of becoming more able to pass the narrative responsibility from one to the other. We did days of that kind of approach work and, indeed, it is hard to keep everybody "together" during such early days because some people are cynical about that sort of work, just as some people are inspired by it. There were a number of the company whose background was in musical theatre, who were genuinely inspired and charged with delight and imagination, and there were some old theatre hands whose concealed response was: "Oh God, do we really have to go back to drama school!" But eventually, of course, the process was unifying because the actors started to create dramatic incidents that were extraordinary and they realized they could be created in no other way. A director has to devise a program of work that's got a shape to it and an end in mind, which helps the actors to go on connecting both with the material and with each other. Then at a later moment in rehearsal you can have another "improvisational" day either to find again what has been lost, or to discover new things. We repeatedly went back and created things quite plastically, as opposed to rigorously, through improvisational methods.

When we did finally start to stage the production, the design of the set was fantastically important.

I've worked with John Napier since 1974. When we started talking about *Les Misérables*, I told him that he needed to design a chase, a way of encapsulating the idea that one man, a fugitive, is on the run from another man throughout the entire work. Therefore I didn't want scenes designed as ends in themselves, but instead we should be looking for something continuous. Of course I started to gesture as I was talking and moving my hands round in a circle and John said "Oh you mean a revolve." We talked about a Berliner Ensemble production of *Coriolanus* that I'd seen many years before where they didn't just use a revolve simply for the mechanics of scene changing, they used it much more inventively, with the revolving stage going in different directions to create effects of travelling. So a revolve became statutory. I told John that the only thing that had to be there physically was a barricade. It's a story theatre evening and I wanted him to give us space that was unmistakeably French, and nineteenth century. Hugo's point is that a barricade is made out of poor people's lives, it's made out of their possessions, their homes, anything they can lay their hands on because ultimately that is all they have and if they die in the process then everything they possess goes with them. John fretted about it for weeks. He devised this wonderful chamber surround with cobbles becoming brickwork and a number of very high little windows. He and I went to Paris with John Caird for a weekend and we went to the Victor Hugo museum and the Victor Hugo house and we strolled around looking at historic places. Then one morning at breakfast when we were talking about something completely different John suddenly shouted "I've got it! I know how to do the barricade." He started to talk about two towers, demonstrating them with the salt and pepper on the table, how they would fold back on themselves as they came in to the center of the stage, requiring a simple hydraulic device. But the idea meant the towers could be hugely high and that they could have been present before to be used as the poverty stricken homes of the slum dwellers of Paris. Therefore, when those self same things come in to form the barricade, the point (Hugo's point) is that it is made out of people's lives. I've always resented that John was criticized for doing another spectacular design dominated show. The show is unusual in the sense that most of its effects employ a bare stage with minimal scenery, like a gate which turns and you're on the other side, or places with just scraps of furniture. The one huge object that John invented is the barricade, which is the single and unchangeable requirement of the piece. To say that the design was spectacle seemed to me to be perverse and dishonest because, in truth, it was a very pure design solution.

When we did *Nickleby* it was a two-evening show. There was never any danger of *Les Misérables* becoming that but there was a danger of it becoming unmanageably long. We had a very problematic period of getting the material cut down to size. Cameron always wanted it to be much shorter and, conversely, I always argued that length is not a finite calculation. Something can be three and three-quarter hours long and everyone will agree they hadn't realized that the time had passed in a flash, and equally something can be two hours long and the audience is desperate to get out after an hour. I've never believed the American formula that no hit musical can be longer than two hours. The point is that Rodgers and Hammerstein didn't believe it; they had very long shows and so did Lerner and Lowe. You can't do *My Fair Lady* in under three hours ten minutes whatever you do; that's the time that masterpiece takes. That's what the writers wanted it to take and you betray the material if you don't do that. But I think when we opened *Les Misérables* at the Barbican for our first preview, we were running three hours thirty minutes and that was too long for its own good. On the other hand I was determined that we should not throw out the baby with the bathwater. So finding the material to cut involved some rewriting and it was tough going but I think eventually we made the right decisions. A lot of the changes we had to make were to do with the Javert plot, and Roger Allam was very long-suffering and generous. He understood the problems and was willing to contribute ideas to find the solutions. But it made a big difference to his story because we had included quite a lot of Javert chasing Valjean to Paris and through Paris. By the time we reached our first night the running time was just under three hours fifteen minutes but it had been tough to achieve that.

But music theatre is a tough discipline. It is really more difficult and more complex to achieve good work in this genre than, say, a straight play. There is so much marshalling of the different departments: musical composition, lyric writing, book writing, choreography, stage movement, scenic and costume requirement, all of which on a new show are constantly changing and constantly developing. So getting all that to cohere is exhilarating but it is phenomenally complex. There is undoubtedly in some minds a false distinction between serious and popular theatre, the legitimate and the illegitimate. I've never seen such a dividing line, I believe the theatre experience is all one fabric and I speak as one who has been involved with all kinds of theatre right from the beginning of my career. I think that Shakespeare wrote the first stage musical—the middle section of *The Winter's Tale*, his pastoral sequence. There's a complete musical structure to the sequence with alternating song and dialogue; he knew that there is something joyous and unifying about harnessing music to language. There was never a dividing line in the eighteenth century or the nineteenth or for much of the twentieth century. There was no problem with Noël Coward writing a serious play like *The Vortex* and then writing music and lyrics for a West End show. No one thought he was betraying his gift; they thought it was proof positive of his wonderful versatility. It seems to have been in the later part of the twentieth century that the critical fraternity got hold of the idea that musical theatre was way beneath them. So what we are dealing with here is intellectual snobbery, which still survives in some quarters. But that snobbery isn't current with audiences. If you stand at the back during a performance of something like *Oklahoma!* or *My Fair Lady* you'll see people present from every social group and background—people who may have come "sniffily" and people who may never have been to a theatre before all stand up together at the end. There's a shared joy and therefore something unifying. And I do believe that *Les Misérables* and *Miss Saigon*, and many shows inspired by *Les Misérables,* have changed the perception of musical theatre and its possibilities.

JOHN CAIRD

John Caird is a well-respected freelance director and writer working in theatre, opera, musical theatre and television. His work on the direction and adaptation of *Les Misérables* with Trevor Nunn has played a significant and continuing role in his life. He was responsible for the transfer of the show into its new London home at the Queens Theatre and the re-opening of the show on Broadway. Prior to working on *Les Misérables,* he and Trevor Nunn directed the highly acclaimed eight and a half hour long RSC production of *Nicholas Nickleby* at the Aldwych in 1980. Their work with an ensemble company on this production was invaluable when it came to tackling *Les Misérables.* Both of these productions have won numerous awards around the world.

John is an honorary Associate Director of the Royal Shake-

Photo by Catherine Ashmore

John Caird

speare Company, where he has directed more than twenty plays including classic works by Shakespeare, Ben Jonson, Shaw, Gorky, Farquhar, Strindberg and Brecht, and new plays by Peter Flannery, Pam Gems, Jonathan Gems, John Berger and Nella Bielski, Richard Nelson, David Edgar, Mary O'Malley, and Charles Wood.

Recent work includes *Macbeth* at the Almeida Theatre and *Hamlet* at the National Theatre, both with Simon Russell Beale, while previous productions at the National include Bulwer-Lytton's *Money,* John's own new versions of Bernstein's *Candide* and Barrie's *Peter Pan, Trelawny of the "Wells," The Seagull* with Judi Dench, Pam Gem's *Stanley* with Anthony Sher and *Humble Boy* by Charlotte Jones with Diana Rigg and Simon Russell Beale. Further recent stage work includes productions of *A Midsummer Night's Dream* and *Twelfth Night,* both for the Royal Dramatic Theatre in Stockholm, Michael Weller's new play *What the Night is For* at the Comedy Theatre with Gillian Anderson and Roger Allam, and *Becket* with Jasper Britton and Dougray Scott at the Theatre Royal, Haymarket.

John's other work includes Andrew Lloyd Webber's *Song and Dance* at the Palace Theatre, Mozart's *Zaide* at the Battignano Opera Festival in Tuscany and the *Siegfried and Roy Spectacular* in Las Vegas and, most recently, Verdi's *Don Carlos* for the Welsh national opera, and *The Beggar's Opera* in Tokyo. His television work includes *Nicholas Nickleby, As You Like It,* his own adaptation of Shakespeare's *Henry IV* plays for the BBC and his Japanese TV version of *The Beggar's Opera.*

John's work as a book writer, adapter and lyricist has also been highly acclaimed and includes the following: a new version of John Gay's *Beggar's Opera* with the composer Ilona Sekacz first performed at the RSC, a new adaptation of J. M. Barrie's *Peter Pan* with Trevor Nunn, *Children of Eden* with composer Stephen Schwartz, and Bernstein's *Candide* with new lyrics by Richard Wilbur and Stephen Sondheim. Caird, together with composer Paul Gordon, also wrote the acclaimed Broadway musical *Jane Eyre,* which won several Tony nominations.

JC: The original French version of *Les Misérables* from the Palais des Sports in Paris was the sort of musical for those who already knew the story. Trevor Nunn and I had to make it into a dramatically cohesive piece of work. It was our avowed intent to adapt the whole novel or at least to include as much of it as we possibly could and to leave nothing out without careful consideration. We had to risk that we were doing something that was of a different scale, a different ambition from what musical theatre was normally trying to accomplish. And there was always a tension between the ambition being the thing that people would approve of when they went to see it and making the thing just too unmanageable to be a commercially viable proposition. Musicals tend to become trivialized by what they touch because of the way they are put together and because of what people expect of them. But keeping faith with the seriousness of the work was made easier because we had already done it with *Nicholas Nickleby* and we knew it could work. We knew we could create something that was both serious and popular.

We had to examine the story as it came to us and try to express a great deal more of it. We worked very closely with Alain and Claude-Michel, and at first with James Fenton and later in great detail with Herbie Kretzmer. A great deal of work was done in consultation with James about the restructuring of the piece. It originally started at the factory gates and we had some difficulty in persuading Claude-Michel that you could start the musical with something other than "At The End Of The Day," the "magic notes" as they were known. That seemed to Claude-Michel to be the only possible way of opening the work because it was how he had first imagined it. But to us it seemed unsatisfactory because it took away the main meat of the story, which is Valjean's progress. In fact we even discussed starting it at the point where Valjean breaks the window and steals the loaf of bread. However, because the first fifteen minutes of the show are a sort of Prologue, the feeling that you're finally beginning the show proper at the factory is still evident.

What Trevor and I felt we had to do more than anything else was to pull the lyrical and melodic structure of the show more into the voices of individual characters. The whole show was too loaded emotionally toward Fantine. She had the two major ballads of the evening back to back: "J'Avais Rêvé D'Une Autre Vie" and "La Misère." And we felt it crucial that Eponine had a song. You can't have a character that central and that heartbreaking without giving her a major song. Quite late on we proposed that we should use the "La Misère" melody for Eponine instead of Fantine. Claude-

Patti LuPone, Barbican Theatre, London, October 8, 1985.

FANTINE: "I dreamed a dream in time gone by/When hope was high/And life worth living."

Ensemble, Palace Theatre, London, 1989.

WOMEN: "Lovely Ladies/Waiting for a bite/Waiting for the customers/Who only come at night."

Barry James, Ensemble, Palace Theatre, London, 1988.

THÉNARDIER: "Everybody raise a glass." MME THÉNARDIER: "Raise it up the master's arse." ALL: "Everybody raise a glass ter the master of the house."

Ensemble, Broadway Theatre, New York, March 12, 1987.

ALL: "Tomorrow we'll discover/What our God in Heaven
has in store/One more dawn/One more day/One day more!"

Michael Ball, Frances Ruffelle, David Burt, Barbican Theatre,
London, October 8, 1985.

EPONINE: "Just hold me now, and let it be/Shelter me,
comfort me."

Ensemble, Palace Theatre, London, December 4, 1985.

FEUILLY: "Drink with me to days gone by/Sing with me the songs we knew."

Colm Wilkinson, Michael Ball, Barbican Theatre, London, October 8, 1985.

VALJEAN: "If I die, let me die/Let him live, bring him home."

Colm Wilkinson, Broadway Theatre, New York, March 12, 1987.

VALJEAN: "I am reaching, but I fall/And the night is closing in/And I stare into the void—To the whirlpool of my sin/I'll escape now from the world/From the world of Jean Valjean/Jean Valjean is nothing now/Another story must begin!"

Roger Allam, Barbican Theatre, London, October 8, 1985.

JAVERT: "I am reaching, but I fall/And the stars are black and cold/As I stare into the void/Of a world that cannot hold/I'll escape now from the world/From the world of Jean Valjean/There is nowhere I can turn/There is no way to go on...."

David Bryant, Broadway Theatre, New York, March 12, 1987.

MARIUS: "Phantom faces at the window/Phantom shadows on the floor/Empty chairs at empty tables/Where my friends will be no more."

Judy Kuhn, Colm Wilkinson, Randy Graff, Broadway Theatre, New York, March 23, 1987.

VALJEAN: "On this page/I write my last confession/Read it well/When I, at last, am sleeping."

Frances Ruffelle, Colm Wilkinson, Randy Graff, David Bryant, Judy Kuhn, Broadway Theatre, New York, March 12, 1987.

VALJEAN, FANTINE, EPONINE: "To love another person/Is to see the face of God."

Ensemble, Theatre Royal Drury Lane, London, September 20, 1989.

ALL: "The heat is on in Saigon/The girls are hotter 'n hell."

Lea Salonga, Simon Bowman, Theatre Royal Drury Lane, London,
September 20, 1989.

KIM: "My name is Kim/I like you Chris."

Simon Bowman, Lea Salonga, Theatre Royal Drury Lane, London, September 20, 1989.

KIM: "You are sunlight and I, moon/Joined by the gods of fortune."

Lea Salonga, Simon Bowman, Theatre Royal Drury Lane, London, September 20, 1989.

GIRLS: "Dju vui vay vju doi may/Dju vui vay vao nyay moy."

Lea Salonga, Simon Bowman, Theatre Royal Drury Lane, London, September 20, 1989.

CHRIS: "What a party that was!"/ KIM: "You're going to leave me now."

Lea Salonga, Simon Bowman, Theatre Royal Drury Lane, London, September 20, 1989.

CHRIS: "It's telling me/To hold you tight/And dance/Like it's the last night/Of the world."

Lea Salonga, Barry K. Bernal, Broadway Theatre, New York, April 11, 1991.

THUY: "I'm here! I'm here! I'm never dead!/I'm here! I am the guilt inside your head!"

Ensemble, Simon Bowman, Theatre Royal Drury Lane, London, September 20, 1989.

CHRIS: "Let me go, John, I can't leave her/Why in the world should I be saved/Instead of her?"

Miss Saigon 8

Claire Moore, Lea Salonga, Theatre Royal Drury Lane, London, September 20, 1989.

KIM: "Then you must take Tam with you."

Jonathan Pryce, Broadway Theatre, New York, April 11, 1991.

ENGINEER: "What's that I smell in the air?/The American Dream."

Jonathan Pryce, Broadway Theatre, New York, April 11, 1991.

ENGINEER: "There I will crown/Miss Chinatown/All yours for ten percent down."

Peter Polycarpou, Claire Moore, Simon Bowman, Lea Salonga, Jonathan Pryce,
Theatre Royal Drury Lane, London, September 20, 1989.

KIM: "How in one night have we come...so far."

Michel said that he could imagine "La Misère" moving to someone else but he could never imagine "J'Avais Rêvé D'Une Autre Vie" not being Fantine's song. So that became a definite thing.

One of the great difficulties in terms of the musical personality of the show was how to keep the musical centrality of "La Misère" with a complete change of lyrics and giving it to somebody who wasn't intended to have it. Of course we couldn't keep it as central in the meaning of the show as it had been in the French because you can't translate the words "La Misère" into a singable English phrase. So finding a place and a raison d'etre for the song's existence was very hard but it eventually became "On My Own." Herbie had had considerable problems with the lyrics. He had been slaving away for weeks and had taken us through all the things it could be about and couldn't be about and Alain had worked on it a great deal. But in the end Trevor and I wrote it out on paper napkins one night at dinner in Joe Allen's because we knew we had to rehearse it with Frances Ruffelle the next day or she would kill us! She had been wonderful about it but it was only three days before we went into technical rehearsals.

When we first heard the French version of the show it was not only Eponine who didn't have a song. Javert didn't have a song, Marius had no song, and Valjean had "Who Am I?" but no song on the barricade. You can't have a principal character in a musical if they don't have a song. They must have the moment where they fully express themselves and you can learn about their raison d'etre. We felt that Thénardier needed that sort of song too. "Master Of The House" is comic and witty but not a very profound way of proposing a character and the Thénardier at the Inn is a very different person from the one that ends the piece, the man who is haunting the sewers.

It was important to the meaning of the piece that Valjean, Javert and Thénardier should have songs that were at the heart of Victor Hugo's philosophy and theology. The philosophical heart of Les Misérables is centered in these three characters. Valjean's story is fundamentally a New Testament Christian tale. It's a story about redemption through suffering. And the God who is represented by the Bishop of Digne is a forgiving God who will understand your suffering and reward you for it in the end. That's at the center of the whole story, and indeed that's what redeems Valjean at the last minute; that's what makes him capable of grace at the end. In competition with that, Javert believes in an avenging God, an Old Testament God with Old Testament language. The avenging God, who strikes you down if you deviate from the social or judicial law, is at war throughout the play with the Valjean God, the forgiving God, and it's the forgiving God who wins. The point at which Javert understands that he's wrong, that it doesn't work that way and that Valjean doesn't respond to type, he can't bear it and takes his own life. But that's only two sides of the triangle. The other side is the Thénardier God. The Thénardier God is dead. The Thénardier God is a God who used to be beneficent but has now proved to be incompetent because the world seems to him quite godless.

In order to represent the world of *Les Misérables* properly you've got to have those three beliefs adequately enshrined. So there are three great songs that represent those beliefs: "Bring Him Home," which is the song about redemption and hope and glory and the possibility of a forgiving God making things right where they had gone wrong in a life and in a moment of crisis; "Stars," which is a statement about order and chaos and a righteous and angry God taking retribution on those who disobey his law; and "Dog Eat Dog," which is a cynical song about how it's actually every man for himself and there isn't such a thing as God and if you look up to the heavens all you see is the moon smiling down on you as if approving your violent and disgraceful behavior. These three songs have no dramatic function whatsoever. You don't need Javert to sing "Stars," you don't need Valjean to sing "Bring Him Home" and you don't need Thénardier to sing "Dog Eat Dog." You could cut all three songs and the story would be completely comprehensible in purely dramatic terms. What you need the songs for is to deepen the emotional experience and understanding of these three characters and to appreciate their positions more clearly. It was a way of trying to represent more faithfully and in greater detail all of the richness of the original novel.

However, there were certain things that we had to get rid of because they overcomplicated the story. We couldn't have Mabeuf, Monsieur Gillenormand, Marius' father and all those other fascinating characters. We toyed for a long time with being explicit about the fact that Gavroche is Eponine's brother, but it doesn't help. There are some things that are useful connections and there are some things that on the stage in a three-hour play seem like ludicrous coincidences and you just don't need to know them. We talked for a long time about dramatizing the early days of Fantine and putting in her lover and student friends, to better understand what's happened to her. But in the end it would have made the show hopelessly long and somehow in the song "I Dreamed a Dream" you get the sense of what has happened to her. It's all about compression. Somehow in the performance you've got to get the audience to a heightened form of concentration in order to get them to appreciate every second. Les Misérables is actually a very simple story, not like a Dickens story, which has got incredible detail and hundreds of different interrelating characters. There are only nine central characters in Les Misérables and very few peripheral characters so there's not a great deal of complexity to deal with in that respect. But it's philosophically complex. That's the difficult thing.

There was a long process of structural negotiation that Trevor and I went through with Alain and Claude-Michel while working in great detail with Herbie about the precise nature of the English adaptation. This went on right up to and even during rehearsals with rewriting the whole structure of the second half, especially the barricade sequence, so that it made cohesive sense, trying to get the dramatic incidents of the barricade in the right order so that they had some degree of narrative and dramatic tension. We gave some scenes Brechtian headlines, putting a date and place up on a screen so that the changes in time and location were clear. There was a great deal of re-working and sculpting that was done partly in rehearsals and partly through discussions with Alain and Claude-Michel. In the end Trevor scripted out a document from those discussions that was like a screenplay, a scenario. From that we could start putting in all the existing bits of music and suggesting other places where we would have to have extra music or a repeated verse in order to get more information in.

As we were rehearsing we were also changing things on the hoof. For instance, in the ABC Café scene it was originally only Enjolras, Grantaire, and Marius that you heard from and nobody else said anything. So we spread many of Grantaire's and especially Enjoras' words among the other students as a way of involving everybody in the piece more. Their solo bits gave their characters more of a chance of life. The carousel scene was Herbie's idea, as Trevor and I were concerned that the women didn't have enough to do. I proposed that the best possible music for a scene about the women of Paris would be the "Lovely Ladies" music, done in a different way, because it's an interesting inversion. You start with the downcast women of a provincial town who have been forced into prostitution and you use the same music and the same concept of an endlessly revolving world with a carousel you can't get off, only this time you apply it to war and revolution rather than prostitution. But actually it's the same carousel and the same women. It was to have been sung by all the women together but again we decided to split it up with a line or two each, like a Greek chorus, making the words mean more by giving them to individual personalities.

At one point we tried to make the whole piece more socialist, radical and political, moving away from Hugo's peculiar brand of French Catholic theology. But in the end we felt we were knocking the stuffing out of the work emotionally if we completely turned our backs on the religion in it. It's actually crucial to an understanding of the work. *Les Misérables* is ultimately a piece about sacrifice. Fantine sacrifices herself for Cosette, Eponine sacrifices herself for Marius, Valjean sacrifices himself for Fantine and Cosette and finally for Marius, Enjolras and the students sacrifice themselves for what they believe in and Javert is sacrificed on the altar of his own vanity and self-deception. It does give the work a marvelous moral spine—that all those characters are related to each other in that way. But there's also a great deal of Romanticism about it, whether it's Eponine preferring to die in the arms of the man she loves rather than go on living without him, or the political Romanticism of students, thinking that it's more important to die on the barricade than to go on living in a world of injustice that they can't abide.

Hugo's vision of life is much bleaker than the modern view that you can overcome all your problems if you want to enough. In those days you only had one shot at life, but Hugo shows how even somebody whose life is destroyed by his experience can achieve some sort of grace. It's not by introspection or trying to improve yourself; it's by trying to help other people. If there's an ultimate message in *Les Misérables* it's that, "To love another person is to see the face of God." (See *Les Misérables* photo insert 12.) To love somebody else and to help them in the most difficult and extreme circumstances is a very unmodern message in a world that seems to be telling us, "To love yourself is to see the face of God." There's something utterly solipsistic about life today. As the great Whitney Houston song has it: "Learning to love yourself is the greatest love of all." Some young women, when auditioning for the role of Fantine or Eponine, sing that song because it's one of their favorites and I think to myself "How can you come to an audition for *Les Misérables* and sing a song about how self-love is the greatest love." What Hugo makes his reader feel is that they can change things. He's a very enabling writer in that sense and I think that one can attribute the huge popularity of *Les Misérables* to the same reaction from the theatre audience. They leave the theatre feeling that they've seen something that has made them feel more positive about the more difficult things in their lives.

The imagery in the novel is very powerful and it was from this that Alain drew the imagery of the original lyrics and indeed the whole lyrical structure. But the way in which the major themes and their reprises are worked out was part of the structural negotiation that we then had to go through. For instance, by structuring the piece anew so that the Prologue existed, Claude-Michel was able to propose that Javert's suicide would be a wonderful way of setting up the character of Valjean. So the music for the soliloquy, where Valjean tears up his ticket of leave, is musically identical to that for Javert's suicide, but in a different key. So the two moments of moral crisis for the two main characters are connected. The audience may not notice it at the time, unless they're musically very sophisticated, but it's there at a subliminal level and, of course some of the lines are nearly the same too. (See *Les Misérables* photo inserts 8 and 9.) And there are other fascinating connections—for instance, between the Bishop of Digne and the Café song: "Come in sir for you are weary," is the Café song. And there's a connection again with Valjean and Fantine: "I've seen your face before" in Act I has the same music as: "M'sieur, I bless your name" at the end of Act II. When Marius, Cosette and Eponine sing "A Heart Full of Love" the music for that is reprised near the end with a different trio, Marius, Cosette, and Valjean. It's the same music exactly, note for note, but a whole tone higher. In the first instance a couple are celebrating their happiness and a jealous outsider is regretting the pain it is causing her and in the second case it is exactly the same only this time the outsider is Valjean.

Some changes have taken place over time, for instance, it was as late as Washington, D.C. that we put in a reprise of "Who Am I?" I felt very strongly that we simply weren't telling the story of the last weeks of Valjean's life adequately. We'd done it pretty well everywhere else in the show but how do you explain how, having rescued Marius, he then cuts himself off in that little room all on his own? We'd left it out in the London version and it seemed inexplicable really. A reprise of "Who Am I?" was the perfect solution because at the point when he least wants to consider his past he is forced to consider it. Within ten minutes of the end of the evening we are reminded graphically of the whole story and it floods the audience with the importance of his whole journey. Listening to Valjean describing the moral difficulties in his journey and the moral difficulties that still haunt him makes you understand why he would cut himself off, that he's still a man flawed by his own beginnings, that he still needs to be redeemed and forgiven.

We all felt that Gavroche's song "Little People" would have to go. Now it's been condensed into just a verse and a half as a way of him having a go at Javert. But at one time it was a stand up number on the barricade. There was a point just before we opened at the Barbican when it seemed like the only song in the evening that people would really enjoy! It was a wonderful number and you'd think "This has just got to bring the house down." But we had always underestimated how passionately the audience would become attached to the story and they couldn't suspend their interest while a kid entertained them with a daft song about being little. The audience just wouldn't sit still for it and in the end we had to cut it. I had long wanted to put in the scene with little Cosette at the well, when she first meets Valjean, which was a logistical nightmare because of the position of the revolve, but we finally managed to do it for the tenth anniversary in New York.

When you make changes they seem significant at the time but within a few months everybody thinks it was always like that. The most important thing is to imbue in everybody that change is possible, that no show is ever perfectible. That's the joy of live theatre, that it isn't ever going to be the same twice over and it's incumbent on everybody to play on its organic and mutable nature. I think that from the beginning the actual creative process was helped enormously by there being, on the one hand, the artistic safety of working with the RSC and on the other hand commercial expectations and financial responsibility. Working within the RSC meant that you could be more daring and more experimental but we also worked within our normal Barbican budget of £150,000 ($285,000). Cameron put in the same amount, so there was a very good even-handed dialogue where both sides needed the other. It worked in both artistic and commercial terms and the legacy of that has never disappeared.

In a show as big as this you need a co-director. One person just can't do it all. You need a co-director to bounce ideas off with the literary and adaptation work as well as with the direction. We made several decisions about how it wasn't going to be the same as *Nickleby*. We wouldn't use a choral style of narration. We would tell the story more conventionally through the characters. But the way it was most influenced by *Nickleby* was in the use of large forces on the stage, a large ensemble of people who were all equal in the telling of the story. That's why all but Valjean and Javert play other parts at some point in the story. For instance, Thénardier plays a farm laborer in the Prologue and Fantine plays an urchin on the barricade. This sort of ensemble playing is crucial to the meaning of the piece. There's a collective responsibility for story-telling that everybody shares.

That's why the right cast was so important. We were looking for people who could sing and act equally well. Finding people who could sing well enough for Claude-Michel's music, people he approved of and whose voices he liked and people who could play those very earthy, poor, peculiar, deformed people was very tricky. Some of the people we had were good actors with reasonably good singing voices and a few of them were great singers who had to be put through an intensive acting course in rehearsals in order to get what we were doing, and they managed it wonderfully.

But casting is an imperfect science. You're not going to find the strongest man in Europe to *play* the strongest man in Europe. Ultimately you cast the man with the best *voice* in Europe to play the part. And we were lucky enough to have Colm Wilkinson as our first Jean Valjean, and he created that role brilliantly. You make your decision as to who should play a role and from that moment they are that person. They must have the freedom to act like they act and to sing like they sing. To a certain extent you can propose changes to them and you can involve them in artistic choices but their body, their face, and their voice is the raw material you are working with. Even when someone takes over a role they must bring themselves to it. They mustn't be told "Oh this is where you hold the rifle in your left hand" or "this is where you put your hand on her shoulder," otherwise you end up with second rate performances. I often tell a cast that it is incumbent on all of them to do three different things in their performance every night of the run, nothing that would throw somebody else or put them in the wrong part of the stage but something original and fresh for themselves. Nothing remains the same in theatre. It must be organic and change all the time. It's going to change anyway so you'd better be in control of the change and not let it happen in spite of you.

The actors have to bring as much of themselves to a part as they can. It was interesting when we started to rehearse the American cast because we did an exercise where we got the company together and sat in a big circle and asked them where they came from, where their parents came from, when they came to America and why. And we found that in most cases their ancestors had come to America from Europe—France, Germany, Russia, Poland—at precisely the time of *Les Misérables* for precisely the same reasons of injustice, poverty and degradation that Hugo is describing. So in that sense the American cast of *Les Misérables* were more truly the children of Victor Hugo than the English cast. And by inference the people seeing the show in New York would be closer to the events too.

The actors not only have to get inside the skin of their character but they've also got to get inside the skin of the music as a musician, not just as a singer. They've got to feel the intensity of the music and let that inspire them. They have to let the musical feel, the rhythm and the content of the lyric define the atmosphere. For instance, in "Bring Him Home" Valjean has got to be passionately praying but he's also got to let that wonderfully elevating melody imbue him spiritually. In "Stars" Javert has this almost mechanical attitude to the world but the song also has a strong "rock anthem" element. A good Javert will feel the rhythm of it coming up through his legs into his body. It's the rhythm of the song that gives it its emotional rigidity and strength.

I think that one of Claude-Michel's greatest gifts as a composer is the rigor of his songs and that comes from their rhythmic structure. He's extremely strong on how the rhythm tells the story of a character. But he also has a very idiosyncratic musical style. Claude-Michel loves spending time with the soloists, just going through their songs with them and getting them to feel the song as he wrote it. Knowing how Claude-Michel sings and breathes and thinks musically is a very important part of the actor's ability to interpret the song. I often say if they can just go away with Claude-Michel for half an hour and work on a song with him they'll understand everything they need to know about it.

John Napier provided us with a very fluid set of design solutions. The design framework was so powerful that you could do a lot of different things within it. We started off knowing how we were going to be setting things up within that basic framework but that didn't stop us from trying different solutions. In rehearsals we started with improvising characters and movement. We improvised sections of the novel, giving the actors a number of different characters, which made them expert at switching from one character back to another in a matter of seconds, so they could do things like the Prologue and other fast moving bits of the show, the Paris beggars scene and so on. It's important to get modern casts to understand what it was like to live then. Kate Flatt did some important work improvising movement with the actors playing prostitutes and convicts. She taught them how to move as if their bodies were being ripped apart by disease or deprivation or how to look like they'd been locked up for fifteen years. We didn't employ a choreographer as we had decided from the beginning that there would be no dancing or rhythmic or stylised movement. Even in the wedding scene the waltzing is naturalistic movement that would happen at a party. But Kate gave everyone in the cast a sense of period style and reality.

Once we'd started on the scenes we began to apply the improvisational work. Before we started on a scene we had a very strong idea of what we wanted, partly in visual terms but mostly in the emotional and character content. We knew what the big picture ought to be, but a lot of the detail we ended up with was discovered in rehearsal. For instance, in deciding how to stage "One Day More," we didn't want everybody just standing around the stage like in a Mozart opera all singing their different lines. We wanted something more dramatic than that. In improvisation we discovered that a crowd rushing toward you down a narrow street was a good image for the onrush of an insurrection. But how do you stage that? How do you stage people running down a street without them constantly disappearing into the wings or running off the front of the stage? Our final solution, with the apparently forward marching crowd with the red flag waving, is one of the strongest images in the show and it created exactly the impression we wanted. (See *Les Misérables* photo insert 4.)

We also made use of slow motion, which helps you distance things, to put them in relief and to change the perception of reality. Some things would seem absurd if you did them at full speed. With slow motion you can heighten moments of violence or moments of movement that would look daft without it, like the Fauchelevent cart, for example. You have a cart colliding with a large group of people and at first it looks like they're moving very fast but the speed is illusory. It's a combination of the revolve moving and David Hersey's lights whizzing round on top of them and you heighten the impact with slow motion. On the barricade, how do you achieve a whole lot of people dying violent deaths, and all in the moment, without there being a lot of blood and so on? By using a device like slow motion the impact is so strong you don't think about the lack of cinematic realism.

As we worked through the scenes for the first time we'd get to the end of the rehearsal day and then have discussions with Alain and Claude-Michel, but usually not with Herbie because he spent most of the time catching up with the lyrics. We might feel that a rehearsal had been pretty good but that there were issues that were not resolved. For instance, when does Fantine get the letter from the Thénardiers? Or what does Marius really think about Eponine? We'd then ask Claude-Michel and Alain if we could have another verse or make a cut or employ some new musical idea. And they would look at each other and hum things together and come up with new music or new lyrics. Or at the end of rehearsals *they* might come up with concerns, such as a piece of music being overused, and we'd then decide to use something else which would mean a different rhythm, different lyrics and a different scenic structure.

So there was a great deal of collaboration going on all the time. It was like a pressure cooker or a hot house. The changes were forced out of all of us. But the work was surprisingly egoless. There was a real sense of artistic democracy between us that was very exciting. At times there would be passionate disagreements where people would have to fight their corner. But there was an understanding between everybody that such passions were allowed and were a necessary part of the process. If an idea got shot down and it was a good idea then it would get argued back in again and if it was a bad idea then it needed to be shot down. It was a fascinating process. Of course there were certain areas of expertise that in the end no one would dare to assail, for instance Claude-Michel might ultimately put his foot down and say "I've thought about what you said, but that song is just like it is and I'm not changing a note of it." Or maybe with staging for Trevor and myself, or with the commercial and producorial aspects for Cameron there would be certain things that were simply not negotiable.

I still enjoy working on it and from time to time I go in and help when there is a new cast in London or I pop in on a production in some other part of the world. I've been working on the Broadway re-opening and I'm very involved still with the Japanese production. The audience response is always interesting and varies from someone who knows it so well they're humming along with the tunes to someone seeing it for the first time gasping out loud when Gavroche is shot. But I think the great commercial value of *Les Misérables* is that it is as potent for somebody seeing it over and over again as it is for somebody seeing it for the first time. Somehow people are able to wring endless enjoyment out of it and endless meaning and I think the reason for that is the intellectual and artistic rigor of the piece. Because it's got such internal strength you can take constant pleasure from noticing how it fits together and how it supports itself in its characters, its themes, its music, and its staging. There's a real enjoyment in admiring its structure. You can sit and enjoy it on all sorts of different levels and the moment somebody different is in it you can enjoy the different way a role is being performed.

I think *Les Misérables* has helped to change the way people think about musicals, and I think it has also somewhat blurred the dividing line between opera and musicals, which is pretty superficial anyway. The relationship of music to drama is the same whether you're doing *Les Misérables* or *La Bohème. Les Misérables* has helped to ensure that musicals can be regarded as a serious art form. I think it's a great show for people who don't much like theatre and a fantastic show for people who don't like musicals. It's the only show I've worked on where people come up to me and say "I haven't seen *Les Misérables* for a while. I must go and see it again." People seem to have a sense of ownership about it and want to inspect their investment on a regular basis!

NICHOLAS HYTNER

Nicholas Hytner gained an early reputation as one of Britain's leading new theatre directors. As a determined and forthright young director, he had received much critical acclaim in directing before he took on the challenge of *Miss Saigon.* He was born in Manchester and his love of theatre was fostered by the excellent drama and music departments at Manchester Grammar School. He made his mark as a director at Cambridge University where, among other things, he directed *Love's Labour's Lost* and *The*

Photo by Hugo Glendinning

Nicholas Hytner

Threepenny Opera. He graduated from Cambridge in 1977 and immediately formed Cambridge Music Theatre and directed Weill's *Rise and Fall of the City of Mahagonny* for the Edinburgh Festival Fringe. After "cutting his teeth" on this production he began as an assistant director in Glasgow and with the English National and Kent Opera companies, before working as a director at the Kent Opera. He has directed productions at the Northcott Theatre, Exeter, the Leeds Playhouse and the Manchester Royal Exchange, where he was Associate Director.

His opera credits include Wagner's *Rienzi*, Mozart's *Magic Flute* and *Don Giovanni*, Verdi's *Force of Destiny*, Tippett's *King Priam* and Handel's *Xerxes*, and *Giulio Cesare*. In addition he has directed opera for the Netherlands Opera, The Paris Opera and the Geneva Opera.

For the theatre in London he has directed *Volpone, The Importance of Being Earnest, Orpheus Descending* with Helen Mirren, *Cressida* with Michael Gambon and *The Lady in the Van* with Maggie Smith. On Broadway he has directed *The Sweet Smell of Success, Carousel* and *Twelfth Night*. In 2006 he won the Tony Award for Best Direction of a Play for *The History Boys*. For the Royal Shakespeare Company he has directed *Measure for Measure, The Tempest*, and *King Lear*.

Nick has a love of big theatre spaces and enjoys the challenge of vast stages like the Olivier at the National Theatre in London. He has had a long association with the National where he has directed *Ghetto, The Wind in the Willows, Carousel, The Madness of George III, The Recruiting Officer, The Cripple of Innishmaan, The Winter's Tale*, and *Mother Clap's Molly House*. In April 2003 he became the Artistic Director of the National Theatre, taking over from Trevor Nunn. As director of the National he has directed *Henry IV Parts I and II, His Dark Materials, Henry V, The History Boys* and *Stuff Happens*. He has won two Olivier Awards, two Evening Standard Awards and two Tony Awards. In addition he has directed several films including *The History Boys, The Madness of King George, The Crucible*, and *The Object of My Affection*.

NH: When I first heard about setting the *Madame Butterfly* story in Saigon I thought it was a very interesting idea. It was quirky and definitely not mainstream, which, at the time, was very attractive to me. I love big spaces and the feeling of a big house responding to a show. I enjoy the creation of an entire theatrical world. I like inventing and re-inventing worlds for plays to take place in. I like doing plays about big worlds, big communities, plays which reach out. So I was delighted to be given a script and a tape of *Miss Saigon* and asked to direct. It's always exciting to work on a new text and you work instinctively rather than to a set program, starting with the storytelling. If you can help a writer in any way and if you're part of bringing a show to the stage for the first time, it's the biggest buzz of all.

It was a very difficult show to cast and there was, inevitably, a very thorough audition process. The three main actors are all so different and they all work in different ways. Jonathan Pryce was a major actor who had never done a musical, but I don't think Cameron has ever used a more charismatic, intelligent, and analytical actor. Jonathan seizes a role with both hands and puts an enormous stamp on anything he does. I would just provoke ideas that might prompt him to find things that would be effective, but he puts his performance together privately and won't deliver it until he knows what it's going to be. Simon Bowman was a very experienced and expert musical theatre performer and I think that there has probably never been as good a Chris as he was. Lea Salonga, on the other hand, had no real theatre experience. She'd been a child star in the Philippines but now she was literally in a foreign country, so it was all very different. But because of the thorough audition process I knew what she would be capable of and her performance was essentially demonstrated to her moment by moment, which is not something you do with trained actors. All the Filipino cast were very anxious to do well. They couldn't have worked harder to adjust themselves to a new culture, a new climate and a new way of working. As a director you just have to find different ways of working with different kinds of actors.

The way rehearsals work is that everything starts at the same time. There may be music being taught in one room, choreography being worked out in another, and intense personal scenes being worked out in another. I don't consciously work out how I'm going to do a scene beforehand, not move by move. But with a sequence like the flashback sequence, then I kind of knew bit by bit how that would be because you can't go into something like that unless you know what you want. But as for who is where, what they're thinking, what they're feeling, you may have an overview but you always want to be surprised. Although visually *Miss Saigon* was completely preconceived, which a show on this scale essentially has to be, exactly how Jonathan Pryce, for example, would end up you just don't know. It wasn't a show where I used improvisations because they were largely a very inexperienced cast. There are circumstances under which I would heavily rely on improvisations but not in this case. It would have been a grotesque abuse of one's position to take sixteen-year-old girls from Manila, who come from an intensely protected middle-class Catholic background and say, "Now improvise being prostitutes." It wouldn't have worked.

The show was not completely fixed when I came on board but there is not a lot of flexibility for change in a sung-through musical. If you're working on a new play you can actually suggest an idea for a new line and the playwright might change it on the spot. You can't do that very easily with sung-through lyrics. What was interesting was that it was one of those shows where a lot of very disparate influences and very different approaches to the business of making theatre and making a show jelled. Sometimes they pull in entirely different directions but here they just came together. So in this show there are bits of me, bits of John Napier, bits of Cameron, and obviously the whole show is by Claude-Michel and Alain with Richard Maltby. It is a much less consistent and coherent piece of theatrical direction than, for example, *Les Misérables* is. *Les Misérables* is so plainly a synthesis of twenty five years of Trevor Nunn's work, in its production style, in the way it tells its story and in the way it arrives in the audience's laps. Whereas this show is much more a synthesis of lots and lots of people. Quite often that's a recipe for disaster but in this instance I think it worked.

I worked with John Napier on the set. Before I came on board he had already done some work with Jerry Zaks, who had been going to direct *Miss Saigon* and the set John had designed then had been much harder and harsher and had a more metallic feel. I had to tell him what I needed in order to do a scene but essentially the visuals are the set designer's. It's the only time I've worked with John; he's not one of my regular collaborators. If I had worked with one of my regular collaborators it would have been a different show. There would have been less that was concrete but I'm not sure it would have been as successful a show. I think it was a very clever synthesis that Cameron achieved by putting me together with John. The white box and the impressionistic feel which John achieved with those blown gauzes, were absolutely his. But the feel of the show, the juxtaposition of the hard with the soft impressionistic, hazily lit, more romantic feel was something we both worked on. At Drury Lane, which is such a big stage, it was essential to use trucks for the creation of small spaces, but on Broadway we managed to create exactly the same effect without the trucks themselves. The helicopter and its mechanics had already been decided on before I came on board. I always felt that that machine was unnecessary and I remain of that opinion today. We could have done the helicopter without producing the machine, because the feel of the show and the whole design is brilliant, but it's impressionistic rather than real most of the time. But you know what—without the helicopter the show would not have been the success it was. It was absolutely the right decision and there it was and there it stayed. But it was pure personal vanity. It was "Oh God—it's the show with the helicopter." However the seven minutes leading up to the helicopter, that's as good as theatre gets, that's good stagecraft, good design, good writing, the whole thing.

One of the first things you do when it's a new show is to work with the writers to make sure that what they're doing is stageable in the terms you can stage it. My starting point for *Saigon* was the notion that you are presenting an intense personal story about three or four people against the backdrop of one of the major historical events of the second half of the last century. So the challenge was moving in for the close up and then cutting out for the epic wide shots. If you've done a lot of big shows you've learned how to do the epic stuff and you know that the emotional high points will be provided every time by one or two people. It was about being theatrically very fluid and being able to wipe a small scene away with a great influx of people. One thing that kept getting better was the introduction to "If you want to die in bed," where herds of people wipe across the stage and there's one little person left, who is the Engineer. Then they all wipe across again and then he's left again. It was very much a conscious part of what we were doing.

It's the director's job rather than the writer's job to visualize how a scene will work. Alain and Claude-Michel put in the flashback scene with the evacuation of the Embassy but they didn't know how it would work on stage. There was a forward-moving beat and it was all there musically but, if I remember correctly, they saw the evacuation as a single scene outside the Embassy compound. However, I wanted to experiment with the idea of presenting it cinematically and cutting from inside to outside. (See *Miss Saigon* photo insert 8.) It was essentially the cinematic technique of editing together a shot and its reverse—his point of view, her point of view. It was something I just thought would be a good idea and it contributed to the storytelling. It's what a movie director does. An event has to be staged and if there's an exciting way of staging it and a new way of telling the story then a director can contribute that. Otherwise the director and the producer both act as editors helping the writers find a way to do something better.

You also have to be aware of how the audience will follow the story, especially when you have sudden leaps in time. But audiences are wise to that kind of thing from all the movies they've seen and they know what's going on. They love working things out for themselves. The first enormous hand is for "I Still Believe" and that's partly because they're giving themselves a big hand for working things out—"Three years have passed, he's got married and that must be the new wife and Kim's still there." There is a great deal of satisfaction for an audience when you let them engage with the story telling in that way. There's always a three-way conversation between writers, actors and audience.

There is one scene, however, that I'm completely ashamed of. It's the Bui Doi film at the beginning of the second act and it was all my idea. When you're putting a show on you become totally overexcited by it, and there are always moments of total tastelessness in everything you do. Gradually you whittle them away and hope by the time they reach the stage that good taste, which is an overrated virtue, has been restored. But the whole business of rehearsals has got to do with pushing taste to one side, otherwise nothing would ever emerge. The idea was that John was making a speech; he was a fund-raiser so he'd be showing a movie. I selected the archive footage and I supervised its assembly. But when I saw it I turned white. I was horrified. I was upset that this fake fundraiser used and exploited the distress of real children, not to raise funds on their behalf but to create three or four minutes of theatre. I believe you should be very careful about exploiting the genuine distress of real people captured on celluloid. The trouble is I think we stole their images. Nobody asked their permission. However, the world being what it is, no doubt they'll be thrilled they were on Broadway! Everybody said the movie was fantastic, particularly in the States. I think it could have been done without that film and I've often tried to cut it but been outvoted. But I've literally never done a thing that I haven't thought could have been better.

One of the great pleasures and great challenges of working on *Miss Saigon* was to integrate the central story with the wider historical story. And by and large the way the two stories are integrated so that the larger historical events are the cause of small personal trauma does work very well. And although we only tell

one personal story you know that with something like the Vietnam War you could move in on any two people you choose and
have an intense story of personal lives entirely marked by the big
public events. It's absolutely what all the big Italian operas are
about. It's how they work, with big public events as the backdrop
to a small personal story created by the big public movements.
And that's how you get the big chorus numbers followed by the
big arias. The historical perspective in *Miss Saigon* has also been
seen to reflect the personal story in as much as America's apparently benevolent but bungled intervention in Vietnam reflects
Chris' action. But I'm not so sure, especially in the light of recent
disclosures, that America's flirtation with Empire is as without
malevolence as Chris is. I think successive US governments are far
more culpable than they'd like to admit.

In *Miss Saigon* we all tried to make the show as truthful as we
could. I was always very wary about being vaguely mystical, vaguely poetic. I'm utterly distrustful of this vague new age devotion to
completely ill-understood, not-studied, not-lived Eastern religion.
It's much more serious than that to me. In the show we used the
image of the sun and moon and that is a good image because both
sun and moon are real, truthful, concrete images that reverberate
beyond the physical objects that the two words denote. It's when
you start using words and images imprecisely to give vague color
that things fall apart. One of the things we worked on was Kim's
background so she can say, "this is where I came from, this is my
village, this is who was killed," which is immediately concrete and
truthful. It is real because it is lived and it's better than the kind
of mystical things you can only imagine a young Vietnamese girl
might say.

Alain and Claude-Michel are French romantics and French romanticism is always tragic, so impossible love is always one of their
themes. It's part of the culture that love is inescapable, glorious
and ultimately doomed. The quintessentially French love song is a
tragic song of love defeated. The quintessential French love poem
is of love disappointed, and that is truthful and real and that is real

in *Miss Saigon*. What's important about *Miss Saigon* is that there is a passionate belief, which comes from the people who wrote it, that what happened between the two protagonists was very, very real and intense and sexual, and that the sexuality of it was the reality of it. Sexuality, passion, and romantic love are much more unified in the French sensibility than they are in ours. The French sensibility is less judgemental about sexual passion than the Anglo-Saxon sensibility tends to be.

The other thing that is so real in the show is the Vietnamese characters' burning ambition not to be Vietnamese any more. Kim's ambition for her son to be American and the Engineer's ambition to be American are real. Alain, Claude-Michel and I are Jews and we understand that kind of ambition; it's in our blood. Kim might be seen in the same way as a Jewish mother who wants her son to be better than she is. The Engineer wants to be a success in America not in the backwater where he is living. The circumstances that he finds himself in aren't good enough for him. He thinks he's better than that and Kim thinks her son's worth more than that. Driving ambition and determination are very true and very real in *Miss Saigon* and that again is because it's completely unforced. The other thing that is unforced, which is part of living in the twentieth century, is the feeling of helplessness in the face of overwhelming public events.

The most difficult scenes to do were those scenes that seemed the most mundane and the least susceptible to musical treatment. The scene in the hotel, with people wandering round a Holiday Inn singing, always felt a problem to me. It seemed no problem that people desperately trying to push through a chainlink fence should be screaming at the top of their lungs and it never seemed a problem with two people in love in a little room with the sun rising. The emotionally high-pitched scenes, the scenes lifted from *Madame Butterfly* and the big crowd scenes were never difficult. The problem was with the scenes for the white middle-class American people.

It's always more difficult to do a contemporary musical because with any musical the biggest problem is to find a reason why they should sing. If the characters are dressed in the clothes of the first half of the nineteenth century, in a place where they're not talking like you and me, then it's easier because it's stranger. If you stage the action in an exotic place then that makes it easier even if it is contemporary. The hardest part in a musical is when they stop talking and start singing. If there isn't any talking at all then you don't have to negotiate that difficult transition from talking to singing. The disadvantage is that banalities have to be sung because it's impossible to tell a story on stage without at some point having to have banal exchanges of information or mundane conversation. Obviously you pare that away as much as possible but every now and then they have to say something like "I'm sorry but am I in the right room?," "I thought you were the cleaner. Yes this is the right room." That kind of thing is always a problem, even in opera.

I think in the case of *Miss Saigon* and all Alain and Claude-Michel's work the advantages of a sung-through musical outweigh the disadvantages because I genuinely believe that they write pop operas. The advantage is that their shows are pitched high emotionally from start to finish. They're pumped up to an operatic pitch and they're pitched high enough for song to be a natural and inevitable way for the characters to express themselves. In a play it's an equivalent and opposite process. When you're speaking lines you're finding the music and you are, as it were, discovering the ebb and flow, the tempo of the piece. What you're doing when you have music is finding a way of making a pre-existing tempo feel natural and unforced. So obviously it helps enormously if what you're working on is a scene where the ebb and flow of the music and the ebb and flow thought by thought, phrase by phrase feels right and unforced.

The difference between musicals and opera is not so great as you might imagine. There are those who say that the only difference is that operas are performed in opera houses and sung without amplification and musicals are performed in theatres and sung with amplification. *The Magic Flute* has become an opera but it was written for the commercial theatre as a musical and Mozart wrote it to earn money. It was commissioned by a comic actor who was not an opera singer and played the part of Papageno. *The Magic Flute* is undoubtedly the very pinnacle of the form. Alain and Claude-Michel's work has gone a long way toward breaking down the boundaries between opera and musicals. I've directed opera and *Miss Saigon* is an opera, a pop opera. It has seriousness of intent and classical symmetries in its structure in the way that *Butterfly* has. Structurally it compares favorably with *Butterfly*, although *Butterfly* is purer and simpler and, if you like, less ambitious. If a story works it's usually a sign that it was structured well. The second half of *Miss Saigon* has always been a problem because less happens than seems to. But you have the flashback, "The American Dream," which is a phenomenal sleight of hand, and the Bangkok number, and it is all done with such skill that you go with it and still feel that gathering sense of tragic inevitability.

Another defining factor in the difference between opera and musicals are the circumstances under which these theatrical events reach the stage. I think what bothers certain critics is the fact that Cameron Mackintosh's shows make a lot of money for everybody involved. Very often entertainment that makes money is concocted only to make money but that is not the case with Cameron's shows. I can bear witness to the fact that Cameron makes his shows to please himself, which is why he differs from his imitators and why he sometimes has the most terrible flops. And to me that is a badge of honor. He has a terrible flop because he liked it. Other people have flops because they're trying to second guess the public. I don't believe Cameron does that and neither do Alain and Claude-Michel. They wear their hearts on their sleeves and that bothers a lot of people here and in France. But they are sincere artists and their work shows that musical theatre can be equally capable of what other forms of theatre are capable of. *Miss Saigon* is a great show and it has profoundly touched many people.

CONALL MORRISON

Conall Morrison is an Associate Director of the Abbey theatre in Dublin, where his work includes a production of Patrick Kavanagh's *Tarry Flynn*, which he adapted and directed and which was also seen at the National Theatre in London. This production won him both a *Sunday Independent* Spirit of Life Award and an *Irish Times* ESB Theatre Award. Other work for the Abbey Theatre includes *The Importance of Being Earnest*, *Hamlet* (a co-production with the Lyric Theatre, Belfast), Boucicault's *The Colleen Bawn*, also seen at the Lyttelton, *The Freedom of the City*, *The Tempest*, *The House*, *A Whistle in the Dark*, *Ariel*, *In a Little World of Our Own*, *As the Beast Sleeps*, *Twenty Grand*, *Savoy*; and a triple bill comprising *The Dandy Dolls*, *Purgatory* and *Riders to the Sea/Chun na Farriage Síos*. Other productions include *Conquest of the South Pole*, *The Marlboro Man*, *Emma*, *Measure for Measure*, *Macbeth*, *Kvetch*, and his own adaptation of *Antigone*.

For the Lyric Theatre in Belfast Conall directed *Dancing at Lughnasa, Juno and the Paycock, Conversations on a Homecoming*, and *Ghosts*. His own plays, including *Green, Orange and Pink* and *Rough Justice*, have had several productions in English theatres.

Photo by Margaret Vermette

Conall Morrison

Conall's play *Hard to Believe* was toured extensively by the Irish Theatre Company, Bickerstaffe and is published by Methuen. His production of the musical *Ludwig II* is running at the Festspielhaus Neuschwanstein in Germany. He has most recently written and directed *The Bacchae of Baghdad* at the Abbey and he directed a new version of *La Traviata*, set in Dublin, with new lyrics by Stephen Clark, for the English National Opera in

London, which premiered in September 2006. Conall enjoys living in Howth, near Dublin in a cottage by the sea.

CM: I felt delighted to be asked to direct *Martin Guerre*. It's a rare privilege to work on something like that because directors and choreographers are only as good as the material they have to work with and as good as the primary artists who have written it. Initially I was very sensitive to the fact that it might be a potential breach of protocol to take over a show that had been directed by Declan Donnellan, who is a supreme director and whose work I hugely admire. But after a meeting with Alain, Claude-Michel, and Cameron in Dublin I realized that they wanted to start from scratch with a completely new team and that they wanted me to be a proper collaborative partner. Before they came to Dublin I hadn't seen the original version so I went over and saw it several times. In many respects I was very impressed and I saw exactly what was going on. The piece had a beating heart and it had some incredible numbers but they had tried to crank it up to the dimensions of *Les Misérables* and *Miss Saigon* and it's really a much smaller story. It's a medium scale musical and the epic canvas they had provided in the large theatre did not accommodate the focused intensity of the piece.

It's been fascinating working with people who have been on such a long journey. I worked on it for two years but Alain and Claude-Michel had been working on it for eight years. So I picked up where other people had left off. It's thoroughly admirable that Alain and Claude-Michel could go back to the story and keep at it until they got it right and maybe that's why they have inspired such loyalty and affection in their audiences. Stephen Clark is a superb writer and he understands how these guys work. I think the combination of Alain and Stephen works very well. Alain has a vast experience and really understands structure, while Stephen is a very sharp lyricist. I enjoyed watching their process at work.

The setting of religious conflict is, of course, something I know about only too well. I do know what the raw element of prejudice is about because I've seen it and lived with it in Northern Ireland.

So in terms of that theme I do understand, rather sadly, what it's like to see a community tear itself apart. However, as a director you are invited imaginatively and professionally to enter into whatever world the script presents and so I should be able to direct a show about Mormons or Eskimos equally well. The most difficult part about staging *Martin Guerre* was striking that balance between a period feel and a contemporary energy. It was about maintaining the integrity of that world and that period of history and still making it completely accessible and worthy of a modern audience's attention and engagement. Spanning the centuries in a seamless way was probably the greatest trick to pull off.

I did a lot of research and reading around that period in France—the broad historical situation, social detail, the nature of the religious conflict, and cultural customs. It was fascinating and it helped to invest the piece with a sociological vigor, creating a free-standing and complete world that you can take an audience into. I introduced the cast to that kind of background material because it helped them get their heads into a different mindset, far removed from the twentieth century. The cast all had to do various bits of reading and research too and then come together and share it. That's not the kind of thing you would need to do in every musical, but it helped to stoke up the stakes of the show when they realized just how important the religious divisions were, what the sexual restrictions were, and how great the power of the Church was. Of course it is basically scaffolding structure and eventually that has to fall away because if a musical smacks of a history lesson then you're in trouble. But it helped access the smell of the period and the texture of life as it was lived then.

I was naturally influenced by watching *Les Misérables* and *Miss Saigon*, studying the mixture of structural rigor, dramatic seriousness and great accessibility and trying to analyze exactly what the guys' formula was and how they were trying to advance that in *Martin Guerre*. So I tried to bring all that to bear, but each show that I do, whether it's a small one man show or a big Cameron Mackintosh musical, must be looked at on its own terms and treated it as if it's the only show you're ever going to do. You're trying to find out what it is in it that is unique and what you can find within yourself that is original. You have to find what is going to give this particular piece its own hallmark, its own stamp and its own individually created world that would be different from every other piece. It had all the qualities of accessibility, the glorious melodic energy that Claude-Michel creates and Alain's nose for a great story and how to tell it. I had to find what would make it original, distinctive, and arresting because it's a dangerous period and you don't want it to become a "men in tights" piece. I wanted to make it true to its period so that the audience got the energy of history and at the same time make it utterly contemporary and compelling, so it would span the centuries.

I worked very closely with David Bolger, the choreographer, to help the actors find the innate choreography of everyday rural life in that period. There are rhythms involved in that kind of existence, in cooking, harvesting, hunting, and playing. It's a very physical outdoor existence so we had to find a way of taking twentieth-century bodies back five centuries to when there was that physical openness. And then find the rhythms, patterns, and gestures within that to create a social, emotional, and physical world for the cast and for the show. You don't know before you start exactly how the final show will be. You know what the writers have given you and you try to ascertain what it is that they want and then you start applying your own imagination, sense of structure, and dramatic values. It was a kind of evolutionary process as we restructured and reworked and Claude-Michel wrote new songs and we worked very closely with John Napier to come up with the look of the piece.

Working with John Napier was not only a highly entertaining experience, it was a wonderful education in terms of set design. There are about thirty fast-flowing scenes that all meld into each other so it wasn't easy to find the right design for the production. We had met a couple of set designers previously, and because John had done *Les Misérables* and *Miss Saigon* we thought that as we were trying to create something new we should bring a fresh eye to it. But although the other designers had very interesting ideas and were very keen to work on it they simply weren't coming up with the right solutions. So we met with John and we would bash things around and at one point he came up with the idea of setting it on two tons of mud—which was brilliant but it wasn't going to work! Eventually as we took him through the story he had various ideas about how it might flow and he reached into his own crazy genius and came up with this idea of a big set with sliding panels and endlessly adaptable wooden structures that could be turned into screens, banqueting tables or a church. And he created a set that could literally catch fire toward the end of each performance. (See *Martin Guerre* photo insert 10.) Then we did some further work, and David and I thought about how we could see ourselves working with the set, and John responded to that. Working with John and with Andy Neofitou on the costumes we really benefited from their years of experience and hopefully challenged them a bit too. It was one of the highlights of the whole process, working with John and tapping into his experience.

Before I start working on a scene I have a general idea of what I want. Of course, with a musical the music is dictating a large amount of it. But if you want to make something fresh and sponta-neous you need to go into that rehearsal room with an open sense of enquiry and a spontaneous energy, especially for this kind of show. If it was a show that was full of tap numbers it would be very tight, with a lot of dance sequences, and a lot more would have to be worked out beforehand. But with this show we were trying to build a community which was composed of definite and differenti-ated individuals. So we needed to keep it as loose as possible and let the overall language emerge and then fine tune it. The best moments were on the floor with the actors, the rehearsal pianist, and Alain and Stephen feeding in. If you have the right cast that can be very exciting—I like to throw things up and see what comes out and then make it into a more focused shape. You try to harness everybody's imagination, because twenty imaginations are better than one, and then the editing process begins.

I'd like to think that the way I work varies from show to show. I like to make each show distinctive and try to find an individual personality for each piece of theatre. No matter what shape or size it is or where I'm working, I always see if I can adapt my working methods. There's obviously some of the same techniques but I like to hold it as an article of faith that in each piece I'm going to take a slightly different approach. Not for its own sake but because I'm looking for something that has its own inimical stamp and its own self identity. If I started falling back on my old techniques and tricks I would probably end up squeezing it into a pre-ordained structure. So although I adhere to various principles I try to embrace a kind of openness that will lead me to something fresh.

What we did in Leeds was to reclaim the show from being a somewhat bucolic affair with lots of dappled leaves and moving trees and we brought it back more toward the world of *The Crucible* where there was that extremity of religion. We ramped up the severity of the social situation and just how violent, dangerous, and loveless the environment was that Bertrande and Arnaud were trying to live in and express their love for each other. (See *Martin Guerre* photo insert 9.) I think it worked very well and made it dramatically pretty potent. But, although the reviews were great, we maybe went a bit too far in terms of the form, the fact that it was a musical. It was a bit too stark, and there were various shades to be explored within it which would help us make the village more engaging. For the American tour, which started at the Guthrie Theater in Minneapolis, we had to re-humanize the village characters a bit so that they were people that you could relate to. Madame de Rols, Bertrande's mother, for example, made great dramatic sense in England because you got to see this overbearing mother and all the pressures that Bertrande was under. But we lost out on having a tug of love there, which we had in America, and which conveyed both great tenderness and the need to show great toughness. We had flattened that out in England, but in America Kathy Taylor gave the part an emotional warmth that any mother could identify with. Also we wanted to create a more physical character with Benoit, so that although he wasn't well educated and a bit left of center mentally, he would be able to express himself with glorious physicality. And Michael Arnold could do that amazingly well, being a marvelous clown, and it worked wonderfully. (See *Martin Guerre* photo insert 6.)

We got back to the characters in the village and gave them individual characteristics which made a richer tapestry. They needed to be more likeable so that you could feel more for them when tragedy struck. Cameron, of course, was keen that we do this. Cameron is a superb diagnostician so he can quickly identify a problem even though he may not have a solution for it. He has an unsurpassed sense of what is not going right and even if his sense of what will make it right is hit and miss, then his energy will make him throw ideas at you. However, when everything is right you might have to leave a little rubbish bit in, just so he can put his finger on that and leave the rest alone!

There was one point when we moved "How Many Tears" to when they came out of church instead of before "The Conversion." I think it was Jude Kelly that suggested it and we realized that it made perfect sense. Sometimes you sit down with a piece of paper and try to work out the structure and the flow of ensemble songs to the solo material and other times when you're working it just becomes self-evident and everything falls into place. Inevitably as you try out the material you road test it, and if you find something doesn't work or needs to be replaced then you find another way. Sometimes people would have different ideas and there would be good fisticuff debates but ultimately the best idea wins and asserts itself. When you're working with a team that size and with that strength of personality and range of experience every decision and every step is worked out and thought through very rigorously. So you're actually making very considered decisions as well as trying to be spontaneously creative and inventive. But it was truly collaborative and that was one of the great joys of working on it.

When you're casting you're looking for that golden formula— people who can sing and act and move brilliantly. We knew it was going to be physically very demanding and we were going to make it a very strong dramatic piece. And, of course, what Claude-Michel writes is musically very demanding. In musical theatre you get a vast range of actors so you have to adapt your approach to each individual. Some might have glorious voices but they're not necessarily the best actors in the world so you have to feed them a lot more than others. Some just have it all, like Joanna Riding, who has a great voice and is also a superb actor, but there are a lot of variations. It's all about assessing each actor's needs and qualities and working out how to bring it all together as a whole so there's no disparity in style or technique, that everybody's in the same team.

The actors have a lot of freedom to create and to bring something of themselves to the role. The job of directing is to make sure that what they're creating and offering up is brought in line with the overall picture, and that it's going to be consonant with what everyone else is doing and how the story is moving along. So what you're trying to do is unlock the creativity of an actor and then channel it so that it's fused into the production aesthetic. In the States there was probably a higher standard of dance ability. But it was slightly more alien to them that we were taking a musical so incredibly seriously dramatically and that we were empowering them to explore every detail within each characterization and asking them for creative input. A lot of them had been used to being told where to go and what to do but David and I wanted to unfold everything they had to offer.

In a musical there are inevitably losses and gains because the music can iron out ambiguity and subtlety, but what you lose you can gain in a heightened sense of feeling and emotional engagement. With the sheer act of singing you're automatically going through the medium of the projected soul, as it were. Speaking is an everyday thing, we take it for granted, it's our normal mode of communication. And it's a tricky thing in musicals, when they just suddenly burst into song when they've been speaking, and that's one of the great joys of the sung-through musical because song is the given language for the evening. By singing you're automatically on a heightened plane of expression so it allows you to say things or access emotions or words that you'd need to build up to over a much longer period of time if speech was involved. So maybe what you lose in terms of detail or complexity you gain in terms of intensity or color of expression.

The soliloquy is always a great moment in drama, where the character speaks truthfully to the audience. The common hallmark of all soliloquies is that the character doesn't lie. They may not be in possession of all the facts but you really get into their heart and their mind and it's incredibly direct and dynamic. The character comes forward and really opens up their heart to you and, in a solo, if the song is good, then it's second to none in terms of its capacity to reach out and communicate with you. Given some of the melodies that Claude-Michel created they were some of the highlights of the show, songs like "How Many Tears" and "I'm Martin Guerre." (See *Martin Guerre* photo insert 5.) They're fantastic standalone songs but they were brilliantly placed within the structure of the show.

Martin Guerre, like all Alain and Claude-Michel's musicals, is about the overwhelming power of love. How love will surface and survive even through something as fearsome as religious wars and sectarian strife, which can tear individuals and communities apart—how you find that even among the rubble, after everyone has ripped themselves apart, that there's a capacity for redemption, that somebody will still light a candle, that people will have learned something from it. In the show there are these little lights of redemption, particularly in Martin's gesture of setting Arnaud free, which throws the more fulsome love and passion of Bertrande and Arnaud into relief. It's not a happy-ever-after ending, it's tragic, but it explores the complexity of love, how it endures, its different forms and shades. One of Alain and Claude-Michel's great themes is that love is only ever interesting when it's set in context. It's always love against a background of conflict, working against the powers of positivity, love and passion.

Another theme is the question of how individuality can survive in a herd mentality or in codified religious structures because society often develops itself in a way which will not allow individuals to express their own sense of faith, passion, or personal loyalty. It's hard to assert your autonomy because society is prescribing your identity. And that's incredibly relevant today as we see the world over that the rise of religious passions is driving world politics. So what was happening then in Artigat is still happening today, only now we have the most terrible modern weapons with which to fight our battles.

You always try to imagine how the audience is going to relate to the show because it's got to engage them, to challenge, excite, and inspire them. But it's not until the previews that you really find out what works and what doesn't, what are the longueurs, what are the bits that are potentially confusing and where are the moments that are really achieving vertical takeoff. In the previews, and indeed through the whole run, you're very much learning from the audience. We may think one bit is brilliant but it may not be landing in the audience's imagination. You have to listen to the audience very closely and specifically, and not just back in the bar afterward, you have to feel the energy in the air and read the atmosphere in the theatre like a weather forecaster. That's ultimately your guide because until that atmosphere is created, sustained, and climaxed, until it feels absolutely right from beginning to end, then you haven't got the show right. The audience is the ultimate critic and the ultimate judge.

Martin Guerre is operatic in as much as it's sung-through, it has glorious melodies that manage to have a contemporary energy to them and at the same time seem to evoke the period quite effortlessly. Of course it takes a lot of effort from Claude-Michel and the lyricists but they make it seem as if it's natural, as if they've managed to access these things from a zone between the different centuries. It's got the historical setting, the great intensity, passion, seriousness and all the high emotion of opera. But it's un-operatic in that it's incredibly accessible all the way through with the melodies, the quality of the voices and the nature of the storytelling. Everything in Alain and Claude-Michel's musicals is designed to be readable by an audience, not in a simplistic or dumbed down way, but not holding anything back, and telling the story in a very engaged and front foot kind of way. Their musicals reach out and grab the audience's imagination more forcefully than opera sometimes does and they're more digestible, comprehensible, and direct than a lot of straight opera.

I was very proud of these productions in England and America and I thought it was a very accessible modern musical that had quite a bit of bite. Everybody was very enthused by the whole thing. Alain and Claude-Michel had genuinely wanted to rework it and Cameron had a passion to drive it through and make it work. Cameron is a guy that has been passion led about musicals all his life. It was a labor of love for him, a show he passionately believed in, and that energy created a great kind of generative momentum for everybody that was involved. ❧

CHAPTER 5

Master of the House

PRODUCER

THE MOST IMPORTANT PERSON in bringing Alain and Claude-Michel's three shows—*Les Misérables, Miss Saigon* and *Martin Guerre*—to life has been their long time producer Sir Cameron Mackintosh. Ever since a young Hungarian director Peter Farago first played him a recording of the original French version of *Les Misérables* he has been the most enthusiastic champion of Alain and Claude-Michel and their work.

But the role of the producer is a complex one. The enormous amount of time, energy and financial involvement in producing a modern-day musical mean that it is essential to find the right work in the first place, not just in terms of instinct for a hit but the producer must really love the project with his heart and soul. And because so much of himself will be invested in it, he must love the *process* of producing a show. Cameron Mackintosh, especially, will never put on a show unless he feels passionately about it. Once he feels that he has got as many rewrites as he can out of the authors, the next essential act is to get together the best creative team to bring the show to life. The director, set designer, costume designer, lighting and sound designers all need not only to be among the best in their field but they also have to be chosen for their suitability to a particular script and an eye to compatibility, and there must be good chemistry between them. Once chosen it is the producer's responsibility to provide the team with the environment to create, to stimulate each other, and to figure out what works and what doesn't. An intelligent producer can make a good writer write better and a creative team more creative. Some producers also like to act as creative directors while others will prefer just to pinpoint what's not working in a production.

Choosing the right theatre for a production is fundamental to its success. The right size is the most important factor, as big shows need near-capacity audiences to break even. For a big musical, if you have a smash hit, you may recoup your investment in about a year, but often it will take longer. As a rule of thumb you shouldn't have a weekly breakeven of more than 60% of the weekly box office potential to cover your running costs. The rest is needed toward recovering production costs. If a theatre is too small for an expensive production it will never recoup even if it's full. The ability to manage a successful marketing campaign is a key skill for any producer, who will need to find ways of keeping the production in the public's eye and catching their attention. Advertising is one of the major expenses in producing whether it be through the press, eye-catching London bus and underground posters, or a gigantic neon Broadway sign.

With ever-escalating production costs, making the budget work is, perhaps, more vital than ever. The producer must find ways to deal in the world of finance and be more and more creative in raising capital. Musicals now come in with exceedingly high capitalization costs; for instance, *The Pirate Queen* will come in at $16 million. The amount it costs to put on the production increases greatly with each year, but the weekly operating costs can be even harder to budget for and have the potential to cut short the run of even the most otherwise popular show. Productions should recoup their investment within a reasonable time for investors to get their money back and hopefully to make a profit to encourage them to invest again in the future. A producer needs to be able to negotiate the potential minefield of Actors' Equity rulings both at home and abroad and also needs nerves of steel in order to ride out any negative or even mixed reviews that, without good word of mouth, can ruin the chances of success. A successful producer needs dedication, commitment, and passion, together with formidable organizational and leadership skills and the ability to charm rather than cajole people into doing what he or she wants.

It's a rare thing nowadays in London and especially on Broadway to see a sole producer's name above a production. But Cameron Mackintosh has not only had phenomenal success in the UK and the U.S., he has internationalized the musical and transformed it into an art form that is seen by as many people as the biggest blockbuster films. In the pursuit of excellence every detail is attended to and the audience response is carefully measured and taken note of. There is a little story that when doing one particular show, Mackintosh wasn't happy with the curtain call and was convinced that the orchestra wasn't hitting the right note to get the audience on their feet. So he plagued the Musical Director until eventually they found this very note and sure enough the whole audience spontaneously rose to their feet. In a theatre auditorium the audience is referred to as "the house" so it can indeed be said that Cameron Mackintosh is the consummate, supremely skilled "Master of the House."

SIR CAMERON MACKINTOSH

Cameron Mackintosh came from a family with some show business connections. His mother was Maltese and his Scottish father was an esteemed amateur jazz musician. But it was his favorite, theatrical Aunt Jean who took the eight-year-old Cameron to see his first musical, Julian Slade's *Salad Days*. He was so mesmerized by the show and especially by the "magic piano" that he persuaded his parents to take him again. This time at the end of the show, full of curiosity as to how the magic piano worked, he marched down to

Photo by Michael Le Poer Trench

Sir Cameron Mackintosh

the pit to speak to Julian Slade, who was playing the real piano there. Slade took the fascinated boy backstage and showed him how everything worked.

From that day on Cameron knew he wanted to work in the theatre. He wrote and put on musicals at home, and at his school, Prior Park College in Bath, he put on the Christmas reviews, showing even at the age of fourteen, a notable flair for organization and an ability to manage a box office to advantage. At seventeen he began a stage management course at the Central School of Speech and Drama in London, but impatient to start work in the theatre, he dropped out half way. He got his first job as a stagehand at the Theatre Royal Drury Lane. The job was initially only temporary and he was paid just seven pounds a week, so he also worked there as a cleaner for another seven pounds. He had to sweep the stage and clean the auditorium between performances of *Camelot*. But he hated early mornings and was ingenious enough to pay someone to plug in the Hoover for him so that the theatre manager would hear the noise and think he was already at work. However, when he was there he made himself so indispensable to everyone backstage that the job lasted several months until he left to be the assistant stage manager on the first national tour of *Oliver!*, rehearsing on the set of the original London production at the then New Theatre, now the Noël Coward theatre, which he owns. It was Cameron's 1977 revival of *Oliver!* that was to inspire Alain and Claude-Michel to write *Les Misérables*.

Other jobs followed, with Cameron progressing from assistant stage manager and deputy stage manager to company manager. In

1967 he achieved his ambition to get his name on posters as a producer, albeit jointly with Robin Alexander. At first, he produced only plays and mostly touring productions with some success. His first musical in 1969 was Cole Porter's *Anything Goes*, and although this was successful at the small Yvonne Arnaud Theatre in Guildford there were huge problems in the bigger theatres on tour, and when it reached the 1,500-seat Saville Theatre (now a cinema) in London, the show was an unmitigated disaster. It closed after eleven days. It was eighteen months before he could get back on the road with his own productions. Undaunted, he was soon back in the West End with Slade's musical *Trelawny* (1972), and Tony Hatch's *The Card* (1973). In 1974 he took over *Godspell* and there were many other shows in between. Cameron's first major success in both London and on Broadway was *Side By Side By Sondheim* in 1976. He followed this with successful revivals of *Oliver!* (1977), *My Fair Lady* (1978), *Oklahoma!* (1979) and the revue *Tom Foolery* (1980). It was in 1981 that he produced Andrew Lloyd Webber's *Cats* at the New London Theatre, a show which, to many people's astonishment, became a runaway success and his first international mega hit, produced in over 400 cities worldwide and the longest running show of its day in both London and New York.

Cats was followed by *Song and Dance* (1982), *The Little Shop of Horrors* (1982), *Blondel* (1983), *Abbacadabra* (1983), and *The Boy Friend* (1984). Then 1985 saw the opening of *Les Misérables*. This, like *Cats*, became an international phenomenon. Hot on its heels was the next blockbuster musical *The Phantom of the Opera* (1986). Next to come were *Follies* (1987) and *Just So* in 1989, a year which also saw the opening of the now legendary *Miss Saigon*. Then it was *Five Guys Named Moe* (1990), *Moby Dick* (1991), *Putting it Together* (1992), *Carousel* (1993) and *Oliver!* (1994). In 1996 *Martin Guerre* opened in London, and some two and a half years later a completely rewritten version opened in Leeds. The next shows were *The Fix* (1997), *Hey, Mr Producer!* (1998), *Swan Lake* (1998), *Oklahoma!*

(1999), *The Witches of Eastwick* (2000), *My Fair Lady* (2001), *Mary Poppins* (2004), and *Avenue Q* in 2006.

Cameron Mackintosh is the most successful theatre producer of all time, having staged more musicals in more cities than anyone else in the entire history of the theatre. He pioneered the globalization of the musical and paved the way for others to follow. He made the British musical *the* major player on the world stage and in 1995 Cameron Mackintosh Ltd. received the Queen's Award for Export Achievement. The 1980s were undoubtedly a golden age for the British Musical with the big four megahits *Cats*, *Phantom of the Opera*, *Les Misérables* and *Miss Saigon*, but among the many successes there have been some failures too, like *Moby Dick*, but such flops are a testament to the fact that Cameron puts on shows because he likes them. That is his first priority, while the expectation of making a profit is very much secondary. One of his many qualities is a gritty, stubborn persistence to fight for a show he loves, as is exemplified by the restagings of *Martin Guerre*.

In 1995 Cameron was awarded a Knighthood for services to British Theatre and for his support for many charities. The Mackintosh Foundation is a charity that in 1990 endowed the Chair of Contemporary Theatre at St Catherine's College, Oxford University, where various notable professors have included Stephen Sondheim, Dame Diana Rigg, Arthur Miller, Sir Ian McKellan, Alan Ayckbourn, Peter Shaffer, Richard Eyre, Lord Attenborough, and Thelma Holt. Cameron is president of the Royal Scottish Academy of Music and Dance and he gives much support to new writers. Over a period of several years, from 1990 onward, the National Theatre received a gift of £1 million from the Mackintosh Foundation to produce classic musicals, and if they transferred to the West End profits would still go back to the National. Cameron is renowned for his generosity and is also legendary for his spectacular parties, whether to celebrate a first night or the long-running anniversary of a show. And the invitations are not just for the big names in a cast but for everyone involved. He owns seven theatres in London's West End: the Prince of Wales,

Gielgud, Queen's, Wyndham's, Noël Coward, Novello, and Prince Edward, and he is committed to the ongoing and exciting process of their renovation. In 2006 Cameron was presented with an award for Outstanding Contribution to Tourism given by Visit Britain, an award previously won by the Queen and Harry Potter!

In 1998, *Hey, Mr Producer!*, a celebration Charity Gala Concert, was held to mark Cameron's thirty years as a producer. The Queen and the Duke of Edinburgh were present and there was a cast of 132 plus 86 children and the Scottish Piper band. Many famous names such as Julie Andrews, Dame Judi Dench, Elaine Paige, Julia Mackenzie, Jonathan Pryce, Colm Wilkinson, and Bernadette Peters performed excerpts from his best loved shows culminating with an eight-song excerpt from *Les Misérables*. It was indeed a fitting tribute to such a producer.

CM: I'd wanted to be a producer since the age of 8 and I was determined to be one by the time I was 25. In fact I made it when I was 20. I knew that in order to succeed I would need to gain experience in every single backstage job, whether it was running the prompt corner, running the sound, or managing the props. When I first worked at Drury Lane I used to tell the guys backstage that I would be a producer one day and they used to send me up. But you have to have a dream. Even today my staff have all worked in the theatre in some way and they understand the business from the inside.

I can only work with something I'm passionate about and then do my best to make it succeed. But you have to have an instinct for what works on stage and what makes a great show, which is something you can't teach. You either have that instinct or you don't. I may not be able to tell you exactly why something works but I usually know when something doesn't work. I've never believed that a producer shouldn't meddle with what is happening on his stage and I always get involved with every aspect of a production. Then if it doesn't succeed you know you've done your best.

I'd like to think that after an audience spends two or three hours in the theatre they leave feeling that they're different from when they came in. Therefore the material that I most enjoy working on has some substance. The music should be able to tell a story as much as the words. The lyrics must emotionally propel the story and characters, without any fat in the writing. You should be unaware that you're watching scenery and actors and feel that you've been totally pulled into another world. That's what I aim for in my productions. So once the audience settles down the first thing you've got to do is to show them the language of the evening that you're going to use to take them on a theatrical journey.

In all the really great musicals there is an amazing craft in the construction of the book and the way the music and lyrics are honed. Musicals need to be larger than life, and while some are simply entertaining there are those that evoke a deeper response. Rodgers and Hammerstein knew precisely how to push the emotional buttons with their wonderful, touching stories. Those kind of stories never lose their contemporary appeal. Of course many of the great plots have been reworked in the way that *West Side Story* was reworked from *Romeo and Juliet*. Great storytelling never fails because the essential truths that these stories embody constantly fascinate us. Many of the shows I've done are based on the works of great writers, who provide the backbone for the musical story and become the inspiration for the authors. It's because these great books have such substance in their ideas that they can take a different interpretation. I like to think with *Les Misérables* and *Oliver!* that these musicals are as much a work of art in their own right as the original novels. They're not better than the novels, they don't compete with the novels, they complement them.

Cats was my first huge international hit. Previously if you had a hit show you could take it to New York and that was it. If anybody else wanted it they would buy the rights and do it their own way. But with *Cats* we had offers from all over the world from people who wanted to do an exact replica of our production. And that had never happened before and it took us by surprise. *Cats* was particularly important because it gave me the financial security to do only shows that I really wanted to do. It was really the first time in my career that I wasn't in debt. It takes maybe three or four years to put together a new musical and it costs a lot to develop it. Now I was able to nurture my shows for as long as necessary. Everyone involved works toward the same end and the inevitable arguments during a production are always about how best to serve the piece. It's so important to get the right size of theatre for the production as I have sometimes found to my cost in the past. In fact I've often felt that in casting a show you really need to cast an auditorium as well as the leading lady. Drury Lane is a wonderful theatre and obviously it is great for me to produce a show there, but not many shows can afford to run there for very long. It is a very hard theatre to fill and you have to wonder if a lot of shows wouldn't have been better in a smaller theatre.

None of us can really know what shows the public will take to but for certain it's nothing to do with the nationality of the writers. There are only two places in the world that you can regularly create musicals: London and New York, because that is where the majority of people involved in musicals work and live. But theatre is made by individuals and not by nation states and a show isn't successful because it's British or because it's American but because it has its own magic. It's interesting though that so many of the great Broadway writers from the 1920s until the 1960s, who were the wonderful tunesmiths of the legendary Broadway musicals, were often Jewish émigrés who had either come as children from Europe or were heavily influenced by Jewish European music. America was the essential crucible of their talent. Alain and Claude-Michel are not really true Parisians, they are good Jewish boys and they're firmly in that tradition of European Jewish writers.

The main thing I'm looking for with a new musical is originality and a good idea, but in a lot of the demo tapes that I get sent most of the music just shouldn't ever be heard on stage. The moment that I heard Alain and Claude-Michel's French album of *Les Misérables* I was knocked out by this incredibly theatrical music, which just cried out to be staged. I didn't understand the French lyrics but there was something about the music that seemed to paint pictures of the story in my mind. The opening "magic notes" just took me and it built and built. In this original French version the tune of "On My Own" was the main theme of the show. It was called "La Misère" and this haunting tune was the third one in. I couldn't believe all these wonderful tunes were coming out one after the other. I had no doubt Alain and Claude-Michel were capable of writing a great show. I knew I wanted to do it; I never had a moment's hesitation. But I could never have imagined the public response to it. I never thought it would last more than a couple of years because it was too serious a subject. To be honest I didn't even know if an audience would sit still for a three hour show. But it seemed to have a life of its own.

Once I get inspired to do a show and I feel I've got the most I can out of working with writers on the structure and material, then it is my job is to bring other collaborators to the work. Musicals more than any other kind of theatre are the sum of very wide-ranging collaborators from the orchestrator through to the lighting designer. It's not just the director, the writer and the producer. I don't consider my chair to be any more important than the director's, the

Photo by Michael Le Poer Trench

Boublil, Mackintosh, and Schönberg in 1996 during rehearsals for *Martin Guerre*.

musical director's, or the costume designer's. The only difference in my position is that I have the ultimate responsibility for making sure that the author's vision is put on stage to the best of its ability. And indeed by doing so, ensuring that the show has a long life and keeps people employed for as long as possible to the highest artistic standards. But I believe in changing the creative mix occasionally, because if the same people work together all the time what starts off as marvelous mental shorthand becomes repetition.

As soon as I decided to do *Les Misérables* my immediate impulse was that this was a piece for Trevor Nunn, and I thought that there would be nobody else who could possibly pull this off. However, it took me nearly two years to get him to agree to do it with John Caird, his collaborator on the marvelous *Nicholas Nickleby*. Working at the Barbican Theatre with the RSC was important to the development of the material, which needed the unique contribution that a great subsidized company can give you in the way that people approach and rehearse the work. We needed the cast of *Les Misérables*, whether drawn from a classical theatre background like Roger Allam and Alan Armstrong or the world of the popular musical like Colm Wilkinson and Michael Ball, to be equally accomplished musical performers, so that musically the show was of the same standard as if it had opened straight into the West End. It couldn't just be a classical piece where actors had a good stab at the singing.

When we've been working on Alain and Claude-Michel's scripts, an additional problem for me has always been getting the right English lyrics. Alain has always been very smart at sensing a good idea and he is a very fine librettist in French but although he speaks English fluently he does not instinctively write in English syntax without the help of a collaborator. When he's working with a co-lyricist he's very shrewd about fine tuning something that's nearly right because his own natural talent as a lyricist will win out. But the final words have always taken longer to be realized than the musical score. Alain and Claude-Michel created *Les Misérables* in French and although the original Paris show was considerably different from the show the world now knows the genius of inspiration was completely theirs. From the outset Alain and Claude-Michel had worked out how to compress the bones of Hugo's story and write the kind of music that was going to make Hugo's epic tale take flight. But it was the combined talents of Trevor Nunn, John Caird, and James Fenton to fill out their original inspiration and the marvelous English words of Herbert Kretzmer that made the show finally come together and fully reflect the tone of Hugo's great novel.

With *Saigon* they started off with a much stronger shape to their first draft. What I do best is to act as a catalyst, throwing up ideas if I think something is not there or if it's wrong. For instance, because I felt a song was missing early on in the show I suggested that Chris needed a song after his first night with Kim, so that the audience could understand his dilemma and emotional journey. This became "Why God Why?" When Nick Hytner came on board he fine-tuned the dramatic structure and suggested we take out one character who was a friend of Kim. She had quite a pretty little ballad but it was unnecessary. We found that the show was overfilled with ballads and Kim had one ballad too many. It was actually one of my favorite songs in the show, "Too Much For One Heart," but the story just couldn't take another solo at that point. However, the lovely tune was kept and became the duet "Please" in the second act.

With *Martin Guerre* I don't think either Alain or Claude-Michel realized how big a problem it is to write a dramatic musical not based on an existing source. They're very skillful at adapting but this time they didn't have a definite story to adapt and they had to invent one. Unusually the story of Martin Guerre is based on a tragic true love story based on lies, deception, and religion; these are difficult subjects for a musical. With the original draft score there was the odd gem but, as Claude-Michel was the first to admit, when story writing is generalized, music often becomes generalized as well. Alain first tried working on the lyrics with the show's director Declan Donnellan and then with Herbie, but I knew when I saw the first drafts that it wasn't going to work out. It just didn't seem the right language for the show and at that point I brought in Edward Hardy to write the lyrics. It took a lot of work from all of us to get the story up on its feet at the Prince Edward. The very reason the show eluded us was that there wasn't a simple storyline. We tried too hard to make it clear by adding too much detail. Despite the problems, I think the score contains some of Claude-Michel's most accomplished music. We made some improvements and it gained a much stronger structure. However, it never finally quite came together in any of the versions I produced, despite the revised version of the London show winning the Olivier Award for the Best Musical in 1997. But I have great hopes that in a few years the authors themselves will come up with a version that finally matches up to their original dream for the show and that with distance they'll find a simple through line that manages to keep the suspense as well as the power of this unusual love story.

Sometimes what makes a musical come together is the unexpected. You often audition with a preconceived notion of how the songs are going to be sung as we did with Jean Valjean. Claude-Michel had written the part as a baritone but when Colm Wilkinson threw the songs into a higher octave because he is a tenor, the music sounded far more thrilling and changed the impact of the score. When we were rehearsing, Jean Valjean had nothing to sing on the barricade, and Claude-Michel quickly came up with a song written with Colm's voice in mind. It was "Bring Him Home." In fact, the first time Colm sang it one of the cast said "We knew this show was going to be about God but you didn't tell us you'd arranged for Him to sing it!" In all, five songs were added for the London production, which had never been in the original Paris version.

However, the position of the song can also make a difference. With "Stars" in *Les Mis*, for instance, during the first year of the show's run it was halfway through Act I, after Valjean makes a bargain with the Thénardiers for Cosette, and before Paris, but the song stopped the show in the wrong way. It broke the back of the act and so you might think: "When is the interval coming?" The moment we moved it to Paris later on in the act it became a showstopper in the best way. But, of course, one of the benefits of having a long run is that you have the luxury of looking at a show and saying, I could do that bit better; why didn't I think of it before?

Casting is usually a joint decision. You go by instinct but, unless we all agree on a performer, there's often something wrong. The few times I've gone against my own instinct and succumbed to a director's choice and not argued the case the results have been a mistake. It's usually easier casting second companies because by then we all have a much more clearly defined knowledge of what we're looking for.

I never have a very strong vision of what a show is going to be like beforehand. I'm not one of those people who can do that. I do have a strong visual sense of when something is right but I need the director and the designer to show me something in a rough form first. What I've discovered about myself is that I'm not a very good innovator. I'm at my best in spotting someone else's originality and making that originality as good as it can be. I have to be reactive before I'm proactive and I love seeing the puzzle come together.

It has always been important to have good eyecatching posters as we've had for *Cats, Les Mis, Phantom,* and *Saigon.* A good poster is an immediately identifiable visual statement. It says everything and nothing, allowing the imagination to take flight and catching the spirit of the show with something very simple. But it is often an extremely complex process to make it simple and that is where I often rely on graphic designers Russ Eglin and Bob King for their expertise. I have worked with the same advertising agency, Dewynters, all my life.

I don't think the public goes to the theatre solely because of great reviews, although they can certainly give you a rush on the box office to start with. The most important thing for any show is word of mouth, that's what propels a long run. The greatest satisfaction for me always is seeing a show being performed in the way I dreamed it would be and seeing an audience react as enthusiastically and emotionally as I have in my dreams. I've never tried to do a show to get a particular reaction from an audience. What I hope for is the audience having the same appreciation of that material as I have because in the end if a piece of theatre doesn't affect an audience, why should they bother to see it? It doesn't matter how big the advance is, it depends on how much the audience likes a show—that's what makes it run and run.

The reaction to *Miss Saigon* over the years has grown, not diminished, the further we get away from the Vietnam war. From the start people who had actually been involved with the Vietnam war have always recognized the truthful way the show dealt with such sensitive subject matter. Many vets have remarked on how it brought it all back to them.

Many of my shows have toured successfully, and I think it is because the public knows I'm not prepared to compromise the standards of a show because it's on tour. I want the show to be as good, if not better, than it is in London or on Broadway. When I was a young producer I used to see shows with cut down scenery and costumes, which made the show on tour a pale imitation of the London original. I vowed to change that and take enormous pride in knowing that I have been instrumental in raising the level of musical theatre around the world as audiences now won't put up with anything second rate. I'm also very proud of the Schools Edition of *Les Misérables,* which has been performed by over 60,000 children in the UK and America. It's fantastic to have all this new young talent always wanting to be in the musicals. I am delighted that musicals have now become "cool" again as a whole new generation of fans grow up.

Les Misérables will probably be the show that I'm best remembered for. And it's partly because Victor Hugo wrote such an extraordinary story. I don't think any other musical is likely to be blessed with such a strong foundation. Hugo's genius was that he wrote a story which touches people in every generation and in every country. The characters that he created back in the nineteenth century have the same power to affect an audience around the world today thanks to Alain and Claude-Michel's masterly musicalization. It's very rare in popular entertainment to have something that is both entertaining, thrilling and moving. The magic of *Les Misérables* will always be personal and I get letters all the time from people who keep finding things to empathize with. It's just inherent in the material and I think that when you get something so powerful that, over twenty-one years into its life, audiences leap to their feet and cry, then you know you've been involved in something very special. It has always been a show for the people and it's the people that make a great success, not the hype and not the producer. The inspiration of the writers is the source of it all. I'm obviously very proud that it has now taken over from *Cats* as the longest running musical in the world.

I have to believe that each musical I do is completely different from the others. *Cats* couldn't be further away from *Les Misérables* in style, *Saigon* couldn't be more different from *Phantom*, and *Martin Guerre* was different again. We all have tremendous disappointments, financial problems, and God knows what in theatre, but you have to take each experience and see what you have learned from it. There's not one show I do that I don't make another new mistake. I try not to make the same mistakes. Every time I do another new production it's really exciting and it's like doing my first show all over again. Though now I rarely do new shows, I still get the same buzz and enjoyment of working on great material, new or old. The big surprise for me is that so many of my productions are still going on around the world decades later. The only challenge I care about is keeping up my enthusiasm. I love what I do and I know I'm terribly lucky to be able to do what I love. ❧

CHAPTER 6

New Horizons

THE PIRATE QUEEN
AND BEYOND

THE PIRATE QUEEN is the exciting new Boublil and Schönberg musical produced by Moya Doherty and John McColgan, who produced the worldwide phenomenon *Riverdance*. The musical is based on the real-life story of the legendary Irish pirate chieftain, Grace O'Malley, who is also known as Granuaile, Gráinne, Grany, and, as she is in this musical, Grania. *The Pirate Queen* combines classic storytelling and a sweeping score with the powerful, vibrant traditions of Irish dance and song to create a modern musical event that is both historic romance and timeless epic. Grace O'Malley's life (1530–1603) has all the high passion and magnificent spectacle of an operatic work—yet it is historical fact. Grania was one of the last Irish clan leaders to resist the Tudor invasion of Gaelic Ireland.

The musical opens as chieftain Dubhdara's ship prepares to set sail. His young daughter Grania is desperate to go to sea with her father, but at a time when women were considered bad luck at sea, this is clearly out of the question. However, Grania disguises herself as a boy and, before long, her courage earns her a place as one of the ship's crew. As she grows up she becomes not only the captain of the ship but also the chieftain of her clan and a formidable political leader. She is an intelligent, independent, and headstrong woman who cares passionately for Ireland and for those close to her. She leads her clan triumphantly through many battles and still remains the admiring and respectful only child of her beloved father, chieftain Dubhdara. She agrees to a marriage with Donal, the son of the chieftain of another clan, whom she doesn't know and doesn't love, for the sake of Ireland, despite being very much in love with her childhood friend Tiernan. Queen Elizabeth I of England is infuriated with Grania's successes in defeating her own ships and men, but eventually she somewhat reluctantly begins to admire the strength and convictions of this other powerful, determined leader. At the end of the show, as happened in real life, they have a truly remarkable meeting.

Alain and Claude-Michel have taken this astonishing true story and made it their own. Inevitably, some elements are changed from real life and some details added in order to develop it into a cohesive, dramatic musical and to endow it with their unique brand of heartrending emotion. Although this is a historical musical set in sixteenth-century Ireland, it has a very contemporary resonance. As in all their other shows, Alain and Claude-Michel seem to have an extraordinary ability to use the past as a mirror through which we can see and examine present-day issues.

This chapter has been written around the time of the musical's World Première at Chicago's beautiful Cadillac Palace Theatre on October 29, 2006. It played to over 90 percent capacity and was noted in *Variety* as one of the most successful out-of-town tryouts. The following pages tell the fascinating story, from the initial conception of the work to its out-of-town opening. As with all new shows, there will inevitably be some changes before the New York opening on April 5, 2007. Richard Maltby, Alain's co-lyricist on *Miss Saigon*, has joined the creative team and substantial rewrites are underway clarifying the story of the two leading ladies, Grania and Elizabeth I, and further developing the characters of Tiernan and Donal. The name of Dubhdara's ship has been changed from the *Ceol Na Mara* to *The Pirate Queen*. A new song has been written and Claude-Michel is refining all the musical links. Graciela Daniele, a long time associate of director Frank Galati, is overseeing the musical staging. The story of the show's creation is again told in Alain and Claude-Michel's own words and those of the co-lyricist, director, producers, and, this time—as dance is such an integral element of the show—also in the words of the choreographers. The Fact File in the next chapter will provide some details of the show and casting, together with a full synopsis of the story and a factual history of Grace O'Malley. It has been remarkable in working on this chapter to discover not only the stratospheric standards but also the passion, the excitement, the absolute enthusiasm, and the total commitment of everyone involved with the show, as they all endeavor to make it the very best evening of musical theatre that it can possibly be.

WRITING *THE PIRATE QUEEN*

THE BOOK

AB: Claude-Michel and I always spend a very long time choosing a subject for a musical. It's something we always do on our own, but in the case of *The Pirate Queen,* for the very first time, it was a project that was brought to us. It was Moya Doherty and John McColgan, the producers of *Riverdance,* who brought the story of Grace O'Malley to us and initially, we were quite sure we didn't want to work on someone else's story. And then we started to think about it and realized that although we hate biographies in musicals we would have liked to write *Evita* if we'd had the idea first. We could see that this story was just as exciting as the story of Eva Peron and, in a way, more interesting to us, because it's in period costume yet is still more modern than the history of any modern woman today. So we knew immediately how to do that; after all, even if our last show, *Martin Guerre,* was named after a man, it is really a story about Bertrande in the same way that *Miss Saigon* is a story about Kim. They're both strong, independent, modern women. Claude-Michel was very uncertain but I could see that here was another chance to mix sounds, in the same way that in *Miss Saigon* we mixed Asian sounds with Claude-Michel's theatrical, operatic music. Here, we could take those incredible Irish sounds, which are similar to the Brittany sounds that

Photo by Joan Marcus

Claude-Michel and Alain at early rehearsals for *The Pirate Queen*.

Claude-Michel is so good at, and mix them with the operatic flow of the story, which is such an epic journey. However, Claude-Michel still said, "No, no, I don't think we should do it"—and the very next day he had composed the overture! When I heard it I said, "Look, we both know we are going to do it."

CMS: At first we were a little bit suspicious about the subject matter, because although the story of Grace O'Malley is a true story and she is a historical figure, there is a lot of legend added to the story. Before, we've always dealt totally with reality in our shows, but this story left us very free to structure it in our own way, and that was very exciting. We knew there would be more dance in this show, not only because of the *Riverdance* connection and the quality of their dancers, but because in sixteenth-century Ireland, every time there was rejoicing or a celebration for a wedding, a Christening, or even a funeral wake, there would inevitably be lots of dancing. At that time, I was reading a lot about Japanese Kabuki theatre and I found that fascinating because in Kabuki you can have everything together and you are perfectly free to mix the language of dance with the language of song and so on. It made me realize how we could mix the storytelling, dancing, acting, and singing all together in the perfect way to build the arc of the full evening. From this vision, I wrote the first twenty minutes of the show. We structured the show instinctively, more like *La Révolution Française*, where we took a historical story and wrote another story inside it, a love story. And this time we have the love story of Grania and her childhood friend Tiernan that is going all through the show.

AB: *The Pirate Queen* is an epic musical with, as usual, a political bias. Grace O'Malley defended her country in a way that was unknown for a woman at that time. Although it was considered bad luck to have a woman on a boat in those days, she was a sailor at the age of ten, became the first woman captain on a pirate ship, taking over as the chieftain of her clan when her father, Dubhdara, died, and she became a formidable political Irish leader. She is probably one of the first ever true feminists at heart, long before the word was invented. She also had a very fascinating love life, torn between duty and passion.

The important thing for us was not only to tell the story as it happened, but also to capture the key moments that shaped such an unusual destiny, and to structure them through an evening of musical theatre. So although, in real life, she had more than one husband and more than one lover, we focused our story on the two most powerful figures: her first husband, Donal, and her lifelong lover, Tiernan. However romantic and operatic her love life was, Grace O'Malley's main calling was to protect and fight for her people to the very end, to the last battle, which she would win with words, with the dignity of a queen: the Pirate Queen. Her meeting with Elizabeth I, recorded in the annals of the English monarchy, makes for an extraordinary, if unusual, moment of musical theatre. The story of Grace O'Malley was suppressed for many years by the male historians who charted Irish and English history, but now it is in history books and taught in schools not only in Ireland, but also in

England and other English-speaking countries. So once again, we were taken by a subject in a way that made us think that we would gladly spend three or more years of our lives in the company of such a driven and modern woman as Grania O'Malley.

For the background of the story, Moya and John gave us many historical documents, including Morgan Llewellyn's book *Grania*, and these were very handy as factual sources of information. We realized early on that the musical form was completely obvious to the story. After reconceiving the story and making it our own, we made a definite commitment to Moya and John to write *The Pirate Queen*. They would obviously be our producers, as they had brought the story to us. Originally we started with the idea that John, who directed *Riverdance*, would direct *The Pirate Queen*, but he soon realized that this project was much too big for anyone to be both producer and director. We started to look for a director together, but fate had it that just at that time Claude-Michel, Moya, John, and I were pre-casting in New York and went one evening to see *Wicked*. We liked the show but just fell in love with the sets and were desperately seeking to meet with Eugene Lee, the kind of visual genius that we had not come across since John Napier. Eugene responded enthusiastically to the project and suggested that we meet his friend Frank Galati, who had directed *Ragtime* on Broadway, and who is one of the resident directors of Steppenwolf, in Chicago. Coincidentally, we had already met Frank briefly years ago—at one time, he had been lined up to co-write with us the screenplay of *Miss Saigon* when Steven Spielberg had wanted to direct the film. Unfortunately, that project had fallen through. So we met Frank again with great enthusiasm. After listening to the demo of the show as it stood at the time, with John Dempsey singing all the parts live, not only did he agree to direct it, but soon after, he gave us a director's script of *The Pirate Queen* which was so incredibly detailed that we definitely wanted him to do it. We had previously approached Julie Taymor, who directed *The Lion King*, regarding the choreography, but she was developing *Spider-Man, The Musical* and wasn't available for the next three years. However, she suggested that Mark Dendy, a choreographer she had been working with on *The Magic Flute* for the Metropolitan Opera in New York, should be considered for the show. We loved Mark's ideas and energy, and he was hired before Frank became part of the team. Fortunately, since then, they have become the best of collaborators and friends.

With hindsight, I realize that all the extraordinary directors we have worked with had one thing in common. Trevor Nunn, John Caird, Nick Hytner, Declan Donnellan, Conall Morrison, and now Frank Galati all belong to that same family of creators with strong intellectual backgrounds; they are eternal students in a way, like us, with an unashamed, deep-rooted love for musical theatre. In the English-speaking world, this duality is not a contradiction in terms, as it could be in France, for example, where musical theatre, in the tradition of Rodgers & Hammerstein, Lerner & Lowe, Kander & Ebb, Lloyd Webber & Rice, vastly unknown to the majority anyway, is alien to the highbrow music connoisseurs.

Grania is the kind of character I relish. She is the kind of person who always falls back on her feet and starts all over again. She has the ability to reinvent herself and turn around a situation with bravery. She behaves like, or better, than the boldest of men. She's a woman of extraordinary competence, who lives up to the challenge of modern women, juggling a career (in her case as a political leader) and a complex personal life. What is very touching in the first part of the story is the father/daughter relationship. Her life is guided by this man that she admires and will admire forever, so that every man in her life has to compare to him. Her father doesn't command her to marry a man she doesn't love but they both share the same feeling that this is the right thing to do in the situation. Fortunately, in Ireland at that time, the Brehon Laws allowed a woman to marry a man and to test him for three years before making a definite commitment. So Grania could dismiss her husband when he behaved badly and be free. The sixteenth-century English considered this a barbaric attitude, but funnily enough, this is exactly what is happening today everywhere in the Western world. Aren't people living together for a few years before committing to any kind of serious bond—if they do?

CMS: Grania is a heroic figure for the Irish people, a bit like Joan of Arc is for the French. Grania is a symbol of resistance against the English and of fighting to save the tradition and the freedom of the culture. She's a strong figure of resistance against colonization in general and against losing your soul. She had been fighting Queen Elizabeth all her life, from when she was a young child on her father's ship, and our show is about the history of these two women. Elizabeth I had a very long reign and lived between almost exactly the same dates as Grania. Elizabeth is a major character in the show and always a counterpart to Grania's action. Ireland was not a unified country at that time and was ruled by the chieftains of the various clans. The O'Malley clan were very rich and powerful people who owned a great deal of land and had many ships trading with Spain and North Africa, and they were in direct competition with English trade. Engaging in piracy, they also attacked English ships.

Lord Richard Bingham is a famous historic character and was a confidante to the queen. He was the other Francis Drake but he was sent to fight the Irish, when he would have preferred to travel the faraway world. He is a very frustrated and complicated character, and Grania's fiercest adversary. When Grania is imprisoned, she loses everything—her ships, her castles, and her lands—and her people suffer great hardships. When she is released, she takes the unprecedented step of asking for a meeting with Elizabeth I. The queen was very much her own person and, although she began her reign by trusting her advisors, she soon realized that there was no one to be trusted but herself. In that respect, she is very similar to Grania. Elizabeth was very powerful, but in many ways she was a very frustrated woman, whereas Grania had a complete love life and children. She was a queen in her own way but with all the advantages of having a real life. When the two women finally meet they have long been sworn enemies, but just when a bitter confrontation is expected, the opposite occurs. It's a moment of harmony. They speak, not about political facts, but simply as one woman to another about life, children, men, and all the problems that concern women. So at this moment, instead of being enemies they're more like accomplices. At the end of the meeting the queen gives back Grania everything she had lost, and Grania promises not to fight anymore.

Tiernan is Grania's childhood companion and as young kids they are in love. But Grania decides to marry the chieftain of another clan so that the clans will be united and in a stronger position against the English. (See *The Pirate Queen* photo insert 6.) Tiernan is the kind of man who, despite the anger and frustration he feels, will still keep his friendship for the woman he loves and will wait for her all his life if he has to, because he cannot love another woman. (See *The Pirate Queen* photo insert 8.) But he is not a victim; he is a fighter—he's strong and he's a winner. Donal, the man Grania marries, is not a very nice man and immediately you know the kind of man he is. There are some funny moments because he is such a jerk that he is sincere. And the confrontation between the men and women in the village also gives rise to some comic moments that are a kind of relief that lifts the tension. Finally Donal is someone who loses his Irishness and compromises with the enemy. With this character we have moved away from historical truth for dramatic purposes and hopefully it won't offend any of his descendants.

THE MUSIC

CMS: When Moya and John first suggested this story to us, I went to see *Riverdance* because I wanted to be surrounded by the Irish atmosphere and music, and I was totally overwhelmed by the quality of the music and the musicians. So I started to play as usual on my acoustic piano, thinking about that music and the life of Grace O'Malley, and trying to find the right kind of atmosphere, and after a week or so I had twenty minutes of music. The more I thought about it the more excited I felt, to have that mix of theatre music, rock and roll and Irish folk music. I started thinking how I might work with the musicians I heard in *Riverdance*, who are very good Irish musicians, and they have that sense of Irish music that is very specific. I soon realized the importance of the peculiar sound I wanted to give to the orchestra and I switched to an electronic Roland piano KR7 so that listeners could understand what I was meaning. It's very specialized music and it's not everyone who can play it. So we will not have the usual theatre orchestra in the pit but a complete Irish band.

I started to structure the show, writing one sequence of music followed by another and reworking and rewriting until we managed to have a score more like musical theatre. But the most original, new thing was the complete freedom in the way you could treat this kind of story and make it exciting and uplifting. The band of eleven musicians gives you a sense of period which is neither very old nor very modern but has a sense of Irish origin in the same way that I achieved a sense of the Far East in *Saigon*, even though I'm not a specialist in Asian music. But this will sound more Irish than *Saigon* sounded Vietnamese because of all the Irish instruments, for example, with the fiddle it's a totally different way to play it and to approach it.

As I was working I found out that I knew a lot more about Celtic culture than I had realized. I was born in Brittany, which has a very strong Celtic culture and, as a very young kid, at every wedding or festivity I used to see all the Celtic bands with the pipes and other Celtic instruments and the Celtic dances. It could be just one or two players or a big orchestra that they call "the bagad." So even though I am a Jewish Hungarian I was raised in this Celtic culture. In Vannes, where I was born, I remember that some people still used to speak Breton rather than French, and, of course, Vannes is only about thirty miles away from Lorient, where they hold the biggest Celtic Festival in the world.

With each of our previous three shows I was moving more and more toward an operatic form, and in *Martin Guerre* I was trying to be very operatic. But in this show I've moved away from that and gone completely back to our beginnings. However, for Elizabeth, because she's a queen, the part has been written for a very classical mezzo-soprano and it has been written completely in consideration of that voice. It's the first time we've used such a classical voice and it will be a real treat, especially as we were spoiled for choice in casting the role since there are so many wonderful classical sopranos who

sing at the Metropolitan Opera in New York. There are, as usual, so-
liloquies, the big solo numbers, which are moments of introspection
for the key characters and reprises, which come in the natural and
obvious places where they are required by the story. Apart from a
few small spoken scenes it's all sung-through and there are a lot of
orchestral moments too, for the dancing. What was very important
was that the music didn't sound like a parody of Irish music or, in
the English scenes, a parody of court music. I think when you listen
to the music you will understand that it's still mine, but with an Irish
flavor because of the instruments and because of the way of writing.
So there was a fine line to follow to be sure that you're not falling
on one side or the other.

I didn't work in the usual way with this show, in as much as I
would normally give the score to an orchestrator only three months
before we started the show. But for *The Pirate Queen* I started working with the musicians in May 2005, eighteen months before the
show opened. And we worked together on a regular basis. Julian
Kelly wrote out the music and has been leading the musicians. I
wanted to give them a lot of freedom to interpret the music in their
own way. They are working a little bit like a rock 'n' roll band. It's
something I enjoy enormously. It's a very exciting way to work, and
it's an entirely different process to anything I've ever done before.
The music is very fresh and energetic and full of enthusiasm—and
it's still very theatrical. We had planned for the orchestra sometimes
to be playing in the pit and sometimes on the stage as part of the
community. There were too many logistical problems to do this in
Chicago, but we are hoping to do it in New York. We want it to sound
like a band rather than the usual pit orchestra. We have some Irish
musicians, and some are American or Irish-American. Although they
have the music on the stands they mostly know the show by heart
and at times they can riff, that is, take off and improvise, just a bit,
in ways that vary from night to night. This is more to create energy
for the band than for technical reasons.

When you listen to the music you already have a vision of what
the story is without any lyrics or voices. But now with the first stag-

ing I've been really discovering the show and checking how it works with the sets, lights, music, lyrics, actors, and everything coming together. You sometimes get huge emotion arising from that combination and I've been surprised by some moments in the show. We hope that this subject and this show will be high entertainment and that's the way we've conceived it.

THE WORDS

AB: This writing experience has been more or less similar to working on *Miss Saigon*, where from beginning to end the story held together very early in the writing process. We don't work in a fragmented way because we devise a whole story, a scene by scene story. Then Claude-Michel writes twenty minutes of music, which usually paints with great precision the result of our discussions. When we have written half an hour or an hour of music and lyrics in French, we go back and look at it, and maybe discover that there is a flaw here or there, that a character lacks depth, that his motivations need to be re-discussed. This happened, especially for the part of Bingham, which went through various stages, very much helped by further discussions with John McColgan and Frank Galati. We analyze endlessly and obsessively the feelings of the characters and the meaning of their actions, as well as their relevance to us, as twenty-first-century writers, and to the first spectators of the show. There is a little more comedy in *The Pirate Queen* than in *Les Misérables, Martin Guerre,* or *Miss Saigon,* and it does have a happy ending. It's wonderful at last to have the opportunity not to kill the hero or heroine tragically.

As usual, I had written the whole of Act I of *The Pirate Queen* in French before meeting with my co-lyricist, John Dempsey. From that point, when we started to work together, I would only sketch most of the lyrical contents of the scenes in Act II, in French or in English, before we started to write the lyrics together. As co-lyricist, John came as a natural, because Claude-Michel had met him when his show *The Witches of Eastwick* was playing in London. The work John had done showed his amazing craft as a musical theatre writer for comedy and off-the-wall stuff and we had long discussions to see if he could work in a more tragic, dramatic field. I soon realized that his knowledge and understanding of musical theatre and his range of craft in crafting a song or a scene for musical theatre was such that he certainly belonged to a much wider range as a lyricist than comedy alone. John has been a delight to work with because, in addition to being a wonderful wordsmith, he keeps at all times a complete vision of the show, and he seems thoroughly to enjoy the process of collaboration. As with each of the writers I've worked with, the show always comes first and to me that's the "First Commandment" of musical theatre. And with John I must say that our alliance of minds works in a very unique, both calm and passionate way, as when two people do a crossword puzzle together. As always there have been a number of re-writes of the show, and we both love doing that. Who said, "You don't write a musical, you re-write it?" Re-writing is that special time when you have to stop being self-complacent and finally make the show an evening that you would want to see at the theatre.

CO-LYRICIST: JOHN DEMPSEY

John Dempsey is a very experienced librettist and lyricist who has often partnered with composer Dana P. Rowe. Together they wrote *The Witches of East-wick*, which opened in London in July 2000, has played in Melbourne, Tokyo, and Moscow, and will receive its American launch in Spring 2007. They also collaborated on *The Fix*, which premiered in 1997 at London's Donmar Warehouse, where it was directed by Sam Mendes.

Photo by Margaret Vermette

John Dempsey

John wrote the book and lyrics for *Circles, Dick Whittington,* and *Zombie Prom,* which played Off-Broadway in 1996 and is currently being developed as a film. He wrote the lyrics for the musicals *A Country Christmas Carol* and *The Reluctant Dragon,* as well as for various editions of *The Ringling Bros. Barnum and Bailey Circus.* John has written several plays including *World Today, The Greater Goode,* and *One Miracle in a Lifetime.* He has received Olivier nominations for both *The Fix* and *The Witches of Eastwick* and is the recipient of an Ohio Arts Council Fellowship for Playwriting. He was born and raised in Youngstown, Ohio, eventually moving to Columbus where he taught second grade at Royal Manor Elementary School. He currently resides in New York City.

JD: It has been a wonderful collaboration working with Alain on *The Pirate Queen.* It was a case of two very different minds trying to come to the same end. Alain and I come from two very different backgrounds, cultures, generations, and lifestyles, so this was a real challenge and a real joy. It took us a little time to find our stride and I've never co-written in this way before. I could liken it to four hands repairing a watch, because lyric writing is intricate, little, detailed work and to have two people trying to do it at the same time can be very difficult and very clumsy. So you have to find your way with each other and know how far you can step on each other's toes. You have to establish boundaries first and then obliterate them so that it becomes a true collaboration in the best sense.

By the time I got the first phone call, Alain and Claude-Michel had already written the book of the musical. Very few people seem to realize that the person who does the heavy lifting on a musical is the book writer. The composer and to a lesser extent the lyricist may get all the glory, but musicals don't succeed in spite of the book, they succeed because of it. Many people—in America especially, when they think of the book they think of dialogue, but what the book is in a musical is the structure: it's the story. In the case of *The Pirate Queen,* the book is beautifully structured and it's breathtakingly simple. What Alain and Claude-Michel do is very specific even within the realm of musical theatre. Many people have tried to write musicals in the style of *Les Misérables* and they've all failed miserably because ultimately I don't think people understand what it is Alain and Claude-Michel do from a book-writing point of view. People often compare their work to Andrew Lloyd Webber's but I think they are of two very different worlds. What Andrew does, musically speaking, is very formal, whereas what Claude-Michel does is very raw and it comes right from the heart, just gushing out on stage. There's nothing studied behind it although it's very accomplished musically.

This is also different for me because I'm more accustomed to working on lyrics first. My style of lyric writing tends to be much more conversational, smaller and more detailed, but Claude-Michel writes broad sweeping melodies, so it's hard to match those up. Sometimes it's limiting because there may be certain things I'm desperate to say and I can't fit it into the melody. Also in the past I've tended to write mainly comic lyrics for the shows I've done, like *The Fix* and *The Witches of Eastwick*.

I did some research by reading Irish books and Irish poetry, purely for background, as I don't think poetry ever works on stage. It was more about understanding the culture even more than the historical facts about Grace O'Malley. Alain and Claude-Michel have taken fact, fable, and legend and dramatised their own story. For me, the whole point was to serve their fictional treatment of a non-fictional character. It's the fable, the mythic scale of this piece that I gravitate toward. I used to be an elementary school teacher and I absolutely adore children's literature. Even though this is obviously an adult musical it still has that primal pull that the best children's literature has, which is the highest compliment.

The first thing I was sent to work on was a song called "I Never Want This Dream to End," and it was a song about two kids in love on a boat. I had an English translation of the French lyrics Alain had written. When I got the music I went to Starbucks and got a gallon of coffee and as it was a nice day I took my Walkman and went to Central Park. I walked around listening to the music for a long time before I started to write. At that time we were going to have two young performers as young Grania and Tiernan but eventually the scenario changed and this song became "Here on this Night." When Alain came over to New York he had the first act in French, a literal English translation and tapes of Claude-Michel la-la-ing to the music, and we worked from that. We started on the opening number and just hammered away at it, but it's still the number that gets re-written the most. But that's usual with opening numbers—they have to land in order for the rest of the show to sail.

Then I went to London and Alain and I had a very productive period working eight-hour days. There was one bit in the first act that had to be re-jiggered. Just after the wedding we had Grania going on a long journey to Rockfleet, and that sequence had been constructed with the original concept of the show in mind, which was to do it in a tent in the way that Cirque du Soleil tours. But it was fascinating because we discovered that the show itself demanded the more traditional structure of a musical and gradually it became less of a tent show and more of a stage show. And so as always happens with shows that succeed, it found what it was meant to be. While the journey would have worked in a tent with the horses going round and round, it simply wouldn't work on a stage; it would just be boring. So that first act was a mix of translation and original material that we worked on together. After that it became more about us both working on material with Alain just telling me about what he'd written in French. And in many ways that was easier because when something is written down it just locks you into the text.

Alain and Claude-Michel's musicals are sung-through rather than composed-through. There is a difference, and composed-through is a term that's often misused. As I understand it, it's where a composer starts to play and never reiterates a theme or repeats a motif, and a lot of modern operas are composed-through. But Claude-Michel writes songs with good strong melodies built on repetition. The biggest advantage of a sung-through musical compared to a song/dialogue one is that it allows the music to be bigger. The hardest trick in writing song/dialogue musicals is getting into and out of the songs. If you have music the size of Claude-Michel's and stopped it for dialogue and then tried to get back into a song, it would be a gargantuan task. Musicals have levels and plateaus; if you think in terms of numbers, if dialogue exists at two or three, Claude-Michel's music is above ten. A sung-through musical allows you to play with emotions on a scale that you could never touch in a standard song/dialogue musical. We do, however, have some dialogue for certain moments. There is one short dialogue scene near the end in *The Pirate Queen,* and it's between Elizabeth, Grania, and Bingham. The way Alain and Claude-Michel handle it is rather clever and for them it is just instinctual. The music comes down to the softest point you've had all evening, and it's broken with a sneeze. That is pure genius as a way of leading to the dialogue. Doing a dialogue scene right before the finale gives it a huge punch.

The timespan of the story is never laid out in precise terms. It starts with Grania being in her early teens and ends with her being about fifty. The story is driven by the romance of Grania and Tiernan, who are childhood friends, but it is constantly thwarted by obstacles and, of course, it is driven by politics and the English/Irish conflict. (See *The Pirate Queen* photo insert 3.) But maybe more than anything, it is Grania that drives the show. I think she is the best female character that they have ever written. At no point in the show does she allow either the men in her life or the political landscape in which she finds herself to determine her fate. Grania acts rather than being acted upon. There are moments in the show where it looks like she's going to step forward and sing a "Woe is me" ballad and both times it starts off in that direction only to career into something entirely different two lines in. In both cases she snaps into something completely unexpected and she totally takes charge of the situation. This subversion of expectation is, to me, thrilling. Although this is a historical piece it's very modern and the music is very rock-oriented. Grania is a very modern character; in fact she's timeless in the truest sense of the word. Women in musicals tend to be relegated to virgins, mothers, or whores, and

Grania isn't defined by any of those things. She defines herself, and it's rare in a musical to have a heroine like that.

The musical does show the tragedy of what happens to Ireland, and while Grania is rotting away in prison we see how Ireland is basically sold out from under her and how the clansmen colluded with the English Government in that. But for me the greatest tragic moment comes with the duet "If I Said I Loved You." Grania marries Donal, a man she doesn't love, for political reasons and for the sake of Ireland. Her father, Dubhdara, goes to her and says here are the options: "The choice is yours/To declare where you stand/To choose to wed/For yourself or your land." The first time Alain played that music for me my first thought was Shakespeare. The idea of this chieftain going to his daughter and saying will you marry for the good of your clan—it's moments like that which are classic storytelling. And when Grania sings "My heart?/My land?/My choice/Is clear," we know what her choice is. But after three years Brehon law allows her to dismiss her husband, which is equivalent to divorce, and Grania and Tiernan are both free. They have this little moment then where they're both on stage but in two separate spaces, looking at each other and thinking: "If I said I loved you/All my life I loved you...I wonder what you'd say/Wonder what you'd do/If I said, my love, I love you?" Two-thirds of the way through the song they finally determine to say it and they move towards each other but at the last moment they change their minds, and it turns out to be their last opportunity to proclaim their love until the end of the show. It's that simple affirmation, just hearing in words that someone loves you that is so powerful and the fact that they can't get to that moment is something I find terribly moving.

One of the most exciting duets, "She, Who Has All," is between the Queen and Grania because they're two women of very different positions and they're contrasting their feelings. Their next duet, "Woman to Woman" when they finally meet, is fascinating and yet the music is beyond delicate; it's so light and sweet and as a result it actually builds the tension more than foreboding timpani and blaring French horns.

Writing musical theatre is all about balance. You need to balance the intimate moments with crowd scenes, the huge emotional moments with gentle ballads, and the dramatic numbers with comic numbers. This is something Alain and Claude-Michel are keenly aware of because you want to keep the audience on that roller-coaster, to constantly raise questions, answering some and raising others in an effort to keep the audience off guard a little bit. If you have ten ballads in a row you'll lose your audience. It wasn't until Alain and I were well into the second act that the cleverness of the show's basic structure dawned on me. The first act is largely about Grania as a daughter and her relationship with her father, and the second act is largely about Grania as a mother and it starts with her giving birth. And then the adoptive father, Tiernan, has to take care of the child while she is in jail. That's a very balanced and symmetrical structure. I think that the musical structure is more traditional in the way they use reprises than in their other shows. It's more along the lines of Rodgers and Hammerstein and it makes the score very rich.

There's very little irony in this show except perhaps in the English court. But I think Alain and Claude-Michel are the least ironic men I've ever met. They don't possess irony in the way that Americans do; they're very blunt and out-front with their emotions and how they feel and think. There's no mask; this is who they are. And that, I suspect, is why their work is so well received. It's the very definition of genuine. However, it is a little shocking for someone like me who lives here in New York, where everyone has a mask twenty-four hours a day.

Tiernan, the boy Grania is in love with, is an interesting character. He's not a traditional leading man. He's heroic but he's not the hero and he's masculine but he takes on many feminine attributes. Throughout the show he's looking after Grania and taking care of her child. He has to be delicate and caring enough to have that nurturing side without being a wimp or a mama's boy and he has to be very much a man in the traditional Irish sense of the 1500s. He's is physically a great warrior, and at times he does take matters into his own hands. It's a really tricky balance because you have to be able to buy him as a hero and at the same time accept that he would be comfortable being subordinate to a woman, because Grania is a captain and a chieftain and he is beneath her in station. It could have been a very difficult part to cast if the perfect guy, Hadley Fraser, hadn't walked in.

Elizabeth is one if my favorite characters, and she's very much in line with my sensibility. She has a very dry sense of humor, a wicked sense of her place in history, and a surprisingly sad inner life. I've really enjoyed writing for this Elizabeth, who varies greatly from all the other fictional treatments we've seen. It's an enormous challenge too, as Claude-Michel has written her in an operatic soprano. When you have a voice singing that high it can be very hard in the theatre to understand the words. The logistic problem is to come up with consonants and vowels that could be sung in those octaves with some clarity. Audiences don't listen much to lyrics to begin with and Elizabeth carries a lot of exposition so it was important to get it right. It is the character that has been rewritten the most because of this built-in difficulty. It's a great role for an actress because she gets to be everything—a raving lunatic, a brat, a sage, a bitch, and a saint. In some ways she's the perceived villain yet, in the end, she turns out to be a very smart woman—which obviously the real Elizabeth was—and she's allowed this beautiful moment of grace. Luckily we found a sensational actress for the role with Linda Balgord. As important as wonderful voices are it's just as vital to get great actors. In sung-through musicals this is imperative. An actor can shade dialogue in ways that you can't shade lyrics. Lyrics chained to melodies may not give you all those levels of subtext that you can get with dialogue, and the actor, aided by the director, of course, has to provide that inner life.

Donal, Grania's husband, has some comic moments but ultimately he is the most villainous character in the piece. When we first meet him he's having his stag party the night before his wedding to Grania and he's getting drunk in what's referred to as a *shebeen*, which is a kind of bar with women of loose morals. (See *The Pirate*

Queen photo insert 5.) He's drinking with the boys and bragging that even though he's getting married nothing is going to change: "Truth is, friends, a conjugal vow/Doesn't change a bull to a cow/ Married man or not the party goes on." So we think how funny he is but there is one point where he says one or two things that are rather disconcerting and then he goes back to being funny. But it's just a hint of a clue to his real character. The more the audience likes this funny rascal the more they will feel the betrayal when he betrays Grania. It's not just that he betrays her with other women because I don't think that would be enough for her to dismiss him, but it is his outrageous, deplorable treason to Ireland.

Bingham is the most villainous character, but I find him a very interesting one. He debases the women of Ireland in a horrific way

Photo by Joan Marcus

John Dempsey, Alain Boublil, and Claude-Michel Schönberg

but, although he is a villain, he also serves as a comic foil to Elizabeth. The best way to get inside a character's mind and to let the audience know what the character is thinking is with a soliloquy. It's what musicals can do that almost no other art form today can do. That sort of playwriting doesn't exist anymore. But musicals do it beautifully, strongly, and simply; we expect it and we revel in it. I find musicals to be the most abstract form of art that exists. And the most amazingly abstract feature of the musical is that it pretends not to be abstract. It's a calculated illusion and that is what we respond to.

My job as a lyricist is to try to make sense of the worlds that Alain and Claude-Michel work in. Half the trick was finding the right language, and I found the simpler the better, especially for the Irish characters. If you think of the characters here in terms of material, then the English are silk and the Irish are cotton or wool. Grania and all the clansmen need a very simple language, a sort of humble poetry as opposed to clever rhyme schemes and puns, and it really works with Claude-Michel's music in a very surprising way. The English have a very specific way of speaking in this musical. It's very arch and it's usually duplicitous. Elizabeth and Bingham, who are well-educated people and have a stunning command of the English language. It was great fun coming up with specific words for them, the kind of words that no one I know would ever use. It's the first time for any show that I've been able to go to a Thesaurus and look for the weirdest choice.

The characters do develop a certain autonomy as you write. They are strongly written and Claude-Michel's music has such a strong identity, he has set the path the character will go on emotionally. A wise man once said, "Music tells you what to feel, lyrics tell you what to think." So as lyricists Alain and I follow the path set by the music. However, with Elizabeth, who has a lot of exposition, some of it is in recitative and for a few little bits of it we did lyrics first. We would write some lines and Claude-Michel would set them to music, including one that had a very funny setting. We just wrote the wackiest dialogue and Claude-Michel set it to music and it's very funny.

The exposition has to come in easily digestible moments. There's a line in *Urinetown* that says too much exposition can kill a show, and it's absolutely true. You have to be very clever where you put it in so it doesn't feel like a character steps forward and explains the plot. The English Court scenes are very big in exposition but in the Irish scenes it's much more character-based and emotion-based. In the scene where Grania's father is explaining that England is over-running the country he tells Grania that the clans have to unite and that it would strengthen their cause if Grania were to marry Donal, who is the head of another clan. That's a great example of how to do exposition in a graceful, necessary way because he's explaining all this to his daughter. So that is perfectly valid and logical and the fact that we get to absorb that knowledge at the same time is a terrific bonus.

There's very much a sense of fate to the show, how Grania takes fate into her own hands. The word "fate" crops up an awful lot in the show. There's a song at the end called "The Sea of Life," and it's all about how life is like being on an ocean with waves and tides that you can't control. The important thing is that you have to bear it and journey on and keep to your destination. It's that sense of recreating your own fate while reconciling it with what the world has planned for you. There's also a theme about parents and children and the notion of growing past your parents into maturity. There's a song near the end of the show for Elizabeth and Grania. Grania is in jail and Elizabeth is miserable and each is thinking about the other one. It's a song about jealousy: "What does she have I don't have?" Elizabeth has thrown this woman in jail and she's been there for years, yet she's still strong. Elizabeth realizes the reason is because Grania loves this man and her child.

Comic songs are always terribly difficult to write and yet they're the ones I gravitate to first. Comedy is based largely on rhythms and situations and in this show the situations are there but the rhythms are not. Claude-Michel's rhythms are not innately comic even though the music is funny in certain comic numbers. Comic songs are all about finessing the vocabulary and the language. You never have any idea what you have on hand until you get in front of an audience, and it's very interesting to see what gets laughs and what doesn't. The court of England has some very funny stuff. They have a song called "Rah-Rah, Tip-Top," which is a song that's about how great everything is and how although the English are losing their navy, they're trying to convince the Queen that everything is fantastic: "Rah-rah, tip-top/Ev'rything's right as rain/Rah-rah, tip-top/Here in the Queen's domain./Once again the news today is joyful to the brink/Fifty ships went out and forty-nine refused to sink." It's all about putting the best face on bad news. We wanted something exaggerated that was a nonsense form, and bit by bit we hammered it into "Rah-rah, tip-top," which we thought sounded completely absurd and like a parody of that sort of proper English. We were both a bit giddy and having fun and it was also great because it didn't need to rhyme, it just keeps getting repeated. But we decided to sleep on it and the next day we both said: "Every time I think about it I laugh." So that's how it ended up but we spent half the time coming up with that phrase and the rest of the lyric came very easily and quickly. It's a song where there has to be that tremendous sense of cleverness, and I tend to go back to it every week and change little bits, which I think aggravates Alain no end. But with a comic song I'm a firm believer that you spend months and months just gently finessing it to get it into good shape.

The song titles usually precede the lyrics. It's often the first thing you come up with and you almost always know where it's going to rest in the song. The title is the thing that the audience takes away and I think it was Tim Rice who said, "If you're really lucky the audience will hear the title." So you spend an inordinate time coming up with the titles. In the case of "Rah-Rah, Tip-Top," once we had come up with the title it was very obvious where it would go as there was a line in the chorus that was clearly the title line.

This show has more love songs than anything I've done before. I usually have a much harder time getting into love songs but interestingly in this show the love songs proved the most rewarding. A song like "If I Said I Loved You" required a great deal of emotional scouring. It was hours and hours of discussion followed by minutes of frantic writing; catharsis by way of a rhyming dictionary. Alain seemed to take great pleasure in pushing me to write what he consistently referred to as "grown-up songs," something he claims I've never written before. I've gotten very good at smiling politely and not acting offended. His point is not easily dismissed, however. Emotions in a show such as this are harder to mine than in traditional American musical comedy, which is terra firma to me.

If there's one thing I've learnt from Alain it's that there's a difference between writing a good lyric and writing the right lyric. Which is not to say that Alain doesn't write good lyrics because clearly he does. But people in America respond to cleverness and they don't respond to simple lyrics well at all. You can get 98 percent right and all they harp on is the 2 percent you got wrong. But the lyrics that Alain writes are correct. They're absolutely correct for the character and that's the hardest thing to get right. It's a huge challenge but it's an obsession with Alain and that is why he is as successful as he is artistically.

We always know exactly what needs to be put across in any one section because Alain and Claude-Michel determine what the plot points are. In fact, Claude-Michel on some of his demos sometimes does a narration track on top of his la-la-ing where he says what the part has to be about. So when you start working on a song you know what it is you want to convey emotionally, not just in terms of character but also in terms of how it sets up everything that is to follow. Sometimes you have to put in little hints or bits and pieces so that they can be referenced later. Sometimes you will even go back and plant the clues so it looks like brilliant foreshadowing but it's actually the opposite. Alain and Claude-Michel always start at the beginning, whereas I've always preferred to start at the end. I like to start with my final image and final number and work backward, the way one would write a mystery novel. You know what the solution is and you construct the crime around it. But this show was largely written in chronological order from the opening number to the closing number with little digressions here and there.

When you're writing music first the music is a structure that gives you limits both positive and negative in which you have to accomplish something. You might have eight syllables and stresses on the third and the seventh and within that you have to say, "I will always love Ireland and Ireland will always love me," or whatever the mission of the song is. So the music is constricting. Claude-Michel's music is written in uniquely French speech rhythms. They're not at all English, let alone American, and so trying to find something that sounds appropriate within English vernacular that fits the music is not easy. There's a lot of rushed phrases that sort of fall off. In England and much more so in America, we build to the end of our sentences, whereas in French the end falls away. So it's quite hard in English to build any sort of dramatic momentum when the phrases are constantly falling away from you. So I just had to find a way to do it with Alain's help, and eventually I found that a phrase can die off at the end if, psychologically, you keep the thought unfinished so that we have a reason to hear the next phrase.

Sometimes it helps to write a dummy lyric. It helps me determine the line structure and to remember the rhythm of the melody. You just write whatever the music brings to mind and occasionally the dummy lyrics end up being the actual lyrics because your initial instinct was right. But 99 percent of the time they're garbage. You just write about the pattern of the carpet or something nonsensical because it helps you to get the structure down. Sometimes you'll do a dummy lyric that has the right content, rhyme scheme, or word but not in the right order. With comic lyrics you have to get the joke down on paper but it's not worded precisely. Then you have to strip away syllable by syllable and it's like dominoes—if you take one syllable out the whole thing collapses and you have to rebuild it. But you need a dummy lyric for comic lyrics more than other lyrics because they're written from an intellectual place rather than an emotional place.

I think a lyric must appeal to the imagination. It's good to leave selective, purposeful gaps. Claude-Michel's music is so descriptive emotionally that you don't even need to speak English to understand his shows. The music says so much that often the words hang off the melodies like ornaments. If you overstate the obvious it just becomes either cloying or like a bunch of sledgehammer blows, which is the last thing you want. You want something that's delicate and has a certain amount of subtext because you have to let the music do its work and you have to let the audience do its work. An audience loves to be engaged and if you give them everything on a silver platter they become a lazy audience and that's not what you want in any show.

To get a line to sing well it helps to be aware of phonetics and the physical mechanism that produces the human voice. The best sound to end a line on, for instance, is "ah," while long "e" and short "i" are very closed and pinched off and long "u" depends on the singer. If you employ clumsy sounds in clumsy places, then the lyric doesn't hit the ear right. It can say the perfect thing but if it doesn't hit the ear right then the audience doesn't hear it; you might as well be singing it in Greek. I look at singability as the delivery system. You can have a wonderful letter that you mail to someone but if the delivery system is faulty then it will never land on their doorstep. Sometimes you have to make sacrifices, and Alain will always sacrifice a good vowel sound for the proper meaning. He and I are very much right brain, left brain, which is why I think ultimately we have forged a good partnership. He's all about meaning and I'm all about craft so where we disagree we have wonderful little arguments and debates that hopefully result in lyrics that are well-crafted and meaningful.

I think that aural satisfaction is hugely important and all the great lyrics that we remember have near-perfect prosody. It's the thing I believe in most – that absolute wedding of music and lyrics, where you cannot imagine one without the other. It's when the music and lyrics don't fight each other but sit perfectly naturally on each other and when it hits the ear just right. If you think of "Some Enchanted Evening," you just can't think of the words without the music or vice versa. Rodgers and Hammerstein have perfect prosody and Stephen Sondheim does, too.

I don't believe in rhyming to the King's English; I believe in rhyming to pronunciation. I don't agree with fake rhymes and I would never rhyme "dream" with "mean," but I rhymed "middle" with "little" in *The Fix* because no American pronounces it as little—although of course I wouldn't do that if I was writing an English character. In this show it's the first time I've rhymed "been" with "queen" and it's for the English characters. I would never do that in America; I would rhyme "been" with "fin" or "begin" to fit in with how we pronounce it. I don't believe in near-rhymes or identities, like "leave" and "believe." There's not a lot of respect for the hard and fast rules of rhyme in pop music today, but it all depends how important it is to you personally and as a writer it is very important to me. Genuine rhymes hit the ear better and if there's a dramatic point you want to make then rhyme is a fantastic way to do it. Near-rhymes glance off the ear, and so the point doesn't get made as strongly. I may be old-fashioned but that's my theory.

Some recitative doesn't require any rhyme at all and sometimes it's more effective if it's not there because rhyme instantly calls attention to itself. There's a little section in the show when Tiernan comes to Rockfleet to fetch Grania because her father is dying. It's only five or six lines and there's no rhyme whatsoever but I like that because emotionally it just feels very honest and direct and that sense of bad news he comes with doesn't feel couched in comfort in any way as there is no rhyme. The queen, Bingham, and the Court have much more rhyme than the Irish characters do. Donal has a bit more rhyme only because he thinks he's clever and he isn't, necessarily, so he plays that pretense of cleverness. Sondheim says that rhyme implies intelligence, and I think that's basically right, so you have to be very careful when and how you use it. I'm a big fan of rhyme, and in musical theatre it is expected. But in a show like this that falls outside the boundaries of conventional musical theatre, it becomes a much trickier subject. Even if the music dictates that there can be a rhyme in a certain place, it's the character and the content that tells you whether or not it should be there.

Sometimes you might fix a rhyme before the rest of the line. For instance, if you are writing about a sailing ship instantly the word "sail" and "gale" pop into your mind so you write those down in the margins. But normally you worry more about the content and you let the content provoke and dictate the rhymes. Alain and I have different ways of working with rhyme as he always writes his first line and then comes up with something to rhyme with it whereas I always try to come up with the second line first and then work backward because I think it's the word that gets rhymed that has the bigger impact. It's two distinctly different ways of working, and ultimately, in the best of all possible worlds, you have two good phrases that just happen to rhyme.

There has to be a large cast because Claude-Michel's music is not for the faint of heart to sing. It's very demanding vocally; it requires huge ranges. So you have this enormous vocal requirement, and at the same time it's a huge dance musical, which requires very specific kinds of dancers. The most expensive thing in this show is not the set, the costumes, or the lighting; it's the numbers. In the old days you could have a big chorus because you paid them pennies and they all had day jobs as waiters but, of course, you can't do that now.

The Pirate Queen has been a great show to work on. It has been a blast writing with Alain, as he's such a nice man and he's fun to work with. But above and beyond that, I found the subject matter compelling. I love the fairytale nature of the story and it deals on a metaphoric level with things that are very important to me. It's an unusual partnership in many ways, but it's been a fantastic time. As the show stands right now I'm thrilled with it. The orchestrations have just got better and better. I think this has the potential to be a remarkable entertainment. Strangely enough, the songs I'm most proud of are the love songs, specifically "If I Said I Loved You," "She Who Has All," and the whole of the last fifteen minutes. I enjoy living the life of a writer, and although it's sometimes hard to get yourself writing, when I start I can't stop. I get completely obsessed with a song. I do have a love/hate relationship with it, but I'm never happier than when I'm writing.

THE DIRECTOR: FRANK GALATI

Frank Galati, born in Illinois, is a Steppenwolf Theatre Company member, a well-known playwright, and an award-winning director. He won two Tony Awards in 1990 for his highly praised adaptation and direction of *The Grapes of Wrath*, which played at Steppenwolf's Chicago space, the La Jolla Playhouse in California, the National Theatre in London, and on Broadway. *Grapes* also won the Outer Critics Circle Award for Best Play and the Drama Desk Award for Best Direction. Steppenwolf is a highly renowned theatre and roughly the Chicago equivalent of London's National Theatre. Frank was also nominated for a Tony Award in 1998 for directing the musical *Ragtime* on Broadway. His screenplay (with Lawrence Kasdan) for *The Accidental Tourist* was nominated for an Academy Award. He has received nine Joseph Jefferson Awards for his work in Chicago theatre: one for acting, five for directing, and three for writing and adapting.

His other Steppenwolf productions include *After the Quake, Homebody/Kabul, The Royal Family, Morning Star, Valparaiso, You*  *Can't Take it with You, Aunt Dan and Lemon, Born Yesterday, Earthly Possessions, As I Lay Dying,* and *Everyman*. At Chicago's Goodman Theatre, where he has been an Associate Director since 1986, Galati has directed *The Government Inspector, She Always Said, Pablo, Passion Play, A Funny Thing Happened on the Way to the Forum, The Winter's Tale, The Good Person of Setzuan,* and the adaptations *Cry, The Beloved Country* and *Gertrude Stein: Each One As She May*. Frank

Photo by Joan Marcus

Frank Galati

has also directed at the Chicago Opera Theatre several times, including *Four Saints in Three Acts*; for Chicago's Lyric Opera he has directed several productions including *The Voyage of Edgar Allen Poe*, *Pelleas and Melisande*, *La Traviata*, *Tosca*, and William Balcom's *View from the Bridge*, seen at the Metropolitan Opera in 2000. Frank Galati is a professor in the Department of Performance Studies at Northwestern University, and he holds many degrees from that institution (School of Speech, 1965, and graduate degrees in 1967 and 1971).

FG: My first impressions of *The Pirate Queen* were when a CD of the music was played for me at Eugene Lee's home in Providence, Rhode Island. Eugene, John McColgan, Moya Doherty, and John Dempsey were poised around a picnic table in a very beautiful garden as I joined them to listen to what Claude-Michel had composed. The overture itself packs a huge emotional wallop so I was immediately engaged and deeply moved. The overture evokes the sea, and it has a tremendous depth and a kind of endless vista: the magnitude of the world, the world ringed by water, water as the fundamental element of life and out of which we're all born; it's just tremendously powerful. I had the script in front of me and John Dempsey valiantly sung all the lines against a piano/vocal performance that Claude-Michel had laid down.

As the show unfolded it was clear even in this very sketchy outline that from a dramaturgical point of view it was extremely sophisticated. It was an epic historical romance that was bringing to light and embodying the story of an exceptional woman, Grace O'Malley—the adventure of her lusty life, the extraordinary heights of leadership that she attained, and, ultimately, her struggle with Elizabeth I. So I found it an absolutely fascinating story; I was completely moved by it and even in tears. It's a story that had been suppressed in Irish history by the patriarchal, male-dominated history community, which would not want to bring forward this heroic woman because they considered it unseemly for a woman to behave like a man. And while it was all right for Elizabeth I, it was not all right for Grace O'Malley. After listening to that CD, I knew immediately that I wanted to direct the show, so I went to Dublin to meet Alain and Claude-Michel. I presented them with an initial concept for the staging of the show. We had to see if we were compatible to work together and if we had the same artistic vision for the show, but we all seemed to feel that it was a good match. Alain and Claude-Michel's musical personalities are grounded in departures from the conventional musical theatre forms. I believe that one of the great achievements of their shows has been their extraordinary hold on the stage as theatre art, and I think that Trevor Nunn was a genius in his conception of *Les Misérables*, both in its magnitude and its relative simplicity.

My starting point on *The Pirate Queen* was the text, the score in its entirety; that is, the poetic text, the vocal text, and the text of the music which is the primal source of all that happens on stage because it's the emotional font from which everything else is drawn. I had to try to get inside that, to understand it, not just rationally but to try and make contact with its inner nature. Then the most important thing was to find a theatrical language that would allow the story to unfold in an authentic theatrical way, not as a glamorous, hi-tech musical with all kinds of contemporary bells and whistles and special effects that had nothing to do with sixteenth-century Ireland. In many ways, the story's real agency is song, and although spectacle is important, it is secondary. We don't want the audience to feel as if they're at a magic show, a Las Vegas Cirque du Soleil performance or a big-budget blockbuster movie.

I felt strongly that theatre in the late sixteenth century was in fact the Elizabethan stage, named after the queen, and it was the stage of Shakespeare. He called it "This little wooden O," which, if you use your imagination, could, as he puts it, "Compass the vasty fields of France." So I thought "Wow! The Globe Theatre." Of course Shakespeare also said, "All the world's a stage," which is why he called his theatre The Globe. So that was a major source of influence for me, the Elizabethan stage with its stage machinery, its trap doors, its spooky effects, and its battle scenes, but all modestly offered, simply produced, spectacle in a teacup. The splendor is in the verse and the music and only incidentally in the magic that is created by sprinkling cut paper to make snow or shaking a piece of fabric to indicate the sea. So springboarding off from the Elizabethan stage, I proposed to Eugene Lee that it might be a conceptual framing device for the show that would take advantage of all of the high-tech options available to us, but that we would present *The Pirate Queen* as if it were the stage of Queen Elizabeth I upon which Grace O'Malley stars.

Eugene Lee is just marvelous. He's the master of American stage design and he's become a kind of senior figure in American theatre art. He's much beloved because he's not only a wonderful collaborator but also a visionary. He has created some truly groundbreaking designs for *Candide, Sweeeny Todd*, and *Ragtime*, on which we worked together, and most recently *Wicked*. Eugene is meticulous in his scholarship and his work is very grounded in the real world in the materials, textures, metals, woods, and glass that he uses. In *The Pirate Queen* there is architectural, real wood and gilded carved ornate forms that are drawn from Elizabeth's world, but we also have water, rain, snow, fog, fire, lightning, repelling, sails that billow in the wind, storms at sea, stars, the zodiac—it's a very complete world of images. I think what is characteristic of Eugene is a grounding of these highly theatrical images in real materials.

Eugene and I work very closely together and we were in constant conversation with each other about every unfolding moment of the story. We went through four scale models of the set of every single scene. We moved from a quarter-inch model, which is a quarter-inch to represent a foot, to a half-inch model, which is very large. We have a model for everything, every theatrical gesture, every prop or piece of furniture, cart, wagon, and in some cases we have structures that come up from below the stage. So we're able to look and shine light in the model in ways that the lighting would produce smoke effects and we could just look at the whole thing.

One of the most critical things for us in our collaboration is devising how we move from scene to scene and this is especially challenging in a work that's epic and panoramic because we can't swipe the action and go immediately to the next scene or cut the way you can in a film. You have to sustain the momentum and the energy of the story while you're changing scenery, in fact to use the scene change as part of the narrative so that it never stops. It has to roll on and be forward moving right through to the end of each act. One of the most difficult aspects of staging, however, is simply getting out of the way. Not interfering with the natural ebb and flow of the story and making sure that whatever physical gesture in staging and stagecraft we achieve is done with a degree of humility so that it just features the story and gets out of the story's way.

The show has a huge cast, with thirty-nine actors and eleven musicians. It includes eight Irish dancers and four swings, who cover a number of roles and never appear unless somebody is out. There is also understudying within the ensemble so that if this one is out, this one goes up and a swing goes in. But to have such a large cast is increasingly more unusual on Broadway because of the cost. It was quite a difficult show to cast in some respects because you want a population that's not typical in the sense that you need people who can dance and sing but you don't want them to look like dancers and singers. You want them to look like fishermen, not pirates per se, but you want them to look like ordinary villagers, clans people from sixteenth-century Ireland and commoners and nobles in the court of Elizabeth I. So you want people that are individually striking and who also have enormous talent.

We had a somewhat ample rehearsal period with the first three weeks just for the dancing, the choreography, and the fights. Then we brought in the whole cast and we started working on it together from the beginning, and those rehearsals were five weeks. Then we had four weeks of tech. So was three months of rehearsals before the first previews and then it's always a big milestone in the evolution of a show the first time it's played in front of an audience. All of a sudden something changes and you have to take into account the way the story lands, the way it feels when it's told and what the receiver does to alter the equation. It's certainly true that it takes an audience to complete a text. You cannot really know how to tell a story until someone is listening to you.

I generally prefer not to work out how I'm going to do a scene beforehand, but with a show as complex as this the job is bigger than the staging of individual scenes. Many things had to be taken into account beforehand, especially these huge shifts and transitions but also things like lighting cues and even to figure out exactly who's in what scene, how many are Irish, how many are English, how many women do I have, how many men, and how many women do I disguise as men because I have to have more men on stage in some scenes. Then maybe I have to have all the people who are English in one scene to be Irish in the next scene and I have no time between scenes for them to change. But when I'm working on individual scenes, I prefer not to have it worked out. I like to do it with the actors and let the choices that the characters make grow from the actors' impulses. I try to be their mirror to respond back to them and tell them what I've gotten and so on. You can do improvisations and make it up as you go to some extent, but—of course—in a musical you can't improvise their lines because they're within a musical structure. But I think that sense of spontaneity and of the unexpected is crucial in the theatre so you are always trying to achieve that.

In rehearsals I try to make the environment safe. I think that actors have to feel comfortable enough to fail so I try to keep them from harm in the rehearsal hall, to be gentle and to be open and to avoid, as much as possible, turbulence and stress. I think a comfortable safe environment is more important than a bunch of actors doing what they're told. It's quite different for actors to be in a musical than in a play because although the music helps to interpret a scene you can't have that same level of subtext in song that you can have in speech. It's easy to say that the subtext is in the music and so you don't have to manufacture that but I think it's tricky because we hide things and music discloses. So an actor in a musical is always having to negotiate between what is expressed in speech that's actually song and what is hidden, which may be in the undercurrent of the score but still has to have the tension of secrecy or concealment from the performer. So although in some ways being in a musical is easier for an actor, in some ways it's more difficult.

In a sung-through musical the measures of music are the ultimate clock and the absolute timekeeper and you don't deviate from that. The advantages of a sung-through musical have something to do with virtuosity and flow, that there's something so dazzling about an endlessly outpouring musical performance, all song, all night long. But, as in opera, there are degrees of musical modalities that are offered. There's recitative, there are places where we're marching along metrically but not melodically, and then we get to the emotional moment when what can be said can only be said in a kind of soaring melody—and then the melody takes off. So there are songs obviously within the sung-through musical form, but there are also stops and structures that lead into and out of song.

The dance and all the choreography have been worked out with Mark Dendy, who is a fabulous collaborator, and the Irish step dance has been choreographed by Carol Leavy Joyce. From my point of view, the director and the choreographers have to become kindred spirits and help each other, guide each other with advice and counsel and encouragement and share, absorb and accept ideas from each other. When you become bonded in that way you have a clear vision together of what the show is trying to achieve and then it's a seamless flow between direction and choreography.

Alain and Claude-Michel have always been interested in history and always used it as the source of their artistic projects, usually going back to a time of terrible conflict, whether it be war-torn Vietnam or Victor Hugo and the civil strife in France, and drawing out of it an immortal love story. The same is true of *The Pirate Queen*, and as they go to the past for their source and reconstitute the past, they create a musical theatre of our time that is very contemporary. So they seem to be using the past as a lens through which we can examine where we are today. *The Pirate Queen* is primarily about the power of love and faithfulness. It's about courage and pride and bravery in the face of overwhelming odds and daunting forces that threaten to divide and defeat a people. It's about the age-old and ageless conflict between clans and tribes and countries and nations that we cannot seem to get ourselves out of. As far as we have come today, where are we?

There's no doubt that Grace O'Malley as a pirate was ruthless and took lives, but to some extent I feel like an apologist for her because she's the hero of my story. Her piracy was born out of need rather than greed—so she could feed her people, clothe the men and women of her clan, and protect them and to keep them from harm in the same way that Elizabeth did for her people. You could say that Elizabeth as a colonist and a dictator was a tyrant, and Grace O'Malley a kind of terrorist, but when they meet they see in each other's eyes a kindred soul a-burning, and they sit down together and relate to each other above all as women.

It is very exciting to work on a new show. When you're doing a classic, something that's already been born and grown up and is what it wants to be and shouldn't be changed or dismantled, your obligation is to find some new vision for it. But when you're working on a new show it's far more complicated and it's much less safe. It's scary because you're trying to invent as well as to interpret and the director and most of the other people who work in creating a new show are not only interpreting but they're involved in all those creative birth pangs. There is a definite collective responsibility for storytelling that draws us together as artists. What we all have in common is the necessity to make the story clear and to try to connect things so that one action leads inexorably to another action. It's a collective obligation whether it concerns costumes, scenery, lyrics, or music.

A new show is constantly undergoing transformation, and we went through several drafts. I was responsible for introducing the stage directions, which describe the physical action, into the text. In the beginning it was difficult to have a preconceived idea of the final show because the work we did together was so transformative. There were sessions with Alain, Claude-Michel, the co-lyricist, choreographer, and producers, where we had to make choices, looking with a very hard, clear examining light at every detail of the lyrics, the position of the songs and so on. At one point we flipped two songs around in the first act, and that was such a huge break-through that we all cheered. It was and is a long ongoing process and we're constantly revising. But working on *The Pirate Queen* is a blast and I couldn't be happier.

THE CHOREOGRAPHERS: MARK DENDY AND CAROL LEAVY JOYCE

MARK DENDY

Mark Dendy is the new talked-about young American choreographer, who was delighted to join the all-American creative team on *The Pirate Queen*. He was the artistic director of *Mark Dendy Dance and Theater* from 1983 to 2000, touring the world and performing in New York at The Joyce Theater, Lincoln Center, Dance

Photo by Joan Marcus

Mark Dendy

Theatre Workshop, and Performance Space 122 to considerable acclaim. He is the recipient of many awards and grants including the prestigious Alpert Award in the Arts. In 1997, he won a New York Dance and Performance Award, "The Bessie," for sustained achievement with his troupe. Since 2000, he has been focusing on a career in musical theatre. In that year he won an Obie Award, The Joseph Calloway Award, and a Drama Desk Nomination for his choreography for Andrew Lippa's Off-Broadway show *The*

Wild Party. Mark then went on to choreograph *Carnivale* for the Radio City Music Hall Rockettes under the direction of Graciela Daniele. In 2003 he choreographed the Broadway musical *Taboo*, and in 2004 he choreographed Mozart's *The Magic Flute* at the Metropolitan Opera under the direction of Julie Taymor, and *Ritual* at The Washington Ballet. In 2005 he choreographed Kirsten Child's new musical *The Miracle Brothers* at the Vineyard Theatre in New York. His regional work includes *Baptiste*, *The Dybbuk* (Hartford Stage) and *Camille Claudel* (Goodspeed Musicals). After *The Pirate Queen* his next project is the Stephen Schwartz *Pippin* revival headed for Broadway in the 2007–2008 season.

MD: Dance is very significant in *The Pirate Queen*, but it is always there as a way of forwarding the story. (See *The Pirate Queen* photo insert 7.) It features in a natural way as part of the life of the people in sixteenth-century Ireland because dance was not a performance entertainment but a ritual with roots in its pagan ancestry. The people danced for the harvest, for good weather, to imbue strength into a newborn baby, to celebrate weddings and births, and to mourn and ward off the evil spirits of death. I always approach dance from story and as a place of ritual. The fact that these dances are "real" dances with dramatic purpose and an integral part of our story has been my source of inspiration for creating the choreography in the celebrations for a wedding or a christening and there is a particular kind of stylised choreography employed in the battle scenes.

The show opens with twelve strapping Irish sailors, rough men of the sea, with their oars. (See *The Pirate Queen* photo insert 1.) They do a pounding percussive dance with the oars and as they come forward, they themselves form the ship. It isn't physically there, there's only a prow that comes up in front of the stage, but they are rowing along to give the illusion of a ship. The movement in general doesn't have an ultra- or über-contemporary feel to it. There's no jazz or pelvis or any traditional show-business dance in it at all. It's very, very physical and of the earth. They're in boots, and you see their muscles. It has a very grounded masculinity to it, and they're very hearty, strong men and women of the earth and the sea.

In one scene there is a pub dance where the men are having their bachelor party for Donal before he marries Grania and there is a lot of jumping, big strong movement and Irish dance in that scene. In the wedding dance, when Grania is betrothed to someone she doesn't love, first the men dance and then the women dance and they switch off and the partners change each time. It's like a round and so eventually Grania is face-to-face with Tiernan as the lights change. So there's this moment at the wedding where she's confronted by the man she truly loves. The new husband Donal, who's basically a lout and a drunkard, taps in, and it almost becomes a fight. Then the dancing goes into this ferocious physical reel that is very virtuosic for the men. At the christening there is a dance that kind of softens the men into candy. They all go to look at the baby and they just melt and do this very soft dance. At the court of Queen Elizabeth there's a court dance for the Elizabethan courtiers.

There's been a lot of research to do and a lot of new things to learn. I have on the team an excellent Irish Step Choreographer Carol Leavy Joyce and a very strong Contemporary Dance Associate Rachel Bress. We've had Elizabethan lessons, square dancing lessons, and Irish dancing lessons, although it's a little late for me to learn Irish dancing. But I work very closely with Carol, and there is so much of the traditional Irish footwork, but in a ritual form and not in that presentational line form of *Riverdance*. In fact, the history of Irish dancing is fascinating because the rigidness and tightness that we have today was actually enforced by the Catholics and then by the English when they took over because they considered any movement in their bodies to be sexual. So the dancers had to maintain stiffness and hold their arms straight, and there was to be no touching. But before that it was very much looser, and that is what we've gone back to.

I spent a wonderful time on the West Coast of Ireland. I stayed in Westport and I went to Clare Island, Clew Bay and all over Mayo. I saw all the castles and actually got into a bog in a marsh by one of Grace O'Malley's castles, and although it was February I just had to feel the water! Then one Thursday night I went into a bar in Westport to have a couple of drinks with the local rowdies but quite late on in the evening various elderly couples arrived. They may have been seventy-five or even eighty years old but they all came in and sat at tables and started talking until the music started. Then they all got up and in formation they were doing this traditional real Irish stepping with patterns and they danced for a couple of hours. They pulled me up and so I joined in and they were just incredible. John and Moya had no idea where they were sending me as far as this goes—that it was dance night on Thursday night for all the locals. But it was really amazing and gave me the inspiration to develop my own vocabulary for the show while incorporating the authentic Irish elements. Together Carol and I have created a truly unique hybrid of Irish and Contemporary dance. But there have been so many little things like that in this whole process where things synchronize and go together so well that it's like God is watching over it all.

There are three major battles in the show and they are stylized and choreographed very specifically. There's one moment especially when Grania has just given birth on board ship and then the English attack. She's obviously incapacitated, but when they are losing she rallies her strength, gets up out of bed, and goes up on the deck to lead the fight. This is a true story, although in real life it was the Turkish they were fighting. She does win the fight but during the course of the battle she's so weak from loss of blood that she's delusional. So all of a sudden at a certain point in the fight the audience sees it through her deluded eyes—things go in slow-motion and there are great lighting effects.

It's wonderful to be working with a director like Frank Galati. We have a complete collaboration choreographically and we've developed a wonderful rapport. He is so intelligent and eloquent and he has such an understanding of the work, both dramatically and thematically, and he is so secure in that that he gives everyone the inspiration to offer their ideas and truly collaborate, to roll up their sleeves and get in there. And that's just a wonderful way to work for me but, of course, chiefly he is the commander of the ship. He's an excellent dramaturge and adapter himself, having adapted *Ragtime*. He brings the knowledge and authority and that experience to this, so it shapes it and it makes it much richer. Ultimately if you work on a great musical you cannot tell where the choreography ends and the direction begins; it's seamless.

It's so good to be working on a real-meat-and-potatoes show like this, because so much on Broadway for a long time has been just dessert. There's nothing wrong with dessert, but I get a lot of cavities after too much. Working on the creative team of *The Pirate Queen* is very exciting. We're working together all the time to forward the story, and when new ideas happen all of a sudden it's like an earthquake; it's so exhilarating for us all.

CAROL LEAVY JOYCE

Carol Leavy Joyce is a teacher and adjudicator of Irish dance. She was a member of the renowned Roddy School of Irish Dance in Dundalk. During her dancing career she has won nine Ulster titles, three All Ireland, and three World titles. She worked as Irish

Dance Director and then Assistant Director on *Riverdance*, and she contributed new choreography to the show. During her eight-year career with *Riverdance*, she was part of the Creative Team that staged the show in the Great Hall of the People in Beijing in China in 2003, and she arranged the *Riverdance* line of one hundred dancers at the Opening Ceremony of the Special Olympics World Games in Dublin's Croke Park. Carol lives in Dublin with her husband Kevin and their two young sons.

Carol Leavy Joyce

Anne Emery, Julia Sutton, Susan Jane Tanner, Sheila Reid, Iain Glen. Arnaud arrives in Artigat. Prince Edward Theatre, July 10, 1996.

Martin Guerre 1

Matthew Cammelle, Stephen Weller, West Yorkshire Playhouse, Leeds, December 8, 1998.

ARNAUD: "Live with somebody you love/Let your love bless each day."

Erin Dilly, Jose Herrera, Hugh Panaro, Guthrie Theater, Minneapolis, September 29, 1999.

FATHER DOMINIC: "In God's name on this day I/Pronounce you man and wife."

Hugh Panaro, Erin Dilly, Guthrie Theater, Minneapolis, September 29, 1999.

VILLAGERS: "It's their wedding day/Their lives have just begun."

Hugh Panaro, Guthrie Theater, Minneapolis, September 29, 1999.

MARTIN: "They all look for someone to blame/But I swear it aloud, I will be proud/That Martin Guerre is my name."

Michael Arnold, Guthrie Theater, Minneapolis, September 29, 1999.

BENOIT: "Not a single cloud up in the sky, Louison/Thank the Lord that it's so dry, Louison."

Martin Guerre 6

Matthew Cammelle, Joanna Riding, West Yorkshire Playhouse, December 8, 1998.

ARNAUD: "Shall we tell them the truth now?/We may never have as good a chance as this." BERTRANDE: "No. They would kill us."

Matthew Cammelle, Joanna Riding, West Yorkshire Playhouse,
Leeds, December 8, 1998.

ARNAUD: "Don't!/Don't let it start/Know in your heart/Each
step we take/Takes us too far."

Stephen Buntrock, Erin Dilly, Guthrie Theater, Minneapolis, September 29, 1999.

BERTRANDE: "Come my love, just one kiss/One kiss before we say goodbye."

Ensemble, Guthrie Theater, Minneapolis, September 29, 1999.

The village of Artigat in flames.

Jose Llana, Erin Dilly, Guthrie Theater, Minneapolis, September 29, 1999.

GUILLAUME: "Bertrande/I'll cut you free/Free from the past."

Erin Dilly, Stephen Buntrock, Hugh Panaro, Guthrie Theater, Minneapolis, September 29, 1999.

BERTRANDE: "Live with somebody you love/May your soul ever rest in peace/As the years slip away/Let our child bless each day."

Jeff McCarthy, Ensemble, Cadillac Palace Theatre, Chicago

DUBHDARA AND CREW: "All aboard the Ceol Na Mara/Duty bound, to sea we sail."

The Pirate Queen 1

Jeff McCarthy, Stephanie J. Block, Cadillac Palace Theatre, Chicago

DUBHDARA: "Was I wrong/To fill your head with tales/Of pirate ships and sails."

Hadley Fraser, Stephanie J. Block, Cadillac Palace Theatre, Chicago

GRANIA AND TIERNAN: "Here on this night our life begins/
Here on this ship our voyage starts."

The Pirate Queen 3

William Youmans, Linda Balgord, Ensemble, Cadillac Palace Theatre, Chicago

ELIZABETH: "Go this day to Ireland."

The Pirate Queen 4

Ensemble, Cadillac Palace Theatre, Chicago

MEN & WOMEN: "Boys are boys/And boys, the party goes on."

Stephanie J. Block, Marcus Chait, Cadillac Palace Theatre, Chicago

EVLEEN: "May God Bless/The bride and groom."

Ensemble, Cadillac Palace Theatre, Chicago

Dancers at Grania's and Donal's wedding.

The Pirate Queen 7

Hadley Fraser, Cadillac Palace Theatre, Chicago

TIERNAN: "I"ll be there/For to me there's no sorrow/Worse to bear/Than a life lived apart."

The Pirate Queen 8

Stephanie J. Block, Ensemble, Cadillac Palace Theatre, Chicago

GRANIA: "Come on, daughters!/Can't you feel your heart beat?/Now's the hour/The time for us to act!"

Stephanie J. Block, Ensemble, Cadillac Palace Theatre, Chicago

CLAN MEMBERS: "A day beyond Belclare/Your father waits for you/Clan O'Flaherty goes/With you to Clew Bay."

Linda Balgord, Cadillac Palace Theatre, Chicago

ELIZABETH: "Why is it in the west/I am constantly defied by this.../Female!"

Stephanie J. Block, Ensemble, Cadillac Palace Theatre, Chicago

EVLEEN: "We welcome you this morning/All of Ireland has a son."

CLJ: It was difficult to research Irish dance in the period of Grace O'Malley because there was so little written down in sixteenth-century Ireland; everything was passed down by word of mouth. For me Claude-Michel's music was a wonderful inspiration, and initially I just listened to it over and over, which inspired the rhythms that you hear in the Irish Dance steps. Mark and I initially work-shopped together in Dublin and then separately in New York and Dublin, respectively, nearer the rehearsal start date. In my Dublin workshop I had sixteen Irish dancers, even though there weren't going to be sixteen in the show, and I put an Irish dance style to it using the rhythms and patterns I could hear in the music. When Mark and I began rehearsals in New York, there were times when my prepared material was too intricate for the Irish dance style of the period or Mark's material was too contemporary for the period.

For the show we had eight Irish dancers who had been part of the *Riverdance* Company for many years, ten modern dancers, a whole ensemble of vocal performers—whose strengths might be singing rather more than dancing, and, of course, all the principals, but what we wanted to see was a rugged, sixteenth-century, west coast of Ireland community dancing together. The primary objective was that you wouldn't see any separation between the groups or different dance styles. We had to find a common vocabulary for the movements so that the different styles would fuse seamlessly to create a complete community dancing together. We investigated many different ways and approaches to each number during rehearsals, but we always kept our main objective as the focus, which was to see a community dancing, celebrating, and mourning together. We wanted dance to tell the story in the same way that the music and lyrics tell the story. At the same time we did not want to disappoint the huge *Riverdance* audience who would expect to see wonderful, virtuosic Irish dancing.

We had a fantastic costume designer, Martin Pakledinaz, who accommodated all our dance needs. He went to the ends of the earth to create a dance boot that was in keeping with his costume design of the period, yet at the same time was soled and heeled to the Irish dancer's hard shoe. Many times when I've done other shows I've been costumed to mid-calf, and then you see our heavy black dance shoes. But that couldn't happen on this show, and he has enabled us to truly blend into the world of musical theatre. When he approached one of the Irish dance shoemakers, they were not that keen to get involved so he found his own shoemaker who poured the fibreglass tip for the boot himself and then had a ballet boot made for the girls to perform their light dancing numbers.

Moya and John, as well as Alain and Claude-Michel, had great faith in what Irish dance could be, and they had the determination to amalgamate it into musical theatre. My background is specifically Irish dance; working with *Riverdance* was a truly wonderful experience, to see Irish dance being introduced to the world stage in what is a full Irish dance show. *The Pirate* Queen has introduced Irish dance yet again to the world stage but this time in musical theatre, where it is very much part of the storytelling. Mark and I have enjoyed enormously this fusing together of the very traditional and much loved Irish dance formations with the fluid, acrobatic, contemporary style, while at the same time including the virtuosic Irish dance technique that exists today.

THE PRODUCERS: MOYA DOHERTY AND JOHN MCCOLGAN

Moya Doherty and John McColgan are the husband and wife team responsible for producing *Riverdance*, the theatrical phenomenon that premiered at Dublin's Point Theatre in February 1995 and has been playing to great acclaim all around the world for the last eleven years.

Moya's career includes theatre, radio, and a distinguished and award-winning track record in television production, both in Ireland and the UK. She is a director of Tyrone Productions, Ireland's leading independent television production company, whose output includes drama, documentary, and entertainment programming.

Photo by Mark McCall

John McColgan and Moya Doherty

She was a founding Director of Today FM and as a member of the Board of the Dublin Theatre Festival, Moya is heavily involved in promoting new and challenging theatrical work in Ireland. Moya has won many awards and accolades over the years. She has been named Veuve Cliquot Business Woman of the Year; she has received the Ernst & Young Entrepreneur of the Year Award and has been bestowed with honorary doctorates from the University of Ulster and from the National University of Ireland in recognition of her success and her ongoing commitment to the world of the arts in Ireland.

John's career as a highly successful television director began in the mid-seventies in RTÉ Television in Dublin. As an award-winning television producer and director he has an international track record. He played a key role in the evolution of *Riverdance*, from the original seven-minute dance number, and went on to direct the full-stage spectacular. John also directed the first video recording of the show, one of the best-selling entertainment videos in the world. He is a former Controller of Programmes at TV AM in London and a former Head of Entertainment with RTÉ Television. John is a founding Director of Tyrone Productions, Ireland's premier independent television production company and is also Chairman of Today FM. In 1999 John joined the Board of the Abbey Theatre. He recently directed a production of the nineteenth-century melodrama *The Shaughraun* at the Abbey, which was critically acclaimed, broke all box office records at the theatre, and then played in London's West End. John's involvement and success in the three key areas of the arts in Ireland—theatre, television, and radio—have been acknowledged by many awards, including an Honorary Doctorate of Law from the National University of Ireland in recognition of his services to the arts and entertainment industry.

MD: After our success with *Riverdance,* John and I wanted to do another production. We had opened up a gateway to the world, to producing something out of Ireland on a global basis, and we felt that the whole profile for organic Irish entertainment was right for following it with something else. But we didn't want to do another Irish dance show. We wanted to do a dramatic musical. We considered a number of mythological and historical stories, but the one we kept coming back to was the Grace O'Malley story. It had a contemporary resonance and a strong female character who lived during a very interesting period in history and had an intriguing relationship with Queen Elizabeth I. The story had an epic nature, and it would also allow us to embrace some of the *Riverdance* elements both musically and with dance.

JMcC: Then we started thinking about who we would like to work with more than anybody in the world. We're both enormous fans of Alain and Claude-Michel and have seen their shows many times. We were at the Barbican on the opening night of *Les Misérables* and I've probably seen it about ten times altogether, in London, New York, Dublin, and a number of places, so you could say I was an Alain and Claude-Michel groupie, really. But it's my opinion that they're the best musical theatre writers in the world. They're the best storytellers and the most eloquent musical writers. They have the most wonderful ability to write and compress a complex historical story and present it with elegance, integrity, and intelligence, to write terrific characters and wonderful melodies and to make it into an accessible evening of musical theatre. So we thought, "nothing ventured, nothing gained," and we approached them with our project.

MD: The first time we met was at Alain's house in London, and Claude-Michel had only seen *Riverdance* the night before. As we rang the bell and waited, John joked, "Well, if they didn't like *Riverdance*, they probably won't answer the door!" So we were laughing when Alain did indeed open the door, just as Claude-Michel came marching up the street clutching a *Riverdance* carrier bag with the souvenir program in it. And yes, they both liked it very much and thought it was a fresh and interesting form of theatre. They liked the idea of working with us, and I think there was a curiosity on both sides as to what we could each bring to the collaboration. However, at one point Alain expressed doubts about this particular story, and my heart dropped a couple of hundred feet, we had so set our hearts on it.

JMcC: They have never taken an idea from anyone before, as they always want to come up with the concept for their musicals themselves. However, we had a series of meetings, and at one point we discussed the possibility of doing the show in an enormous, purpose-built tent, which would be a sophisticated mobile theatre. It was an ambitious concept, but one which excited them because it was so different.

Claude-Michel wrote fifteen minutes of music, and they invited us to go and hear it. But they hadn't said they were going to do it. We sat in Alain's house while they played us the tape, and it was just glorious, wonderful, and we were absolutely thrilled. I think what happened at that point, with Claude-Michel in particular, is that he became hooked on the subject matter—he had fallen in love with Grace O'Malley and with the idea. It had become a passion with them, even though they still weren't sure they were going to do it. They wanted to go away for a few months and see if they could develop the idea into a major piece before they finally decided. After six months they had the first act, and again it was fantastic and we loved the way it was progressing. So we were all happy to go ahead with the project. The relationship between us is growing, and we enjoy enormously the process of working with them. They're very elegant in the way they work and they're very confident. They're very clear about what they're doing and they are so skillful. They understand the world of musical theatre very well.

MD: The story of Grace, or Grania O'Malley, spans six decades, and it has to be made sense of for the musical theatre. So some license has been taken in the telling of the story, as the real Grace had a number of husbands whose characteristics have been encapsulated in one husband in our story. Grania's lover, Tiernan, is based on a fictional character who was introduced by Morgan Llywelyn in her historical novel *Grania*. As producers, we have acquired the underlying rights to this book and we also have the historian Anne Chambers as consultant.

But producing a musical is not for the fainthearted! I think the title of producer is open to interpretation, as sometimes people who are the major investors in a musical call themselves producers. John and I are co-producing *The Pirate Queen* and, as well as funding and investing in it, we provide creative producing, which is what we really want to do. We cast the creative team, we are very close to the piece and work very closely with the authors. We've set up a creative forum that has worked very well with the four of us, and we have a very good relationship. We bring all the key creative decisions to the forum and we discuss what's important so that we are very much a unit. And then the director, set designer, and choreographer are all crucial to the next stage. So we have both a financial and a creative role as producers. Then there is managing the marketing structure, and it was especially important that we get right the first footprint for the show, the first public impression, because there is a lot of uncertainty about what kind of show it will be—from the producers of *Riverdance* and the creators of *Les Misérables*? What *is* that? But, although we're best known for *Riverdance*, we are first and foremost producers.

JMcC: In order to produce musical theatre you have to really love it, because it's a huge challenge creatively, financially, and logistically. The success rate is poor because 60 to 70 percent of musicals fail. It's a huge high risk, so you wouldn't want to do it unless you were passionate about it. And I think it's the same for most musical theatre producers, we all fell in love with *West Side Story*, *Oklahoma!*, and *South Pacific* when we were kids. Moya and I wanted to produce this show because we love the worlds that Alain and Claude-Michel have created and we thought it would be so exciting to go on a journey with them and see the process from the beginning, right from the blank page through to resolution. It can sometimes be a

Photo by Joan Marcus

John Dempsey, Alain Boublil, Moya Doherty, John McColgan, and Claude-Michel Schönberg

bit intimidating working with them because they have such high standards and they interrogate every idea thoroughly, but it's also invigorating and stimulating.

In some ways it is quite different working on a musical compared to working on *Riverdance*. There's a book, there's a play, and it's sung-through, but the principles are the same and the logistics are quite similar. We've been fortunate enough to have *Riverdance* opening, touring, and playing around the world for eleven years. So we've gained huge logistical and managerial experience. We're used to the scale of a big show, we have good relationships with theatre owners and promoters in North America and around the world, and we have a good reputation. We try to imagine productions that will get to the broadest possible audience but still have integrity and a rooted-ness. When *Riverdance* started, we never imagined it would be as successful on the scale it was, and I think if we had imagined that we might have made it different in some way. But it was because we cared about the subject that we created something that we believed in, and it is exactly the same with *The Pirate Queen*. I would like to think that audiences who came to see *Riverdance* would absolutely equally enjoy this, and audiences who had already been to *Les Misérables* and *Miss Saigon* would love this, too.

MD: *Riverdance* evolved from a seven-minute television presentation for the Eurovision Song Contest to a hugely successful full-scale production so rapidly and in a very public way. It was a very mad, exciting, and fantastic time, but this is a saner experience and, in some ways, it's more enriching because we have had the time to nurture the piece, to get to know it, and to watch it evolve out of the spotlight.

JMcC: When this new journey began, the first major question was where we should open the show. We talked about the Point Theatre in Dublin where *Riverdance* opened, and Alain and Claude-Michel found that idea attractive. But the theatre wasn't available at the time we needed it, and after discussing the UK, we finally decided to open in America. They'd never opened there before, but we had produced and toured *Riverdance* there for a number of years. We wanted to open out of town before going to Broadway, and we decided on Chicago, which has a wonderful tradition of theatre and a very sophisticated theatre.

We put together an incredible array of creative talent including the director, Frank Galati, the set designer, Eugene Lee, and the costume designer, Martin Pakledinaz—who are all Tony Award winners. And one of the principal reasons they agreed to work on the project was when they heard the music. They wanted to work with Alain and Claude-Michel, and they wanted to work on a Boublil and Schönberg musical. So we cast the creative team very easily. In musical theatre the creative team is as important as and maybe even more important than the talent that goes on stage. This show is very complex and it's a difficult concept to put on stage, with sea battles and castles, as well as the court of Queen Elizabeth. There is a lot to achieve, so just to come up with a language, a style, and a look that would accommodate this huge vision for the show could, for a lot of people, be intimidating.

MD: We had to consider the creative team very carefully and to decide what the piece required—what intellectual, creative, and imaginative approach. And we had to get people who would understand the piece, who could bring an energy and a sympathy with it along with some left-of-field thinking. Frank Galati brings from his background an intellectual thinking to the piece and a sensibility for good storytelling. The authors can tell a good story but then the director has to fully understand and stage that story. Eugene Lee is himself almost a set designer-director; his sets alone tell a story and he creates a whole world on stage. His set design triggered so many other things for us. He brought with him a wealth of experience and he instantly saw what the piece was and was excited by it.

There was really only one choreographer in North America who was absolutely right for the piece. Mark Dendy comes from the world of Martha Graham, from an avant-garde, non-Broadway voice, but his understanding of movement and choreography is such that he can create a language of movement for these people that isn't imposed upon them but that comes from within. And he collaborated with our Irish Dance Choreographer Carol Leavy Joyce, who was the Irish Dance Director on *Riverdance*.

JMcC: As producers what we try to do is to is to put together and create an environment where creative people can do their best work collaboratively, where there is an atmosphere of respect and admiration for each other's work. We try to find the best people in the world who are creatively right for the project and chemically right for each other because we're all going to work together for a very long time. I don't believe that creative tension or conflict is the way to work. We try to create harmony and an affectionate and inter-supportive, nurturing environment for the piece to grow in. And that's what we've managed to do in this case. Through diligence and good fortune we've managed to assemble a wonderful creative team and each of them are extraordinarily nice people. But the glue that holds them together is the work. They all love the piece and believe that they are working on something really special and they're thrilled to be working together.

MD: It has been a challenging show to cast but there were five moments throughout the auditions when people completely blew us away and we have those five people in the show. Those auditions were so far out on their own for this particular show at this moment in time and I believe we have a very strong cast. We have no stars but we have people who are such excellent actors and singers that they will hopefully become stars as a result. Queen Elizabeth is a marvelous role and we have a wonderful soprano, Linda Balgord; we have a fantastic Grania, Stephanie Block; and we have a young English actor, Hadley Fraser, as Tiernan. We had to negotiate that with Equity, but Hadley is a unique talent, and when he did the audition for us he just displaced the air with his interpretation of Tiernan. In my view he's a sort of younger Colm Wilkinson in the early days of *Les Misérables*; he has that very special quality, and it would have broken my heart if we could not have negotiated to have him in the show.

JMcC: Aside from Hadley we cast the show out of North America because of Equity ruling as we're opening there. There is a huge cast and we are used to big numbers, but we just have to make sure we can afford to pay for them. It's hugely expensive and it's very high risk, but I'm quietly confident because I think this is Alain and Claude-Michel's best work. The casting decisions are collaborative; although theoretically the director has the final say, we discussed the artists we'd seen and we all agreed. It was quite difficult to cast because we needed strong singers, excellent actors, and great dancers. We actually divided it up scientifically. Claude-Michel said that you need this many singers—this many male singers and this many female singers for the ensemble and chorus work, and obviously the leads have to have wonderful voices in addition to being fine actors. Every dancer has to be able to sing. There are a number of different styles as we have Irish dancers, acrobatic dancers, and

Photo by Joan Marcus

Claude-Michel Schönberg, John McColgan, and Stephanie J. Block

show dancers, and we have to work very hard to blend all these styles. We advertised for dancers who can sing, and some of them are terrific singers and some of them are adequate singers but they're brilliant dancers. Sometimes it was heartbreaking if there were some really brilliant dancers who couldn't sing and so we couldn't cast them.

MD: The trickiest thing was securing the right Broadway theatre for this show. Big shows were circling, waiting to get in. Some shows had gone into theatres where they thought they were only going to be there for a limited run, yet they became hugely successful, while other shows we thought would stay for longer failed, leaving the theatre dark with a need to put things onstage in the interim. We needed a big theatre of at least 1,600 seats for it to make financial sense, and due to the fact that the show is so huge in concept. We needed a large stage with flys and wing space for the scale of what's being attempted. We needed to know what theatre we were going into on Broadway before we signed off on our set for Chicago, so they could make the set work in both theatres. It's probably the most nerve-wracking time for any producer, but we finally managed to get the right theatre: the 1,800-seat Hilton on 42nd Street.

JMcC: With a big theatre you normally have to have a big orchestra. The musicians' unions stipulate that you have to have a certain number of musicians for a specific-size theatre and that even if you don't use them, you have to pay for them. But we have just eleven Irish musicians, as we have been able to negotiate the exact number we require for this show because it has a specific ethnic sensibility. Claude-Michel has been working with these musicians for a very long time. It's not like the normal case when the musical theatre orchestra arrives a couple of weeks before, and they just read the music and play it. Julian Kelly, the musical director and orchestrator, wrote down the music, and Claude-Michel encouraged the musicians to bring their own emotion, skill, and interpretation to it. He came to Dublin and worked with them on fifteen minutes of music at a time, and they found it a really exciting way to work. Each of them has brought something of themselves and something of their tradition to it, and so it's incredibly Irish and at the same time incredibly modern. Some of it sounds like rock 'n' roll, some of it sounds like lush cinematic ballads, and some of it even sounds like it was written by eminent Irish composers. I think a sound is being created that has never been heard before in a theatrical musical.

It's not easy producing on Broadway because of the union situation. It's very difficult and very expensive rehearsing and putting on a show there. You have to decide what your budget is and where you're going to pitch the show, and that's based on a number of things: the size of the cast, the size of the set, and the world environment that you create. You can only mount a show that you can get a return on. You can only go so far and after that it doesn't make economic sense. There's a judgement to be made, and I believe that audiences who come to the theatre and pay the sort of prices that you now have to pay both expect and enjoy spectacle, and enjoy something different that they haven't seen before, so that they will gasp with astonishment. The capitalization for *The Pirate Queen* is around sixteen million dollars. But there are three full-scale battles, there's a ship set on fire, there's thunderstorms, there's rain, there's lightning, and so on. Scale and spectacle costs money, but at the same time if you get that right—and when it's put together with a fantastic book, lyrics, and music, then people are excited by that. The operating cost is very high, too, and that's something you have to watch very carefully; it's a nightmare balance. You need to be sure that even if you do have a hit, you can still afford to keep running. It's happened in the past that even with a hit show that the weekly operating costs are so high that it's impossible to make a profit; that's not good for anybody. So there's a very tight line between the scale of the show and the ability to sustain that. With most really big shows you need to be doing at least 70 percent business for a show to last.

MD: It's interesting that this show is a truly international work with Irish producers, an Irish-based story, French authors, and an A-class American creative team. *The Pirate Queen* has huge integrity, it has a sense of place and authenticity, and it has its own unique voice. I knew from early on that there were moments on the page that, to the ear and the imagination, would make people laugh and make people cry, and that's not an easy thing to do in the theatre. Some people seem to think that the day of the epic historical musical is over, but I completely disagree. I think if you give the audience a good piece of musical theatre—no matter what the subject is, if it's a good story, well-told, with well-written music and lyrics; well presented, with high production values; and if people are brought on an emotional journey, then at the end of the evening—we hope— they will leave the theatre feeling absolutely satisfied. There are some moments in the show that are so extraordinarily beautiful and so *good*, and I really believe that Boublil and Schönberg have written a true classic.

MARGUERITE—THE NEXT PROJECT

There is another work in progress: *Marguerite*, which is set during World War II at the time of the Nazi occupation and the dark hours of the French collaboration. It is loosely based on *The Lady of the Camellias* (*La Dame aux Camélias*) by Alexandre Dumas, fils, which in turn provided the story that Verdi's opera *La Traviata* is based on. This will be Claude-Michel and Alain's first book, or song/dialogue musical. They have written the book and dialogue together, but the world-famous composer Michel Legrand is writing the music, and Alain the French lyrics. So, for the first time, it will be a team of three working together from the start. The English adapters of the book and lyrics are still being decided upon.

The project of *Marguerite* started with Michel Legrand's wish to write a musical for Marie Zamora, the French soprano and actress with whom Michel has been touring the world in concert for the last five years. Marie also happens to be Alain's wife. So, naturally, Michel asked Alain to work with him on this project, but during friendly discussions, Claude-Michel himself came up with the idea of updating *The Lady of the Camellias* for Marie. He very generously offered the idea to Alain and Michel, but it appeared very quickly to Alain that he could not take the project too far without his usual accomplice. So Claude-Michel decided that he would join the team, although he would not be writing the music because of his admiration for Michel Legrand's work. Also, both Alain and Claude-Michel felt that it would be exciting to do something as different as a song/dialogue musical, as well as collaborate with Michel Legrand. They believe, though, that the end result will be very much part of the same family.

It's a project they have been developing for the last five years with Jonathan Kent, the co-founder of the Almeida—and a successful director in his own right—who has kept a constant dialogue with the authors over this period. *Marguerite* will be a smaller show, and is planned to open in London in 2008, as well as in France in the same year; with Marie in the title role, the show will be co-produced by Alain and Claude-Michel. ❧

CHAPTER 7

Showcase

A FACT FILE ON THE PRODUCTIONS

Alain Boublil, Cameron Mackintosh, Trevor Nunn, and Herbert Kretzmer at the 1987 Tony Awards.

T HE AMAZING GLOBAL SUCCESS of Boublil and Schönberg's musicals has led to the accumulation of a mass of interesting facts and figures as well as some intriguing trivia. Some of these, inevitably, are constantly changing, and the following facts are up to date as of spring 2006, with later additions for *The Pirate Queen*.

Les Misérables is the world's longest-running international musical, and has been seen by more than 54 million people all over the world. It has been translated into 21 different languages and played in 38 countries and 249 cities. Sixty-four professional companies have opened *Les Misérables*, and the production has played over 42,000 professional performances worldwide in places as disparate as Sheffield to Shanghai, Boston to Berlin, and Helsinki to Honolulu. The Schools Edition of *Les Misérables* has played over 1,400 school productions in the UK and U.S. *Les Misérables* has won over 50 major awards including 8 Tony Awards, 1 Olivier Award, 2 Grammys, as well as the BBC Radio 2 Award for The Nation's Most Popular Musical. There have been 33 cast recordings.

Miss Saigon has been seen by over 32 million people worldwide. It has been translated into 11 different languages and played in 23 counties and 240 cities. Twenty-six companies have opened *Miss Saigon*, and the production has played some 20,000 performances all over the world from Memphis to Melbourne, Philadelphia to the Philippines, and from Wales to Warsaw. *Miss Saigon* has won 30 major theatre awards including 3 Tony Awards and 2 Olivier Awards. There have been 11 cast recordings.

Martin Guerre, both the original and the revised version, played in London for 675 performances before the completely new second production opened at the West Yorkshire Playhouse and went on a very successful tour, first in the UK and then in the U.S. The revised first version won Best Musical and Best Choreography at the 1997 Laurence Olivier Awards. *The Pirate Queen* is a completely new musical which opened in Chicago on October 29, 2006 before transferring to Broadway, opening there on April 5, 2007.

In this chapter you will find all the details of everything you might want to know about the productions in London, on Broadway, and worldwide, with details of the creative teams, casts, musical numbers, reviews, cities played, awards, a discography, synopses, themes, and some fascinating facts and trivia. In addition to *Les Misérables*, *Miss Saigon*, *Martin Guerre*, and *The Pirate Queen*, there are also details of their very first musical, *La Révolution Française*, the original French production of *Les Misérables*, Claude-Michel's ballet, *Wuthering Heights*, and the concert *One Day More*.

The reviews form an extremely interesting part of the production history of the musicals. The excerpts included show briefly the general mood of the reviews, and there are a few longer excerpts where critics have given particularly perceptive and valuable insights. In London, critics do not write their reviews until after the first night performance. Some papers, such as *The Daily Mail*, print them the following day, while other reviews do not come out until the day after that. On Broadway there is a different tradition, and critics write their reviews in the late preview period so they come out immediately after opening night. Early editions of the papers can, therefore, make or break the mood of an opening night party!

LA RÉVOLUTION FRANÇAISE

Alain and Claude-Michel's very first musical, *La Révolution Française*, premiered at the Palais des Sports, Paris on October 2, 1973. It played for forty-five days, filling a lucky cancellation slot by Rudolph Nureyev at the venue. It was the perfect place for such a large-scale musical.

CREATIVE TEAM
The creative credits are:
A musical by Alain Boublil & Claude-Michel Schönberg
Music   Claude-Michel Schönberg & Raymond Jeannot
Lyrics   Alain Boublil & Jean Max-Rivière

Orchestrations   Jean-Claude Petit & Martin Circus
Director   Michel de Ré
Choreography   Brigitte Le Fèvre

CAST
(as on the original concept album)
Général Bonaparte   Antoine
Général Kellerman   Cyril Azzam
Robespierre   Alain Baschung
M. de Lafayette   Jean Bentho
Charlotte Corday   Françoise Boublil
Isabelle de Montmorency   Noëlle Cordier
Danton   Martin Circus
Marie-Antoinette   Franca di Rienzo
Marat   Jean-Max Rivière
Charles Gauthier   Jean-Pierre Savelli
Louis XVI   Claude-Michel Schönberg
Fouquier-Tinville   Jean Schultes
Madame Sans-Gêne   Élisabeth Vigna
Soloist—La Terreur   Gérard Layani
Soloist—Les Chouans   Jean-François Michael

MUSICAL SCENES
1. **Ouverture**   Choeurs
2. **Les Etats Generaux:**
(5 Mai 1789)
Le Roi (Louis XVI)   Claude-Michel Schönberg
La Noblesse: Oui, Sire   Système Crapoutchick
Le Clerge: Ainsi soit-il   Choeurs
Le Tiers Etat: Francais, Francais   Martin Circus
3. **Charles Gauthier**   Jean-Pierre Savelli
4. **A Versailles**
(14 Juillet 1789)   Les Enfants de Bondy
5. **Retour De La Bastille:**
Francais, Francais   Alain Baschung et Choeurs
Il s'appell Charles Gauthier   Noëlle Cordier
6. **A Bas Tous Les Privileges**
(nuit du 4 Auot 1789)   Martin Circus
7. **Declaration Des Droits De L'homme Et Du Citoyen**
(26 Aout 1789)   Jean-Pierre Savelli

8. Ça Ira, Ça Ira
(5 et 6 Octobre 1789)   Système Crapoutchick, Jean Bentho, Mario
    d'Alba, Claude-Michel Schönberg
9. Quatre Saisons Pour Un Amour   Noëlle Cordier
10. Serment De Talleyrand
(12 Juillet 1790)
Fete de la Federation (Talleyrand)
(14 Juillet 1790)   Les Charlots et Choeurs
11. Crieurs De Journaux
(21 Juin 1791)
La patrie est en danger
(11 Juillet 1792) Danton   Martin Circus
12. L'Exil (10 Aout)   Noëlle Cordier
13. Valmy (General Kellerman)
(20 Septembre 1792)   Cyril Azzam et Choeurs
Proclamation se la Rebpublique
(22 Septembre 1792)
14. C'est Du Beau Linge, Mon Général
Madame Sans-Gêne et le Général Bonaparte   Elisabeth Vigna,
    Antoine
15. Le Procès De Louis XVI
Réquisitoire (Fouquier-Tinville)   Jean Schultes
Louis XVI (10 Decembre 1792)   Claude-Michel Schönberg
Exécution (21 Janvier 1793)   Choeurs
16. Chouans En Avant!
(Juin 1793)   Jean-Francois Michael
17. La Terreur Est En Nous   Systeme Crapoutchick
18. L'Horrible Assissinat Du Citoyen Marat par la Perfide
    Charlotte Corday
(13 Juillet 1793)   Françoise Boublil, Jean-Max Rivière
19. Fouquier-Tinville   Jean Schultes
20. Au Petit Matin
(Marie Antoinette)
(16 Octobre 1793–25 Vendémiaire An 11)   Franca di Rienzo
21. Robespierre
Que J'aie Tort Ou Que J'aie Raison
(Avril 1794-16 Germinal An 11)   Alain Baschung
22. La Fete De L'Être Suprême
(Robespierre)
(8 Juin 1794-20 Prairial An 11)   Alain Baschung et Choeurs

23. Gardien De Prison A La Conciergerie
(8 Juin 1794-20 Prairial An 11)   David Gauthier
24. Révolution (Final)
(8 Juin 1794-20 Prairial An 11)   Noëlle Cordier, Jean-Pierre Savelli

DISCOGRAPHY
La Révolution Française
CD ©1973 Editions Musicales Alain Boublil
©1985 Exallshow Ltd.
Awarded Gold and Platinum Discs

LES MISÉRABLES

ORIGINAL FRENCH PRODUCTION
The original French version of *Les Misérables* premiered at the 4,500-seat Palais Des Sports in Paris in September 1980. It was staged by the renowned French director Robert Hossein in three Acts and an Epilogue. The production was seen by 500,000 people in the three months that it played.

CREATIVE TEAM
The creative credits are:
A musical by Alain Boublil & Claude-Michel Schönberg
Music   Claude-Michel Schönberg
Lyrics   Alain Boublil & Jean-Marc Natel
Orchestrations   John Cameron
Director   Robert Hossein
Musical Director   Jean-Michel Defaye
Choreographer   Arthur Plasschaert
Set Designer   Jean Mandaroux
Costume Designers   Sylvie Poulet, Martine Mulotte
Sound Design   Claude Wargnier

CAST
Fantine   Rose Laurens
Jean Valjean   Maurice Barrier
Inspecteur Javert   Jean Vallée
Cosette (enfant)   Sylvie Camacho, Maryse Cédolin, Priscilla Patron
Mme Thénardier   Marie-France Roussel

M Thénardier   Yvan Dautin
Gavroche   Cyrille Dupont, Fabrice Ploquin, Florence Davis
Éponine   Marianne Mille
Marius   Gilles Buhlmann
Enjolras   Christian Ratellin
Cosette (jeune fille)   Fabienne Guyon
M Gillenormand   Dominique Tirmont
Mlle Gillenormand   Anne Forrez

SCENES
Acte I
La jeune Fantine, abandonee par son amant, a fui à Paris. Elle emporte
   avec elle Cosette, l'enfant née de cet amour déçu.
Fantine, chemin faisant, confie Cosette aux Thénardier, aubergistes à
   Montfermeil.
Scene 1: Sortie des Usines Madeleine à Montreuil-sur-Mer
Scene 2: Sur le port
Scene 3: M. Madeleine répare l'injustice commise envers Fantine
Scene 4: La charrette
Scene 5: Tempête sous un crâne
Scene 6: Chez les Thénardier
Acte II
Scene 7: Place du puits aux mendiants
Scene 8: Les amis de l'ABC
Scene 9: 21, rue Plumet
Scene 10: Marius et Eponine
Scene 11: Recontre de Marius et de Cosette
Scene 12: L'attaque de la rue plummet
Scene 13: Demain
Entr'acte
Acte III
Scene 14: La barricade de la rue de la Chanvrerie
Scene 15: Chez M. Gillenormand
Scene 16: Mariage de Marius et Cosette
Scene 17: Les Thénardier chez M. Gillenormand
Epilogue
Scene 18: La chambre de Jean Valjean

MUSICAL NUMBERS
Acte I

La Journée Est Finie
L'Air De La Misère
Les Beaux Cheveux Que Voila
J'Avais Rêvé D'Une Autre Vie
Dites-moi Ce Qui Se Passe
Fantine et Monsieur Madeleine
Mon Prince Est En Chemin
Mam'zelle Crapaud
La Devise Du Cabaretier
Valjean Chez Les Thénardier
La Valse De La Fourberie
Acte II
Donnez, Donnez
Rouge Et Noir
Les Amis De L'ABC
A La Volonté Du Peuple
Cosette: Dans Las Vie
Marius: Dans La Vie
Voilà Le Soir Qui Tombe
Le Coeur Au Bonheur
L'Un Vers L'Autre
La Faute A Voltaire
La Nuit De L'Angoisse
Demain
Entr'acte
Acte III
Ce N'est Rien
L'Aube Du 6 Juin
Noir Ou Blanc
La Mort De Gavroche
Marius et M Gillenormand
Le Mariage, "Soyez Heureux"
L'Aveu de Jean Valjean
Marchandage Et Révélation
Épilogue
La Lumière

LONDON PRODUCTION

Les Misérables premiered at the Barbican Theatre in London on October 8, 1985. It was a co-production with the Royal Shakespeare Company and designed for a transfer to the West End at the Palace Theatre. However, the reviews, with a few exceptions, were appalling and sounded a death knell for the production. If it had not been for the courage and conviction of Cameron Mackintosh, the two-month run at the Barbican could well have been the end of *Les Misérables*. After the reviews came out, the owner of the Palace Theatre, Andrew Lloyd Webber, offered to return the £50,000 ($95,000) deposit as he had, after all, a planned production of his *Phantom of the Opera* to find a home for. The decision had to be made in twenty-four hours, and Cameron Mackintosh decided to go ahead. In the meantime, the general public had defiantly made up their own minds about the show and proved that word of mouth was a greater power than critical response. Within three days of opening, the Barbican production was sold out.

The transfer to the beautiful Palace Theatre went ahead. After a rather slow start the ticket sales gathered momentum, and the show was soon playing to full houses. It played for a total of 7,602 performances, and on January 10, 1994 it became the longest-running production at the Palace Theatre. On April 3, 2004 it transferred to the Queen's Theatre, where it is still playing. On October 8, 2006 *Les Misérables* celebrated its twenty-first birthday, becoming the longest-running international musical of all time, overtaking *Cats*, which closed on May 11, 2002 after running for twenty-one years.

CREATIVE TEAM

The creative credits are:

Written by   Alain Boublil & Claude-Michel Schönberg
Music   Claude-Michel Schönberg
English Lyrics   Herbert Kretzmer
Original French Text   Alain Boublil & Jean-Marc Natel
Additional Material   James Fenton
Directors   Trevor Nunn and John Caird
Musical Supervision   John Cameron
Orchestrations   John Cameron
Musical Direction   Martin Koch
Musical Staging   Kate Flatt
Designer   John Napier
Costumes   Andreane Neofitou
Lighting   David Hersey
Sound   Andrew Bruce

ORIGINAL LONDON CAST

Jean Valjean   Colm Wilkinson
Javert   Roger Allam
Fantine   Patti LuPone
Marius   Michael Ball
Cosette   Rebecca Caine
Eponine   Frances Ruffelle
Thénardier   Alun Armstrong
Madame Thénardier   Susan Jane Tanner
Enjolras   David Burt

SUBSEQUENT LONDON CASTS

Jean Valjean   Dave Willets, Craig Pinder, Peter Carrie, Stig Rossen, Phil Cavil, John Owen Jones, Simon Bowman, Michael Sterling, Jeff Leyton, J. Mark McVey, Mark McKerracher, Robert Marien, Hans-Peter Janssens, Dudu Fisher, Wiik Oystein

Javert   Clive Carter, Don Gallagher, Davis Burt, Paul Leonard, Andrew C. Wadsworth, James Staddon, Michael McCarthy, Ethan Freeman, Tim Morgan, Hal Fowler, Peter Corry, Jerome Pradon, John Cornell, Hartwig Rudolph, Phillip Quast

Fantine   Jackie Marks, Kathleen Rowe McAllen, Rebecca Storm, Grania Renihan, Siobhan McCarthy, Jenna Russell, Ruthie Henshall, Lindsay Danvers, Claire Moore, Silvie Paladino, Rebecca Thornhill, Carmen Cusack, Joanna Ampil, Carola Haggkvist, Kerry Ellis, Ria Jones, Gunilla Backman

Marius   Simon Bowman, Martin Smith, Graham Bickley, Mario Frangoulis, Stifyn Parri, Darryl Knock, Tony Rouse, Mathew Cammelle, Alistair Robins, Graham Mackay-Bruce, Tom Lucas, Niklas Andersson, Jody Crossier, Hadley Fraser, Jon Lee, Garry Tushaw, Hayden Tee, Mike Sterling

Cosette   Gail Mortley, Jacinta Mulcahy, Mary-Louise Clark, Lisa Hull, Sarah Jane Hassell, Megan Kelly, Nicky Adams, Myrra Malmberg, Annalene Beechey, Zoe Curlett, Philippa Healey, Sarah Lane, Helen French, Lydia Griffiths, Julia Moller

Eponine   Jayne Draper, Laura Hamilton, Linzi Hately, Meredith Braun, Silvie Paladino, Stephanie Martin, Gemma Wardle, Jacinta Whyte, Amanda Salmon, Joanna Ampil, Laura Michelle Kelly, Caroline Sheen, Sophia Ragavelas, Shonagh Daly, Jenna Russell, Lea Salonga

Enjolras   Martin George, Christopher Howard, Michael Cantwell,

David Greer, Keith Burns, Graham Bickley, David Malek, David Morris, David Bardsley, Glyn Kerslake, Mathew Cammelle, Mark O'Malley, Paul Manuel, Jason McCann, Oliver Thornton, Ramin Karimloo, Shaun Escoffery

Thénardier Stephen Hanan, David Delve, Barry James, Martyn Ellis, Peter Polycarpou, Mark White, Philip Cox, Hilton McRae, Chris Langham, Nick Holder, Teddy Kempner, Cameron Blakely, Tony Timberlake, Stephen Tate

Madame Thénardier Myra Sands, Gay Soper, Sue Kelvin, Rosemary Ashe, Katy Secombe, Jenny Galloway, Mandy Holliday, Harriet Thorpe, Liz Ewing, Joanna Mays, Claire Moore

MUSICAL NUMBERS

The musical numbers on opening night were:

ACT I

Prologue The Company

Soliloquy Valjean

At The End Of The Day Unemployed and factory workers

I Dreamed A Dream Fantine

Lovely Ladies Ladies and clients

Who Am I? Valjean

Come To Me Fantine and Valjean

Castle On A Cloud Cosette

Master Of The House Thénardier, his wife and customers

Thénardier Waltz M. and Mme. Thénardier and Valjean

Stars Javert

Look Down Gavroche and the beggars

Red and Black Enjolras, Marius and the students

Do You Hear The People Sing? Enjolras, the students and the citizens

I Saw Him Once Cosette

In My Life Cosette, Valjean, Marius and Eponine

A Heart Full Of Love Cosette, Marius and Eponine

One Day More The Company

ACT II

On My Own Eponine

A Little Fall Of Rain Eponine and Marius

Drink With Me To Days Gone By Grantaire, students and women

Bring Him Home Valjean

Dog Eats Dog Thénardier

Soliloquy Javert
Turning Women
Empty Chairs At Empty Tables Marius
Wedding Chorale Guests
Beggars At The Feast M. and Mme. Thénardier
Finale The Company

LONDON REVIEWS

The first night of *Les Misérables* was greeted with an enthusiastic response from the audience and a long, emotional standing ovation, so it came as something of a shock to all concerned that most of the reviews were terrible and, in some cases, quite savage. It is interesting to note, however, that the response to the musical was much the same as that to Hugo's novel. While his highly controversial novel received tremendous popular acclaim, it was condemned by the critics of the day, who wrote hostile reviews. The novel, nevertheless, has become an enduring classic, read throughout the world, consistently receiving the highest critical praise. So it's a case of history repeating itself. Critics, of course, are not infallible.

The critics reviewing the London first night variously described it as "a load of sentimental old tosh" (Lyn Gardner, *City Limits*, 10.18.85), "a turgid panorama" and "a crude cops and robbers epic" (John Barber, *Daily Telegraph*, 10.10.85), and "a banal digest" (Kenneth Hurren, *Mail on Sunday*, 10.13.85). Critics further complained that it was "the reduction of a literary mountain to a dramatic molehill…a lurid Victorian melodrama" (Francis King, *Sunday Telegraph*, 10.13.85), or that Hugo's novel had been reduced "to the level of a comic strip" (Clive Hirschhorn, *Sunday Express*, 10.13.85). They simply talked of "the major failure of the piece to engage our emotion" (Suzie Mackenzie, *Time Out*, 10.17.85), and even said that "it commands respect but it does not inspire affection" (David Nathan, *Jewish Chronicle*, 10.18.85). Michael Ratcliffe believed that they had "emasculated Hugo's Olympian perspective and reduced it to the trivial issues and tearful aesthetic of rock opera and the French hit parade of ten (fifteen?) years ago," and he called it "a witless and synthetic entertainment" (*Observer*, 10.13.85). He continued this tirade even when reviewing other shows. The late Jack Tinker famously christened *Les Misérables* "the Glums" and felt that "it leaves one curiously uninvolved" (*Daily Mail*, 10.9.85).

In light of the amazing global success of *Les Misérables*, such reviews now seem astonishing. But there were some critics, albeit only a few, who loved the show and championed it not only in the British press but even more significantly in international publications. Sue Jameson commented that "the whole evening has that unusually uplifting sensation when you realize you've witnessed a very special event, an evening of the best in British theatre" (*London Broadcasting*, 10.9.85). John Peter wrote about the show's "masterful theatricality...outshining everything else on offer" (*Sunday Times*, 10.13.85), while Benedict Nightingale wrote "*Les Misérables* is more pop opera than musical and more phenomenon than either...I don't think that even the RSC has more successfully combined an assault on the eyes with one on the tears ducts behind them" (*New Statesman*, 10.18.85). Michael Coveney wrote an excellent and lengthy review that was notably full of praise but also full of instructive analysis and insights and suggested that "the show is an important one, bridging the gaps between musical and opera...the unforgettable Act I finale is one of the best I have ever seen...this is an intriguing and most enjoyable musical, fully justifying the meeting of commercial resources with RSC talent and personnel...It is also an emotionally demanding evening. If you are of a marginally susceptible nature, take the Kleenex" (*Financial Times*, 10.9.85). Sheridan Morley's review was also very perceptive: "We have the musical of the year, if not the half decade...the greatness of *Les Misérables* is that it starts out to redefine the limits of musical theatre...it tackles universal themes of social and domestic happiness in terms of individual despair...there is an energy and an operatic intensity here which exists in the work of no British composer past or present...*Les Misérables* is everything the musical theatre ought to be doing" (*Punch*, 10.16.85).

WASHINGTON/BROADWAY PRODUCTION

Les Misérables first opened in America at the Kennedy Center Opera House in Washington, D.C. The show played there for six weeks before transferring to the Broadway Theatre, New York on March 12, 1987. This production was technically improved from that at the Palace Theatre due to computerized control of the moving barricades and revolve, and the set alone cost half a million dollars more than in London. It was altogether a much more expensive production with a budget of $4.5 million compared to the London budget of £1 million ($1.9 million). The show opened with two stars from the London production, Colm Wilkinson and Frances Ruffelle. At first, Actors' Equity objected to the use of British actors, but Cameron Mackintosh let it be known that if the British Jean Valjean could not go on then the show would not go on. The New York production opened with a $12 million advance and received great critical acclaim, consistently playing to full houses and recouping its investment in 23 weeks, a remarkably quick rate of return for such an expensive musical. In October 1990 it transferred to the Imperial Theatre in order to make room for *Miss Saigon* at the Broadway Theatre.

In 1996, in preparation for the 10th Anniversary on Broadway, it was decided that substantial cast changes were necessary. In *Les Misérables*, Valjean and Javert are the only two principals, as all the other actors play more than one role and are technically classified as chorus. American Equity rules that all chorus members must have run-of-show contracts and can stay with a show until it closes. But with such a long-running show, this resulted in some performers in their late thirties who, having been with the show for years, were no longer suitable to be playing young students in their early twenties. In order to protect the high standards of the production and to re-energize it, almost half the cast was sacked. They were, however, offered very generous severance packages and some were even invited to re-audition.

Les Misérables is currently the third longest-running musical in Broadway history. On January 25, 2002, it overtook *A Chorus Line* to become the second longest-running Broadway show, a record it held until February 4, 2004 when it was overtaken by *The Phantom of the Opera*. *The Fantasticks* was the longest running Off-Broadway show with 17,162 performances before it closed in 2002; it then re-opened in August 2006. *Les Misérables* closed on Broadway after sixteen years on May 18, 2003. However, as part of the *Les Misérables* "Coming-of-Age" celebrations it re-opened at the Broadhurst Theatre, with its 6,681st Broadway performance. Previews started on October 24, 2006, with the official opening night on November 9.

ORIGINAL WASHINGTON/BROADWAY CAST

Jean Valjean   Colm Wilkinson
Javert   Terrence Mann
Fantine   Randy Graff
Marius   David Bryant
Cosette   Judy Kuhn
Eponine   Frances Ruffelle
Enjolras   Michael Maguire
Thénardier   Leo Burmester
Madame Thénardier   Jennifer Butt

SUBSEQUENT WASHINGTON/BROADWAY CASTS

Jean Valjean   Gary Morris, Tim Shew, Donn Cook, Philip
   Hernandez, Robert Evan, William Solo, Craig Schulman, J. Mark

McVey, Mark McKerracher, Frederick C. Inkley, Ivan Rutherford, Keith Randal, Robert Marien, Dudu Fisher

Javert Michael McCarthy, Norman Large, Anthony Crivello, Robert Westenburg, Robert Cuccioli, Merwin Ford, Christopher Innvar, Robert Gallagher, Philip Hernandez, Gregg Edelman, Shuler Hensley, Herndon Lackey, Robert DuSold, Richard Kinsey, Chuck Wagner, David Masenheimer, Joseph Mahowald

Fantine Maureen Moore, Laurie Beechman, Mary Gutzi, Rachel York, Andrea McArdle, Paige O'Hara, Jacquelyn Piro, Melba Moore, Florence Lacey, Juliet Lambert, Jane Bodle, Lauren Kennedy, Susan Dawn Carson, Christy Baron, Donna Kane, Alice Ripley, Susie McMonagle, Lisa Capps, Jayne Paterson, Susan Gilmour

Marius Ray Walker, John Leone, Eric Kunze, Michael Sutherland Lynch, Craig Rubano, Marsh Hanson, Ricky Martin, Peter Lockyer, Kevin Oderkirk, Kevin Kern, Hugh Panaro, Mathew Porretta, Tom Donoghue, Rich Affanto, Stephen Brian Patterson

Cosette Tracy Shayne, Melissa Anne Davis, Jennifer Lee Andrews, Christeena Michelle Riggs, Tobi Foster, Sandra Turley, Jacquelyn Piro, Tamra Hayden, Kate Fisher, Stephanie Waters

Eponine Kelli James, Natalie Toro, Debbie Gibson, Brandy Brown, Lea Salonga, Tia Riebling, Sarah Uriarte Berry, Kelli Rabke, Megan Lawrence, Sutton Foster, Kerry Butler, Dana Meller, Catherine Brunell, Jessica Boevers, Russell Arden Koplin, Josie Langel, Michelle Maika, Gina Feliccia, Christeena Michelle Riggs, Dawn Younker, Rona Figueroa, Diana Kaarina

Enjolras Joseph Kolinski, Joe Mahowald, Lawrence Anderson, Ron Bohmer, Robert Aaron Tesoro, Paul Avedisian, Stephen R. Buntrock, Christopher Mark Peterson, David Gagnon, Joe Locarro, Gary Mauer, Brian Herriott, Ben Davis

Thénardier Ed Dixon, Adam Heller, Allen Fitzpatrick, Nick Wyman, Drew Eshelman, J.P. Dougherty

Madame Thénardier Cindy Benson, Evalyn Baron, Tregoney Shepherd, Ann Arvia, Jean FitzGibbons, Fuschia Walker, Betsey Joslyn, Kathy Santen, Gina Ferral, Diana Rogers, Aymee Garcia

WASHINGTON/BROADWAY REVIEWS

When *Les Misérables* opened in Washington and on Broadway, the critical response was altogether different from that which greeted the show in London. Some critics had already seen the London production and were aware of the international potential of the show, while others acknowledged the differences in form from the traditional Broadway musical. That *Les Misérables* opened in the wake of a series of Broadway flops—*Grind, Big Deal, Smile,* and *Rags*—did nothing to allay fears that the "British" musical was taking over. *Cats* and *Me and My Girl* were already hugely successful, with *Starlight Express* about to open and *Phantom of the Opera* and *Chess* due the following season. So *Les Misérables* opened amid great speculation about the future of the Broadway musical and gave rise to some interesting debate about the nature and form of musical theatre. The *Washington Times* review concentrated on the show's adherence to Hugo's novel: "The most difficult part of pulling off this far-fetched notion of a musical *Misérables*—and the most successful—is the compression of plot and fluidity of movement that takes us through Hugo's 1,200-page tome with such ease and clarity...the directors succeed at keeping *Les Misérables* a passionate, pulsating, human saga" and concluded that "if you agree that the musical theatre can take on important themes and lofty source material, or are open to being so persuaded, head to the Kennedy Center Opera House. *Les Misérables* is as satisfying and spectacular a show as you may see for years to come. It dares to be ambitious, reaches out for the heart and the soul, and touches them both. Don't go without a hanky, but go" (12.29.86).

Jack Curry and Jeannie Williams discussed the different form of the musical. "Audiences who attended the Kennedy Center premiere of *Les Misérables* over the weekend no doubt are still trying to categorize what they saw. Billed as a musical, the three-hour, $4.5 million production defies conventional notions about the most popular form of stage show. There's no dialogue, there aren't any real dance numbers, there's little outright humor...In an era in which lasers and high-tech gizmos have zapped the heart out of musical theatre, the newcomer asserts the musical's capacity for lofty emotions and epic drama...Valjean's demise ends the tale satisfyingly...if you're doing a death scene with ghosts, lead up to it with a crackling good story. *Les Miz* has that as a base, goose bump thrills throughout, and music to march you happily out of the theatre...*Les Miz* stands out because it extends the bridge that Stephen Sondheim has begun to construct between theatre and opera" (*USA Today*, 12.29.86).

In the *Washington Post*, Joseph McLellan reviewed the music of the show with tremendous insight: "Despite its flaws, *Les Misérables* is nothing less than a masterpiece. But to see the redeeming qualities of this opera (yes, that's what it is), you have to search carefully and rather deeply.

And the place to look is in the music...Some who see *Les Misérables*, people who do not usually go to the opera, leave the show moved—but puzzled at what has moved them. They are not used to or prepared for the deep, subtle, subliminal work of music used with operatic skill to redeem a theatrical piece that might otherwise be laughed off the stage. They find the music haunting them days, even weeks, after the final curtain, after most of the plot and visual effects have faded from the memory. And gradually the impression grows that the essence of *Les Misérables* is the music. But it is not the music alone; it is music working synergistically with the other elements of the show—pulling them together, giving them structure, above all making connections between apparently unrelated parts of the show and arranging them into thematic clusters...The major characters all have motifs that recur occasionally in the orchestra and constantly in their vocal music...The repeated use of these motifs gives depth and complexity to the show." In drawing attention to the parallel between Valjean's decision to leave his old life behind and Javert's suicide McLellan comments: "Thus, at the beginning and end of the show, its two towering symbolic figures are brought together, paralleled and contrasted, and their characters explored in moral explanation of their decisions. The fact that both so-liloquies use the same music and that there is parallel wording at the climatic points—the resolution of each identity crisis—increases the power of the scenes even for those who are not consciously aware of what is being done...Beyond its ingenious use of musical texture for dramatic purposes, the score of *Les Misérables* also has a freshness, vitality, and variety that show the hand of an expert composer"* (1.15.87). (See *Les Misérables* photo inserts 8 and 9.)

When it reached New York, the show gained the approval of the much-feared drama critic of the all-powerful *New York Times*, Frank Rich, who was particularly enthusiastic about the Act I Finale: "If any-one doubts that the contemporary musical theatre can flex its atrophied muscles and yank an audience right out of its seats, he need look no further than the Act I finale of *Les Misérables*...The opera-minded com-poser Claude-Michel Schönberg, having earlier handed each character a gorgeous theme, now brings them all into an accelerating burst of coun-terpoint titled "One Day More." The set designer John Napier and light-ing designer David Hersey peel back layer after layer of shadow—and a layer of the floor as well—to create the illusion of a sprawling, multilay-

---

* © 1987, *The Washington Post*. Reprinted with permission.

ered Paris on the brink of upheaval. Most crucially, the directors Trevor Nunn and John Caird choreograph the paces of their players on a revolving stage so that spatial relationships mirror both human relationships and the pressing march of history. The ensuing fusion of drama, music, character, design, and movement is what links this English adaptation of a French show to the highest tradition of modern Broadway musical production...Mr. Schönberg's profligately melodious score, sumptuously orchestrated by John Cameron to straddle the eras of harpsichord and synthesizer, mixes madrigals with rock and evokes composers as diverse as Bizet (for the laborers) and Weill (for their exploiters). Motifs are recycled for ironic effect throughout, allowing the story's casualties to haunt the grief-stricken survivors long after their deaths. The resourceful lyrics can be as sentimental as Hugo in translation. Yet the libretto has been sharpened since London, and it is the edginess of the cleverest verses that prevents the Thénardiers oom-pah-pah number, "Master of the House," from sliding into *Oliver!*...By the evening's end the company need simply march forward from the stage's black depths into a hazy orange dawn to summon up Hugo's unflagging faith in tomorrow's better world."* (3. 13.87)

Clive Barnes, however, wrote a review in the *New York Post* that seems to be strangely at war with itself. He opens with: "Make no bones about it. *Les Misérables*, the Anglo-French import that opened at the Broadway Theatre last night, is simply smashing. This is magnificent, red-blooded, two-fisted theater. Start fighting to see it. You will not be disappointed. This is something like the Grand Canyon. Every expectation is fulfilled. It lives up to its hype." Yet he then goes on to complain about the monotony of the music and, in comparing it with *Nicholas Nickleby*, he states, "*Les Misérables* is superbly served, instantly disposable trash." He then concludes, "On stage the whole saga, this wonderful human pageant, falls satisfyingly into place...like a jigsaw...*Les Misérables* is the stuff of theatrical legend. Go with the proper expectations and you will have a lovely evening."

WORLDWIDE PRODUCTIONS

Les Misérables has been opened by 64 professional companies worldwide: London, Washington/Broadway, Tokyo (3 Companies and Japan Concert Tour Company), Tel Aviv (2 productions), Budapest (2 productions), US National Tour 1, US National Tour 2, US Bus & Truck, Syd-

---

* © 1987, *The New York Times* Co. Reprinted with permission.

ney, Reykjavik, Oslo, Vienna, Toronto, Gydnia, Melbourne, Stockholm, Montreal, Amsterdam, Odense, Paris, Prague (2 productions), Madrid, Copenhagen, UK Tour (2 companies), Manila, Duisburg, South East Asia, Karlstad, Aalborg, Australia National Tour, Antwerp, Aarhus, Helsinki, Buenos Aires, Gothenburg, Malmo, Bonn, Sao Paulo, Chemnitz, Estonia, Gyor, Detmold, Shanghai, Korea, Mexico, Saarbrücken, Dessau, Bolmo, Berlin, Danish Tour, Luneburg, Regensburg, Trondheim, Tecklenburg, Staatz, and Mastodonterne.

These productions have played in 38 Countries: England, United States of America, Japan, Israel, Hungary, Australia, Iceland, Norway, Austria, Canada, Poland, Sweden, Holland, Denmark, New Zealand, France, the Czech Republic, Spain, Northern Ireland, Eire, Scotland, Wales, Bermuda, Malta, the Philippines, Mauritius, Singapore, Germany, Hong Kong, Korea, South Africa, Belgium, Finland, Argentina, Brazil, Estonia, China, and Mexico.

Les Misérables has been translated into 21 different languages: English, Japanese, Hebrew, Hungarian, Icelandic, Norwegian, German, Polish, Swedish, Dutch, Danish, French, Czech, Castilian, Mauritian Creole, Flemish, Finnish, Argentinean, Portuguese, Estonian, and Mexican Spanish.

CITIES WHERE *LES MISÉRABLES* HAS PLAYED:

UK: England: London, Birmingham, Bournemouth (concert), Bradford, Bristol, Chelmsford (concert), Exeter (concert), Liverpool, Manchester, Newcastle, Plymouth, Romsey (concert), Sheffield, Southampton, Windsor. **Wales:** Cardiff (concert). **Scotland:** Edinburgh. **N. Ireland:** Belfast (concert). **Argentina:** Buenos Aires. **Australia:** Adelaide, Brisbane, Melbourne, Perth, Sydney. **Austria:** Vienna. **Belgium:** Antwerp, Brussels (Schools Ed). **Bermuda:** Hamilton. **Brazil:** Sao Paulo. **Canada:** Calgary, Edmonton, Hamilton, Montreal, Ottawa, Regina, Saskatoon, Toronto, Vancouver, Winnipeg. **China:** Shanghai. **Czech Republic:** Prague. **Denmark:** Aalborg, Aarhus, Copenhagen, Haslev, Herning, Odense, Varde, Vejle. **Ireland:** Dublin. **Estonia:** Tallinn. **Finland:** Helsinki. **France:** Paris. **Germany:** Berlin, Bonn, Chemnitz, Dessau, Detmold, Duisburg, Heidelberg, Luneburg, Regensburg, Saarbrücken. **Holland:** Amsterdam, Scheveningen. **Hong Kong. Hungary:** Budapest, Gyor, Szeged. **Iceland:** Reykjavik. **Israel:** Haifa, Jerusalem, Tel Aviv. **Japan:** Chiba (concert), Fukuoka, Hiroshima (concert), Ichihara (concert), Kawasaki (concert), Kobe (concert), Kochi (concert), Matsudo (concert), Matsuyama (concert), Nagoya,

Osaka, Sapporo, Sendai, Tachikawa (concert), Takamatsu (concert), Tokyo. **Korea:** Seoul. **Malta:**Valletta. **Mauritius:** Mahebourg. **Mexico:** Mexico City. **New Zealand:** Auckland. **Norway:** Oslo, Bolmo. **The Philippines:** Manila. **Poland:** Gydnia. **Singapore. South Africa:** Cape Town. **Spain:** Madrid. **Sweden:** Gothenburg, Karlstad, Malmo, Stockholm. **U.S.:** Washington, D.C., New York. **US Tour 1:** Baltimore, Boston, Chicago, Detroit, Los Angeles, Philadelphia, Washington, D.C. **US Tour 2:** San Francisco. **US Tour 3:** Akron, Albuquerque, Amarillo, Atlanta, Augusta, Austin, Bakersfield, Baton Rouge, Birmingham, Bloomington, Boise, Buffalo, Calgary, Champaign, Charleston, Charlotte, Chattanooga, Cincinnati, Clearwater, Cleveland, College Station, Colorado Springs, Columbia, Columbus, Corpus Christi, Costa Mesa, Cupertino, Dallas, Dayton, Denver, Des Moines, Duluth, East Lansing, El Paso, Escondido, Eugene, Evansville, Fayetteville, Flint, Fort Lauderdale, Fort Myers, Fort Wayne, Fort Worth, Fresno, Gainesville, Grand Rapids, Green Bay, Greensboro, Greenville, Hartford, Hershey, Honolulu, Houston, Huntsville, Indianapolis, Iowa City, Jackson, Jacksonville, Kalamazoo, Kansas City, Kitchener, Knoxville, Las Vegas, Lincoln, Little Rock, Long Beach, Louisville, Lubbock, Madison, Melbourne, Memphis, Miami, Milwaukee, Mobile, Muncie, Myrtle Beach, Nashville, Newark, New Haven, New Orleans, Norfolk, Oklahoma City, Omaha, Orlando, Palm Desert, Pasadena, Peoria, Phoenix, Pittsburgh, Portland, Portsmouth, Providence, Raleigh, Rapid City, Reno, Richmond, Roanoke, Rochester, Rockford, Sacramento, Saginaw, Salt Lake City, San Antonio, San Diego, San Jose, Sarasota, Savannah, Schenectady, Scranton, Seattle, Shreveport, Sioux City, South Bend, Spokane, Springfield, St. Louis, St. Paul, St. Petersburg, State College, Syracuse, Tallahassee, Tampa, Tempe, Thousand Oaks, Toledo, Tucson, Tulsa, Wallingford, West Palm Beach, West Point, Wichita, Wilmington.

AWARDS RECEIVED BY *LES MISÉRABLES*
UK
London
LONDON CRITICS' CIRCLE AWARDS 1986
Best Musical
OLIVIER AWARDS 1985
Best Actress in a Musical: Patti Lu Pone—Fantine
RADIO 2 AWARD 2005
NATION'S MOST POPULAR MUSICAL

Manchester
MANCHESTER EVENING NEWS AWARD 1992
Best Visiting Production
Liverpool
LIVERPOOL ECHO ARTS & ENTERTAINMENT AWARDS 1999
Best Touring Production (large scale)

RECORDINGS

ORIGINAL LONDON CAST RECORDING
Silver and Gold Discs 1986
Platinum Disc 1988
Double Platinum Disc 1992
Triple Platinum Disc 1997
COMPLETE SYMPHONIC RECORDING HIGHLIGHTS
Silver Disc 1993
Gold Disc 1995

UNITED STATES

Broadway
8 TONY AWARDS 1987
Best Musical
Best Book: Alain Boublil and Claude-Michel Schönberg
Best Score: Music—Claude-Michel Schönberg, Lyrics—Herbert Kretzmer and Alain Boublil
Best Director: Trevor Nunn and John Caird
Best Featured Actress in a Musical: Frances Ruffelle—Eponine
Best Featured Actor in a Musical: Michael Maguire—Enjolras
Best Set Designer: John Napier
Best Lighting Design: David Hersey
NEW YORK DRAMA CRITICS AWARD 1987
Best Musical
5 DRAMA DESK AWARDS 1987
Best Musical
Best Featured Actor: Michael Maguire—Enjolras
Best Music: Claude-Michel Schönberg
Best Orchestrations: John Cameron
Best Set Design: John Napier
NATIONAL BROADWAY THEATRE AWARD 2001
Best Score (Marius Company)

Washington
HELEN HAYES AWARDS 1987
WASHINGTON THEATRE AWARDS SOCIETY 1987
Best Non-Resident Production
Best Actor in a Non-Resident Production: Colm Wilkinson—Valjean
Best Supporting Performer in a Non Resident Production: Frances
    Ruffelle—Eponine
Los Angeles
DRAMA-LOGUE
Drama-Logue Publisher/Critics Award: Cameron Mackintosh 1988
**THE LOS ANGELES DRAMA CRITICS CIRCLE AWARDS
    1988**
Costume Design: Andreane Neofitou
Lighting Design: David Hersey
Original Music: Claude-Michel Schönberg

RECORDINGS
Original Broadway Cast Recording Gold Disc 1989
Les Misérables Symphonic Recording Gold Disc 1992
Les Misérables Symphonic Recording Highlights Gold Disc 1996
GRAMMY AWARDS
For Best Original Broadway Cast Recording 1988
Les Misérables Symphonic Recording 1991

CANADA
Toronto
DORA MAVOR MOORE AWARDS 1989
Best Lighting: David Hersey
Best Set Design: John Napier
DORA MAVOR MOORE AWARDS 1999
Outstanding Male Performance in a Musical: Colm Wilkinson
    Valjean
Montreal
ADISQ AWARD 1990
Best Musical Production

ARGENTINA
ACE (Asociacion Cronistas del Espectaculo) AWARDS 2000
Best Musical
Best Production

BRAZIL
PREMIO QUALIDADE BRAZIL AWARD 2001
Best Musical

MEXICO
HERALDO AWARDS 2003
Best Musical
Best Direction: Ken Caswell
Best Theatre Actor: Carlos Vittori—Valjean

JAPAN
ARTISTIC FESTIVAL PRIZE 1987
awarded by the Agency for Cultural Affairs in Japan

AUSTRALIA
Sydney
SYDNEY THEATRE CRITICS CIRCLE AWARDS 1987
Best Musical
Best Actor of the Year in a Musical: Philip Quast—Javert
SYDNEY MO AWARDS 1988
Female Music Theatre Performer: Debbie Byrne—Fantine
Male Music Theatre Performer: Philip Quast—Javert
Supporting Musical Theatre Performer: David Campbell—Marius
Melbourne
GREEN ROOM AWARDS 1990
Best Production: Cameron Mackintosh
Best Direction: Trevor Nunn, John Caird & Gale Edwards
Set Design: John Napier
Costume Design: Andreane Neofitou
Male Lead: Rob Guest—Valjean
Female Lead: Marina Prior—Cosette
Male Performer in a Supporting Role: Anthony Warlow—Enjolras
Female Performer in a Supporting Role: Robyn Arthur—Madame
    Thénardier

RECORDINGS
Original London Cast Album
Gold Disc in Australia 1989
Double Platinum Disc in Australia 1991

SWEDEN
Stockholm
AWARDS 1991
Best Male Leading Role: Tommy Korberg—Valjean
Best Female Leading Role: Maria Rydberg—Eponine
Best Male Supporting Role: Claes Malmberg—Thénardier
The Jury's Special Prize (for translation of the text)—Ture Rangstrom

FRANCE
Paris
THE MOLIERE AWARD 1992
Best Musical 1992
Alain Boublil and Claude Michel Schönberg
LES VICTOIRES DE LA MUSIQUE 1992
Meilleur Spectacle Musicale
Alain Boublil and Claude-Michel Schönberg

CZECH REPUBLIC
Prague
THALIA MUSICAL AWARD, 2003
Jiri Korn—Thénardier
Recording
GRAMY 1992

HUNGARY
LISZT PRIZE 1988
MUSICAL SINGER OF THE YEAR 1990
Gyula Vikidal—Valjean
MUSICAL SINGER OF THE YEAR 1991
Sandor Sasvari—Marius
GASZAIMARI PROZE 1992
Aniko Nagy—Eponine
HONOUR CROSS OF THE HUNGARIAN REPUBLIL 1994
Gyula Vikidal—Valjean

DENMARK
ENTREPENØR PRISEN 1993
Morten Grunwald—Producer
SÆLGERNES PRIS 1994
Morten Grunwald—Producer

DET BERLINSKE FONDS HÆDERSPRIS 1994
Morten Grunwald—Producer
WILHELM HANSON FONDENS ÆRESPRIS 1995
Morten Grunwald—Producer

GERMANY
Duisburg
GOLDENEN EUROPA AWARD 1996
Musical of the Year
IMAGE AWARD 1997
Best Supporting Actress: Anne Welte—Madame Thénardier

ESTONIA
Tallin
CULTURAL ENDOWMENT OF ESTONIA
MUSICAL AWARD OF THE YEAR
Jassi Zahharov—Jean Valjean

ISRAEL
Tel Aviv
ISRAELI THEATRE AWARDS 1999
1st Prize for Musicals

DISCOGRAPHY
LES MISÉRABLES—Original French concept album
Album, Cassette and CD
©1980 Editions Musicales Alain Boublil
Disques TREMA
2 x RC 230 310086/76
CD 710217
Awarded Gold Disc
1980
Single
LA FAUTE A VOLTAIRE Fabrice Bernard and ROUGE ET
    NOIR the Company
© 1980 Editions Musicales Alain Boublil
Disques TREMA
RC 110 2410151 and 2548013
1980

Single
L'AIR DE LA MISERE Rose Laurens
©1980 Editions Musicales Alain Boublil
Disques WEA Filipacchi
WE 101 11603
1980
LES MISÉRABLES—Highlights
Compilation from the French Concept Album
©1980 Editions Musicales Alain Boublil
First Night Records
Scene 2 Scene C2 Scene CD2
1985
Maxi Single
I DREAMED A DREAM Rose Laurens
©1980 Editions Musicales Alain Boublil
I DREAMED A DREAM Patti Lupone
WHO AM I? Colm Wilkinson
ACT 1 FINALE, the Company
1st Night Records ©1985 Exallshow
Score L1
1985
LES MISÉRABLES—London cast recording
Double Album—Cassette and CD
1st Night Records ©1985 Exallshow Ltd
Encore 1 Encore C1 Encore CD1
1985
In UK awarded Silver Disc May 1986, Gold Disc September 1986
Platinum Disc May 1988, Double Platinum Disc 1992
Triple Platinum Disc 1997
In Australia awarded Double Platinum Disc, 1991
Single
I DREAMED A DREAM and ONE DAY MORE
Patti LuPone and the Full London Company
1st Night Records
P. 1985 Exallshow Ltd.
Score 1
1985
Single
ON MY OWN Frances Ruffelle and
DO YOU HEAR THE PEOPLE SING? the Company

©1985 Exallshow Ltd
1st Night Records
Score C2
1985
Cassette
ON MY OWN Frances Ruffelle,
I DREAMED A DREAM Patti LuPone,
DO YOU HEAR THE PEOPLE SING? Ensemble and
PROLOGUE Colm Wilkinson, Roger Allam and Ensemble
©1985 Exallshow Ltd
1st Night Records
Score C2
1985
Single
BRING HIM HOME Colm Wilkinson
©1985 Exallshow Ltd
1st Night Records
Score 7
1985
LES MISÉRABLES—**Broadway cast recording**
Double Album, Cassette and CD
Geffen Records ©1987
GHS 24151 (record), M5G 24151 (cassette)   1987
GHS 24151-2 (cd)

Grammy Award, New York, Best Cast recording, 1988
Gold Disc, USA, March 1989
LES MISÉRABLES—**Japanese cast recording**
ON MY OWN and THE PEOPLES SONG
Single and cassette
Pony Canyon 7AO704, 10P3093
1987
LES MISÉRABLES—**Israeli cast recording**
Hed Arzi Ltd. ACUM Can 15292
1987
LES MISÉRABLES—**Hungarian cast recording**
©Radioton 1988 SLPM 14111-B
1988
LES MISÉRABLES—**Original French concept album**
Album Cassette and CD

Re-released in United States and Canada only
©1980 Editions Musicales Alain Boublil
Relativity 88561-8247-2
1988
LES MISÉRABLES—**Viennese cast recording**
©Polydor GmbH 1988, 2LP 83770-1, 2CD 837770-2,
2MC 837770-4
1988
Single
I DREAMED A DREAM and BRING HIM HOME
Sona Macdonald and Reinhard Brussmann
©Polydor GmbH 1988 887 953-7   1988
LES MISÉRABLES
The Complete Symphonic Recording
1st Night Records, ©1988 Exallshow Ltd
MIZ 1, MIZ C1, MIZ CD1
1988
Grammy Award, New York, 1991
Gold Disc, USA, 1992
Silver Disc, UK, 2002
LES MISÉRABLES—**Stockholm cast recording**
CBS Records LP 467870-1, CD 467870-2, MC 467870—3
1990
Single
I DREAMED A DREAM and ON MY OWN
Karin Glenmark (Fantine), Maria Rydberg (Eponine)
COLUMBIA COL 656641 7
1990
LES MISÉRABLES—**Amsterdam cast recording**
PHONOGRAMB.V. 1991 Mercury CD 848 598-2
©Mercury 848-599-4
1991
LES MISÉRABLES—**French Cast recording**
TREMA 1991
DCD 710 369/370 PM 541
DC 110 369/370 PM 427
DA 310 369/370 PM 524
1991
LES MISÉRABLES—**Highlights from the Complete Symphonic**
   International Cast Recording

©1988 Exallshow Ltd
Cast C20 Cast CD20
1992
Gold Disc, UK, 1995
Gold Disc, USA, 1996
LES MISÉRABLES—**Czech cast recording**
Bonton Records
71 0096-2 311 (CD)
71 0096-4 311 (cassette)
71 0096-1 312 (disc)   1992
LES MISÉRABLES—**Danish Cast Recording**
BMG ARIOLA A/S 1992
09026615332 (CD)
09026615334 (cassette)
1992
LES MISÉRABLES—**Manchester Company**
Highlights
1st Night Records, ©1992 Exallshow Ltd
Score CD34
Score C34 (cassette)
1992
LOS MISERABLES—**Madrid Cast Recording**
BMG ARIOLA SA/RCA VICTOR
74321 17570 2 (CD)
74321 17570 4 (Cassette)
1993
LES MISÉRABLES—**Japanese Live Cast Recording**
TOSHIBA/EMI
TOCT-8375.76 (Takeshi Kaja as Valjean)
TOCT-8377.78 (Sakae Takita as Valjean)
1994
LES MISÉRABLES—**UK 10th Anniversary Concert Recording**
ENCORE CD 8
ENCORE C8 (Cassette)
1996
Gold Disc, UK, 1998
LES MISÉRABLES—**Duisburg Cast Recording**
Highlights
POLYDOR GMBH and STELLA GMBH
1 CD 531 238-2

1996
LES MISÉRABLES—Musikteatern I Varmland, Karlstad
RFM Records
RFM D6081
1996
LES MISÉRABLES—Antwerp Cast Recording
Highlights
Arcade Music Company
CD 2102417
1998
Awarded gold disc on the first day it was launched
LES MISÉRABLES—Berlin Promotional Recording
Highlights—4 tracks only
Universal Marketing Group for Stage Holding
1 CD 980 032-1
2003
LES MISÉRABLES—Japanese Cast Complete Recordings
2 CDs   TOHO.E-03081S (Kazuataka Ishii as Valjean)
2 CDs TOHO.E-03081M (Kiyotaka Imai as Valjean)
2 CDs   TOHO.E-0308B (Tetsuya Bessho as Valjean)
2 CDs   TOHO.E-0308Y (Yuichiro Yamaguchi as Valjean) 2003
LES MISÉRABLES—Prague Cast Complete Live Recording
Cernoch/Jezek/Ulicnik, Bartunek/Hulka/Stagr
3 CDs Goja 401 324 023-2
2004

LES MISÉRABLES VIDEO/DVD
STAGE BY STAGE—The Making of *Les Misérables*
1988 Polygram CFV 04272
VHS 1hour
LES MISÉRABLES—THE DREAM CAST
Les Misérables in Concert for the 10th Anniversary at the Royal Albert
   Hall
1995 VCI-VC6528
VHS 160 minutes
LES MISÉRABLES—THE DREAM CAST
The 10th Anniversary Concert
2000 VCI—VCD0047
DVD 150 minutes

LES MISÉRABLES—DOUBLE DISC COLLECTOR'S EDITION

The 10th Anniversary Concert + Stage by Stage + Commemorative Booklet
2004 VCI
DVD Disc 1—150 minutes   Disc 2—57 minutes

SYNOPSIS
ACT ONE
Prologue: 1815 Digne

Javert releases Jean Valjean from prison after 19 years. However, he is on parole with a yellow ticket of leave, which he always has to show and which makes him an outcast. Only the Bishop of Digne treats him kindly, but Valjean, embittered by years of hardship, betrays his trust and steals his silver. When the police catch Valjean and bring him back, the Bishop lies to save him but makes him promise to become an honest man.

1823 Montreuil-sur-Mer

Valjean has broken his parole and now, eight years later, he has become a mayor and a factory owner. Fantine, who works at his factory, has an illegitimate child, Cosette. When this is discovered she is dismissed. She believes that her daughter, who is lodged with the Thénardiers, is dying, and she is desperate to get money for her medicine. She first sells her locket, then her hair, and finally joins the whores in selling herself. Fantine, who is sick herself and utterly degraded, fights with an unpleasant prospective customer. She is arrested by Javert, but Valjean intervenes and demands that she be taken to the hospital instead. When Valjean rescues a man pinned under a runaway cart, Javert is reminded of the strength of convict 24601, who broke his parole and for whom he has been searching for years. But he claims that this man has just been recaptured. Valjean faces a moral dilemma, realizing that this would finally set him free from the repercussions of his broken parole, but he cannot bear to see an innocent man go to prison in his place. Valjean confesses that he is prisoner 24601. He then flees to the hospital and promises the dying Fantine to find and care for her daughter Cosette. Javert arrives to arrest him, but Valjean's superior strength ensures his escape.

1823 Montfermeil

Valjean finds Cosette at the Thénardiers, who have treated her cruelly while spoiling their own daughter, Eponine. They drive a hard bargain with Valjean, who pays them substantially so that he can take her away.

1832 Paris

Nine years later, Valjean and the grown-up Cosette are helping the poor when they are set upon by Thénardier and his gang. The attack is interrupted by Javert, who does not recognize Valjean until Thénardier enlightens him, by which time Valjean has escaped. During the scuffle of the attack, the student Marius and Cosette have literally bumped into each other and fallen in love at first sight. There is much unrest in the city, and the politically-minded students of the ABC café plan an insurrection. After the death of General Lamarque, the only man left in the government who shows any feeling for the poor, the students see this as a sign to raise support for an uprising. Thénardier's daughter Eponine proves how much she loves Marius by unselfishly helping him to find Cosette. Marius and Cosette declare their love, and Eponine, waiting outside the gate, prevents an attempt by her father's gang to rob Valjean's house. Valjean, convinced that it was Javert spying outside his house, decides they must leave the country.

ACT TWO

The students prepare to build a barricade, and Marius asks Eponine to take a letter to Cosette. This is intercepted by Valjean, who learns of his daughter's true feelings. The barricade is built, and the students defy an army that warns them to give up or die. The little street urchin Gavroche sees through Javert's disguise and exposes him as a spy. Eponine returns to the barricade to be with Marius, but is shot and dies in his arms. Valjean joins the students at the barricade in order to find Marius, and although he has the opportunity to kill Javert, he lets him go. The students rest, and Valjean prays that Marius will be saved. Gavroche is shot while trying to gather ammunition behind the barricade, and then everyone else except Valjean and Marius are killed in the fighting.

Valjean escapes into the sewers with the unconscious Marius, avoiding Javert, who is still in pursuit. Thénardier is robbing corpses in the sewer, including Marius, who he thinks is dead. As Valjean and Marius emerge from the sewer, Javert is waiting for them. But after Valjean pleads for time to take Marius to the hospital, Javert lets him go. Shattered by the overturning of his black-and-white beliefs, Javert takes his own life. Marius finds it hard to accept that he is still alive when all his friends have died. Unaware of the identity of his rescuer, he recovers in Cosette's care. Valjean confesses the truth of his past to Marius and insists that he must go away, believing that his past might threaten Cosette's security.

At Marius and Cosette's wedding, the Thénardiers try to blackmail Marius. Thénardier claims that Cosette's father is a murderer and as proof he produces the ring which he stole from the "corpse" on the night the barricade fell. Marius recognises the ring as his own and suddenly realizes that it was Valjean who rescued him from the barricade that night. Valjean, sadly alone and dying, is joyfully reunited with Cosette before he dies. Cosette then reads the letter he has given her and learns the truth about her past as the spirit of Valjean joins the spirits of Fantine, Eponine, and all the students who have died.

THEMES

The universal themes dealt with in *Les Misérables* are Justice and Mercy, Human Goodness, Impossible Love, and Personal Identity. Javert's concept of justice is governed by the letter of the law. He is implacable and merciless, seeing justice only in terms of black and white. His soliloquy, "Stars," illustrates his sense of an ordered universe—of constancy, pre-ordained place, and his unwavering belief in Old Testament judgement: "Mine is the way of the Lord/Those who follow the path of the righteous/Shall have their reward/And if they fall/As Lucifer fell/The flame/The sword!" The stars of the night sky are in fact a metaphor for the policemen, the "sentinels" who are the guardians of the law: "You are the sentinels/Silent and sure/Keeping watch in the night." In contrast, the Bishop of Digne is guided by Christian mercy and a belief in the power of good. His generosity frees Valjean from the hatred that has governed his life and turns him from a sense of "an eye for an eye" justice towards Christian love. The theme of Mercy is linked to that of Human Goodness and self-sacrifice, and it was so important to Hugo that he wrote of *Les Misérables*: "In a tale wherein goodness is the pearl of rarest price, the man who was kind comes almost before the man who was great." In the show, there are many examples of how human kindness can have a "ripple" effect: The Bishop of Digne's original act of kindness changes Valjean so that he helps Fantine, he brings up Cosette as his own daughter, he saves Fauchelevent's life when he is trapped under the cart, he risks imprisonment by admitting his identity to save a wrongly accused man, he risks his life at the barricade to save Marius, he saves Javert—who in turn allows Valjean to save Marius, and he finally gives up his life with Cosette and Marius so they are not endangered by his presence. Fantine gives her life trying to save Cosette, and the students give their lives trying to win a better life for the poor. Eponine suffers bitterly from her unrequited love of Marius, but she puts his happiness before her own so that he can be with Cosette. Ultimately, she sacrifices her life to be with him on the barricade. It is through Eponine that the theme of Impossible Love is chiefly developed, but also through Fantine who had been deserted by her lover.

The theme of Personal Identity is developed mainly through Jean Valjean. His identity is killed off twice, first when he is sent to prison ("They gave me a number and murdered Valjean"), and second when he tears up his ticket of leave ("Jean Valjean is nothing now/Another story must begin"). Taking on a new identity as the mayor of Montreuil-sur-Mer, he is only prepared to disclose who he really is in order to save an innocent man ("Who am I?'/I'm Jean Valjean") and, at the end, to Marius in order to save potential problems for Cosette if he were to be discovered. The students also have an identity crisis as Enjolras tells them, "It is time for us all/To decide who we are." Disguise is another way of exploring the theme. Javert is disguised as a rebel, Eponine as a boy, and the Thénardiers as the Baron and Baroness de Thénard. Personal identity, then, is shown to be confirmed in a variety of ways: by name, by moral character, by appearance, and by the perceptions of oneself and others.

FACTS AND TRIVIA

Victor Hugo's novel, published in 1892, was originally titled *Misères* and then *La Misère*. The Bishop of Digne, Monseigneur Myriel, was based on a real-life Bishop of Digne, Monseigneur Miollis, and the hero, first called Jean Tréjean, was inspired by a meeting with a desperate man who had been arrested for stealing a loaf of bread. The episode of Fantine's arrest was also based on a true experience, which Hugo personally witnessed, and he was able to intervene in the same way Valjean does. The novel was very popular, but it was considered a threat to social order and was on the Vatican's banned list for several years. However, it has been translated into almost every language and, after the Bible, is one of the world's bestselling books.

The now famous lithograph of little Cosette was designed by Emile Bayard, Hugo's favorite illustrator. This full motif of little Cosette with a broom was used on the cover of the original French concept album. For the London production, it was brilliantly reworked by the Dewynters

advertising agency with the French
flag added as a background. Many
adapted versions have been appropriately created as *Les Misérables*
travelled around the world or celebrated the various milestones in
its production history.

Les Misérables has been seen
by 10,953,665 people in London. It has grossed £206,689,372
($393,887,609) at the London Box
office and over $2.7 billion world-
wide.

The famous revolve has made
216,275 complete turns in London alone, equating to over 4,168 miles or
the distance from London to Chicago. If you add the complete revolves
worldwide, it is a staggering 39,851.33 miles! (The circumference of the
earth is only 24,859.82 miles.)

The London Jean Valjeans have stolen over 8,000 loaves of bread, and
the London cast have fired more than 60,000 gunshots. The drummer
for *Les Misérables* in London was at the very first orchestra rehearsal at
the Barbican in 1985 and is still playing in the show to this day!

There are approximately 101 members of the cast and crew directly
involved in every performance of *Les Misérables*. This does not include
front-of-house staff and the huge backup services including ticket sales,
advertising and publicity, wardrobe staff, set contractors, maintenance,
and office personnel.

Although there was an initial costume budget of only £40,000
($76,000), each performance entails some 392 complete costumes con-
sisting of 1,782 items of clothing and 31 wigs. All the cast, with the exception of Valjean and Javert, play more than one role, and due to the many
costumes involved backstage, at times, seems more like a quick-change
fashion show. It takes 4 people to change Cosette from her black dress
to her wedding dress in less than a minute.

During the 21-year run of the London production, the wardrobe department has washed 81,900 loads of laundry, used 4,914 kgs of detergent, 13,104 cans of spray starch, and ironed 327,600 shirts. The wigs
department has used 2,184 cans of hairspray and 1,092 bottles of wig
glue.

The enormous success of Les Misérables has enabled its debt to the

Royal Shakespeare Company (RSC) to be amply repaid. The RSC receives a royalty, and a proportion of the worldwide profit goes back, in perpetuity, to the RSC. Over the years this has provided a vital financial resource for the company. By 1995 this had totaled over £10 million ($19 million), and is now considerably more.

Over 500 children have played the roles of Gavroche, Young Cosette, and Young Eponine in London. The Sylvia Young Theatre School, which is the most successful London theatre school for children, has provided most of the young Gavroches and Eponines, as well as the Tams for *Miss Saigon*, throughout the history of the productions. For the touring productions in the United States, the children have their own personal tutor to enable them to keep up with their schoolwork.

The biggest single live audience for *Les Misérables* to date was 125,000 at the 1989 Australia Day Concert in Sydney. This free live concert was staged as part of Australia's bicentennial celebrations and featured an international singing cast, symphonic orchestral accompaniment, back projections of stills, and close-up, monitored camerawork. A huge video screen relayed everything to those too far away to see anything on stage, and many of the audience slept in Domain Park the night before to be sure of getting seats. The biggest broadcast audience was when 250 *Les Misérables* cast members sang at the 1996 European football championships, televised to 400 million viewers in 197 countries.

Les Misérables celebrated the 10th Anniversary of its World Premiere on October 8, 1995 with a Gala Concert at the 5,000-seat Royal Albert Hall in London. The Concert, which sold out in just a few hours of the box-office opening, starred the original Jean Valjean, Colm Wilkinson, who led a company of 250 artists and 100 musicians. The specially-arranged finale featured 17 different Jean Valjeans, accompanied by 17 Gavroches, from around the world, singing in many of the languages in which the show has been performed.

The 10th Anniversary concert was filmed for television and has since been seen by over 4 million viewers in the UK. The video has gone on to sell over 1.7 million copies worldwide. A special double-disc Collectors Edition DVD was released in the UK in November 2005.

In 2002, *Les Misérables* was the first Western musical to play in China. It ran for several sold-out weeks, setting new records in China, where a theatrical production would ordinarily only play for 3 or 4 performances. Cameron Mackintosh now has an exclusive arrangement to co-produce with the Shanghai Grand Theatre Chinese-language productions of some of the world's greatest musicals. The first production chosen by the Shanghai theatre will be a Chinese-language version of *Les Misérables*, which is scheduled to open in 2008, making it the first-ever major production of a Western musical in Chinese. The selection and training of the first group of professional musical performers in China has already started, with the ultimate goal of one day creating a Chinese musical.

On November 18, 2004, a special concert performance was given at Windsor Castle in the presence of the Queen, other members of the Royal family, Jacques Chirac, Madame Chirac, Tony Blair, and Jack Straw. The concert was given in honor of the President of the French Republic to celebrate the Centenary of the Entente Cordiale. For this one special occasion the part of Gavroche was played by Adrien Boublil, Alain's son, and sung in French, while the rest of the extracts for the evening were sung in English.

In the summer of 2005, on Elaine Paige's BBC2 Radio program, *Elaine Paige on Sunday*, which regularly attracts over two million listeners, *Les Misérables* was voted "The Nation's Most Popular Musical." Elaine takes up the story:

EP: The listeners were given a short-list of fifty musicals from which to choose. Nearly half a million votes were cast, with *Les Misérables* scooping nearly half—a massive 41 percent of the vote. The remainder of the top ten were: 2. *The Phantom of the Opera*, 3. *Seven Brides For Seven Brothers*, 4. *The King and I*, 5. *Sunset Boulevard*, 6. *Evita*, 7. *Chess*, 8. *The Rocky Horror Show*, 9. *Follies*, 10. *Hair*. The diversity of the top ten reflects the broad spectrum of listeners, whose interests ranged from Sondheim to Rodgers and Hammerstein, and from Lloyd Webber to ABBA's Benny and Bjorn. The public clearly loves *Les Misérables*, which has helped it become such an established part of London's West End. Victor Hugo's book is a classic and it remains a very powerful read. *Les Misérables* has it all, and I think the reasons the musical has retained its popularity are the wonderful haunting melodies, the highly emotional story line, some great comedic moments and its groundbreaking staging—simple but extremely effective. After a while I think there was a real momentum behind the show—it's an event—people go back to enjoy the complete experience again and again and of course many of the songs have become classics.

In 2005, Guinness World Records confirmed that *Les Misérables* has had more concurrent productions (15 at one time) than any other musical in history.

On October 8, 2005 the 20th Anniversary of *Les Misérables* was celebrated at the Queen's Theatre with champagne for the audience and talented excerpts from the various Schools Edition productions in the UK. For the 21st Anniversary in 2006 an appreciative audience was given a special surprise. At the end of the show after the current cast had taken their bows in front of the barricade, the revolve turned to reveal the original cast with Colm Wilkinson singing "Bring Him Home." Then, as the barricade parted, Patti Lu Pone's "I Dreamed a Dream" was followed by Elaine Paige singing "Memory," after which she took off her *Cats* coat and laid it in little Cosette's arms, symbolically passing the mantle of the longest-running musical from *Cats* to *Les Misérables*. In addition, a specially-edited 90-minute version of the show was recorded with the BBC Concert Orchestra and the current London cast, and was broadcast on BBC Radio 2 on October 8.

LES MISÉRABLES SCHOOLS EDITION

Les Misérables has been specially adapted to meet the needs of young performers. This Schools Edition has been carefully abridged by the authors to a running time of just over two hours. The cast must be full-

Photo by Margaret Vermette

The current and original casts in the finale from the 21st anniversary performance of *Les Misérables* in London.

time school students and under nineteen years of age. Schools working on the project have access to an introductory CD and a Rehearsal Set which includes vocal books, musical score, director's script, study guide, and production slides. The Schools Edition was launched in the U.S. on May 10, 2001 at Holy Trinity High School in Hicksville, New York, and in the UK on October 14, 2002 at Stanwell School, Cardiff. Since then, there have been over 1,000 schools productions in America and over 400 schools productions in the UK with over 76,000 students making the show their own. It is the most successful schools edition ever. Alain, Claude-Michel, and Cameron have seen some of the productions and have been delighted with them.

SONGS

The universal popularity of *Les Misérables* has led to some of its songs being used for official events and some special occasions:

Excerpts from *Les Misérables*, including "Do You Hear The People Sing?," "The Prayer," and "One Day More," were performed at the closing ceremony of the Euro 96 Football Championships at Wembley Stadium. Fourteen Jean Valjeans and fourteen Gavroches took part, together with 176 members of the choir.

"One Day More" was used for Bill Clinton's 1992 US Presidential Campaign, and 7 US Presidents have seen *Les Misérables*: Nixon, Ford, Carter, Reagan, Bush, Clinton, and Bush.

"Do You Hear The People Sing?" was played at the Olympic Games Opening Ceremony in Sydney on September 15, 2000 in front of a live audience of 100,000 and a TV audience of four billion people in 197 countries. The Australian band, attempting to select an appropriate number for each country, played "Do You Hear The People Sing?" as the French team entered the stadium. It's a fact that makes Claude-Michel smile, because everybody in the world except the French team knows where it comes from, as the French people have never really taken to musical theatre.

"Bring Him Home" was played at the funeral of the famous footballer George Best, on December 3, 2005 at Stormont, Northern Ireland. This song together with "Empty Chairs At Empty Tables" is often used at funerals, especially in the U.S.

GUEST APPEARANCES

There have been some intriguing guest performances in the London production of *Les Misérables*:

In February 2004, Jerry Hall appeared in *Les Misérables* as part of her "six shows in one night marathon," which gained her a place in the Guinness World Records. She took part briefly in the "Lovely Ladies" chorus, and although she loved her colorful whore costume, they didn't have any boots to fit her and so she did the scene in knee-length black suede boots! It was all in aid of promoting London Theatre, and her whistle-stop tour, travelling on the back of a motorbike, took her first to *Phantom of the Opera* at 7:40, then *Les Misérables* at 8:04, followed by *Fame* at 8:35, *Blood Brothers* at 8:55, *Anything Goes* at 9:25, and finally at 10:09 to *Chitty Chitty Bang Bang*, where her two youngest children were in the audience.

In May 2004, it was the turn of Dame Judi Dench to appear in the barricade scene as the one-time character of Madame La Farge. She was appearing as the Countess of Rossillion in the RSC's *All's Well That Ends Well* at the Gielgud theatre next door to the Queens, and as the barricade scene coincided with her being offstage in her own play, she and Cameron Mackintosh, who owns both theatres, decided that it would be great fun for her to appear in *Les Misérables*. Of the experience she says: "It was absolutely wonderful to be in *Les Mis*. Now I can look Trevor Nunn in the eye and say, 'I've done it.'"

MISS SAIGON

LONDON PRODUCTION

Miss Saigon premiered in London at the Theatre Royal, Drury Lane on September 20, 1989 after 14 previews. This theatre is London's oldest and most historically important, and it is arguably the most famous theatre in the world. Its name is synonymous with popular, spectacular shows, and with its huge stage and seating capacity of over 2,200 it was the perfect theatre for *Miss Saigon*. It was a very special moment for producer Cameron Mackintosh, as this was the theatre where he began his career as a teenager, working as a stage hand and sweeping the stage between performances. The excitement generated by a new show from the creators of *Les Misérables* ensured that it was fully booked for months and opened with a five million pound advance. On December 19, 1994, *Miss Saigon* overtook *My Fair Lady* to become the longest-running production at this theatre, an event marked by a special celebration with champagne for the audience and the *Miss Saigon* cast performing fully-costumed extracts from *My Fair Lady* after the main show. The tenth anniversary on September 20, 1999 was marked by yet another lavish celebration before the show finally closed in London on October 30 the same year after a total of 4,263 performances.

CREATIVE TEAM
The creative credits are:
A Musical by Alain Boublil & Claude-Michel Schönberg
Music Claude-Michel Schönberg
Lyrics Richard Maltby, Jr. & Alain Boublil
Adapted from original French lyrics by Alain Boublil
Additional material Richard Maltby, Jr.
Director Nicholas Hytner
Musical Supervision David Caddick and Martin Koch
Orchestrations William D. Brohn
Musical Staging Bob Avian
Designer John Napier
Costumes Andreane Neofitou
Lighting David Hersey
Sound Andrew Bruce

ORIGINAL LONDON CAST
Kim Lea Salonga
The Engineer Jonathan Pryce
Chris Simon Bowman
John Peter Polycarpou
Ellen Claire Moore
Thuy Keith Burns

SUBSEQUENT LONDON CASTS
Kim Monique Wilson, Meera Popkin, Jenine Desiderio, Jamie
  Rivera, Joanna Ampil, Roanne Monte, Riva Salazar, Maya Barredo,
  Ma'Anne Dioniso, Cezarah Campos
The Engineer Hilton McRae, Junix Inocian, Leo Valdez, Derek
  Griffiths, Robert Sena, Raul Aranas
Chris Jerome Pradon, John Barrowman, Graham Bickley, Mike
  Scott, Glyn Kerslake, Peter Joback, Scott Anson, David Shannon
John Antoni Garfield Henry, Clinton Derricks Carroll, Milton
  Craig Nealy, Colin Charles, Richard Lloyd King
Ellen Ruthie Henshall, Nikki Ankara, Jacqui Scott, Sarah Jane
  Hassell, Jacinta Whyte, Gunilla Backman, Grania Renihan
Thuy Miguel M. Diaz, Robert Sena, Jo Jo De La Cerna

MUSICAL NUMBERS

The musical numbers on opening night were:

ACT I

Saigon—April 1975

The Heat Is On In Saigon   The Engineer, Girls, Marines and Company

The Movie In My Mind   Gigi, Kim and Girls

The Transaction   John, The Engineer, Chris and Company

Why God Why?   Chris

Sun and Moon   Kim and Chris

The Telephone   John, Chris and The Engineer

The Ceremony   Kim, Chris and Girls

The Last Night Of The World   Kim and Chris

Ho Chi Minh City—April 1978

The Morning Of The Dragon   Company, Thuy, and The Engineer

I Still Believe   Kim and Ellen

Back In Town   Kim, The Engineer and Thuy

You Will Not Touch Him   Kim and Thuy

If You Want To Die In Bed   The Engineer

I'd Give My Life For You   Kim and Company

ACT II

Atlanta—September 1978

Bui-Doi   John and Company

Bangkok—October 1978

What A Waste   The Engineer and Company

Please   John and Kim

The Truth Inside Your Head (The Fall of Saigon April 1975)   Thuy, Kim, Chris, John and Company

Sun and Moon (Reprise)   Kim

Room 317   Ellen and Kim

Now That I've Seen Her   Ellen

The Confrontation   Ellen, Chris and John

The American Dream   The Engineer and Company

The Sacred Bird   Kim and Tam

LONDON REVIEWS

When *Miss Saigon* opened, the reviews were generally very good, aside from a few poor ones from critics who seemed puzzled that a musical could tackle such a serious, dramatic subject and wrote comments such as: "An all-singing, all-dancing, laugh-a-minute musical this is not"

(Lester Middlehurst, *Today*, 9.21.89); "Quite why such a melodramatic, weepy storyline is so popular is a mystery to me. Whatever happened to musicals with jokes?" (Jane Edwardes, *Time Out*, 9.27.89); "It gives the impression of being cynically concocted—with lavish, high-tech décor as the most important ingredient—merely to fill theatre seats" (Charles Osborne, *Daily Telegraph*, 9. 21.89); "Fergie will absolutely love this expensive new musical because the biggest star of the show is a helicopter...Kim shoots herself in a very anti-climactic last scene because the authors obviously can't think what else to do with her after Chris has returned with his American wife" (Maureen Paton, *Daily Express*, 9.21.89).

The majority of reviews, however, were excellent, and many of the critics who disliked *Les Misérables* were full of praise for *Miss Saigon*. The late Jack Tinker's view was that "it has the power to move one to tears at the mess Mankind can inflict upon itself and also to fill the heart fit to burst with the simple nobility of its heroine's capacity to rise above it. I can think of few modern musicals which can make this claim, and I speak as one of the few that found *Les Miz* most mizzable." He concludes that it is "An evening of shattering dimensions" (*Daily Mail*, 9.21.89). Michael Billington, who is often highly critical of musicals, wrote that *Miss Saigon* "is a first-rate piece of popular theatre: moving, spectacular, even witty. It comes from the same creative team that gave us *Les Misérables*, but it is in every way superior...The show's point could hardly be clearer: that the Americans never remotely understood the people they were supposedly protecting, while the South Vietnamese had an image of America based on celluloid fantasy...What makes this superior entertainment, however, is that it constantly reminds us that the personal drama we are witnessing is only part of a larger tragedy... *Miss Saigon* may not be high art, but it proves that a popular musical can address a serious theme with sincerity, emotion, and integrity" (*International Herald Tribune*, 9.27.89).

Lydia Conway wrote in a very perceptive review that "The creators of *Les Misérables* have come up with an operatic masterpiece...Alain Boublil and Claude-Michel Schönberg have proved that the musical, over and above the stylization of opera, can reach beyond a simple romantic love story to a political realism that packs a powerful and relevant punch...Like the city, the lovers are doomed, and within their relationship all the misunderstandings between East and West are embodied. Achieving a balance between the epic and the intimate, every aspect of the fall, from the sleazy clubs and hotels to the sheer desperation of a people trying to escape to a better life in America, is represented in a seamless flow of songs and scenes proving that you can create realism within the musical genre without recourse to dialogue...Using documentary footage and almost filmic realism, *Miss Saigon* is a superlative example of where the new, socially conscious musical should and can go while retaining its unique ability to entertain. I cannot begin to recommend *Miss Saigon* enough" (*What's On*, 9.27.89).

Mark Steyn's review posed some discerning questions on the relative merits of the sung-through musical: "The most interesting question in musical theatre today is whether 'singing everything' automatically means abandoning reality. The written-through musical gets by on subjects like *Phantom* because we're prepared to accept lush declarative tunes, flowery lyrics, and general swanning about from larger-than-life figures sufficiently remote from our own lives. But...can the form grapple with contemporary characters who speak normally and wear modern dress?...*Miss Saigon* takes the grand passions of opera and sets them to the less florid and self-conscious musical idioms of the everyday world. That it works so well is due to self-effacement and restraint on Schönberg's part. His melodies may not be, in the purest sense, as good as Puccini's, but what seems to me indisputable is that they are better attuned to the needs of situation and character...*Miss Saigon* gives us an absorbing and moving love story and packs a considerable political punch. For those of us worn down by the simple-minded pop pageantry of British musicals, it marks a significant advance for the form, and a stunning achievement for Cameron Mackintosh...By fusing the sweep of opera with the naturalism of the musical play, *Miss Saigon* is the best of the new school of the British musicals" (*Independent*, 9.22.89).

BROADWAY PRODUCTION

Miss Saigon opened at the Broadway Theatre in New York on April 11, 1991 with a record $37 million advance. But this was only after a major dispute with the Actors' Equity Association. They had refused permission for Jonathan Pryce to play the role of The Engineer, which he had created in London, as they could not "appear to condone the casting of a Caucasian actor in the role of a Eurasian," which they considered to be "an affront to the Asian community." Although, at the time, *Miss Saigon* already had an enormous advance of $25 million, on August 8, 1990, Cameron Mackintosh cancelled the production, announcing in a *New York Times* ad that the creative team of *Miss Saigon* found the AEA decision to be "a disturbing violation of the principles of artistic integrity and freedom," continuing, "we passionately disapprove of stereotype casting, which is why we continue to champion freedom of artistic choice." Members of the public were invited to return their tickets for a refund. The furor that ensued, and the huge support from the media and Equity members alike, led to the decision being reversed a week later. Eventually a formal agreement was drawn up on October 10, 1990, with an assurance from Equity that it would not allow any of its members to continue the campaign. The auditioning process began straight away, an ad in the *New York Times* announced "The heat is back on!" and advance sales of tickets resumed. Of the 50 roles up for audition 34 were intended for minorities, 25 of which were for Asians.

So New York's illustrious Broadway Theatre, which had previously been the home of *Les Misérables*, now became the new American home of *Miss Saigon*. However, due to the smaller stage size, some aspects of the set had to be substantially amended. It was decided to dispense with the trucks that had been necessary to create intimate spaces on the vast Drury Lane stage. The Ho Chi Minh statue had to be scaled down, and a smaller version of the American Dream Cadillac had to be specially built in place of the real Cadillac in the London show, which had been bought for $6,000. As in London, *Miss Saigon* opened with great critical interest on Broadway, and this time with rather more mixed reviews. Jonathan Pryce went on to win a Tony Award for Best Actor as did Lea Salonga for Best Actress in her role of Kim. The production had become the sixth-longest-running show on Broadway when it finally closed after almost ten years on January 28, 2001. It had grossed more than $266 million and had been seen by 6 million people.

ORIGINAL BROADWAY CAST

Kim   Lea Salonga
The Engineer   Jonathan Pryce
Chris   Willy Falk
John   Hinton Battle
Thuy   Barry K. Bernal
Ellen   Liz Callaway

SUBSEQUENT BROADWAY CASTS

Kim   Leila Florentino, Rona Figueroa, Joan Almedilla, Melinda Chua, Deedee Lynn Magno
The Engineer   Francis Ruivivar, Herman Sebek, Alan Muraoka, Luoyong Wang

Chris   Sean McDermott, Christopher Peccaro, Jarrod Emick, Pat McRoberts, Tyley Ross, Michael Flanigan, Eric Kunze, Matt Bogart, Will Chase

John   Alton F. White, Norm Lewis, Timothy Robert Blavins, Keith Byron Kirk, Leonard Joseph, Billy Porter, Charles E Wallace, C.C. Brown

Ellen   Jane Bodle, Candese Marchese, Margaret Ann Gates, Tami Tappon, Misty Cotton, Anastasia Barzee

Thuy   Jason Ma, Yancy Arias, Welly Yang, Juan P. Pineda, Michael K. Lee, Edmund Nalzaro

BROADWAY REVIEWS

Miss Saigon opened on Broadway in the wake of the casting controversy, a huge amount of hype, and the knowledge that, with the $37 million advance—the largest advance that Broadway had ever seen, the show was virtually critic-proof. Much was made of the $10 million capitalization and the $100 top-price ticket. Of the total Broadway gross the week *Miss Saigon* opened, forty percent was derived from just four shows: *Cats, Les Misérables, Phantom of the Opera*, and *Miss Saigon*, all British imports and all Cameron Mackintosh shows. Of the shows on the road, a staggering sixty percent was attributable to only three shows: *Cats, Les Misérables*, and *Phantom*. That the reviews were mixed is maybe not surprising.

Many reviews seemed more concerned with the helicopter than the show, and Howard Kissel began with, "As everyone knows, British musicals are less about music than they are about scenery. *Les Miz* was about The Barricades, *The Phantom of the Opera* was about The Chandelier, and *Miss Saigon*, theoretically about the consequences of America in Vietnam, is really about The Helicopter...Apart from some impressive performances, there's not much else to make *Miss Saigon* worthwhile...the music is staggeringly banal, the lyrics insultingly predictable. They don't allow for human chemistry. So you feel the whole thing is mechanical and manipulative...It is hilarious to think the show that raised Broadway ticket prices to a new high is an anti-American, allegedly anti-materialist musical whose second most impressive visual image is a stage-high statue of Ho Chi Minh" (*Daily News*, 4.12.91). Clive Barnes also started with the helicopter ("The chopper has landed"), before going on to complain about "Schönberg's unoriginal and almost unquotable score" and the lyrics which "vary from the plain unvarnished and schmaltzy to the grotesquely inept and grossly insensitive." But he did praise the performances: "*Miss Saigon* is unquestionably a triumph for its cast, particularly the priceless Pryce, but also the mothlike Butterfly of Lea Salonga, incidentally a triumph for the producer, Cameron Mackintosh, whose adamant insistence on them coming over from London now seems fully justified...Pryce is an actor of extraordinary intent. He takes a role, walks into it, and closes the door behind him. He then acts from within the character. As the Engineer, his sleazy sense of self-preservation, his cartoon version of the American dream ideal, and his expressionist way of throwing everything into a glance, gesture, or a pose, has a Brechtian dimension and totally transcends the show's basic material" (*New York Post*, 4.12.91).

Even the better reviews seemed obsessed with the helicopter. Linda Winer saw the helicopter as the major performer in the show: "The helicopter finally landed at the Broadway Theatre yesterday, and, as promised, it is the very best helicopter that ever played a Broadway house. What we did not expect from *Miss Saigon*, perhaps, was the awful power of the scene, the stunning agony of the Saigon evacuation in 1975, with soldiers scrambling into the big chopper and Vietnamese rioting to climb aboard, only to be left clinging and sobbing on the chain fence of the US embassy. The impact of the moment was broken by the audience, which applauded the high-tech special effects as if an acrobat had done a whiz-bang somersault. But in those shocking couple of seconds, *Miss Saigon*—the success and the ferocity of the controversies—finally made sense...The world's first Vietnam mega-musical...dances on a sliver of a line between exploitation and the showbiz equivalent of passionate commentary about exploitation. It steps over that line, in one direction or another, about as often as it stays in balance. It is engaging. It is insulting. It is never boring" (*New York Newsday*, 4.12.91). The *Variety* review also begins: "The chopper has landed. Attended by several controversies and the kind of media scrutiny that says more about the dearth of activity on Broadway than anything else, *Miss Saigon* has finally arrived in New York...With a fleeting, doomed romance at its core, *Miss Saigon*'s heart-tugging elements can be affecting...Big, ferocious, and raw, frequently challenging whatever sense of propriety might remain in the tattered Broadway environs, *Miss Saigon* is in-your-face from start to finish, and it's here to stay" (4.15.91). David Richards' Sunday review stated, "What Mr Boublil and Mr Schönberg are striving to reproduce, as they did in *Les Misérables*, is the grandeur of opera in popular garb...The doomed love between Kim, the innocent Vietnamese bar girl, and Chris, the burned-out G.I. who finds regeneration in her arms before losing her in the chaos of the American withdrawal, is played out on an epic scale. *Miss Saigon* puts the lovers into Cinemascope decors, wraps them in Mr Schönberg's lush music, and then, when their passion is white-hot, throws a chain-link fence between them and exiles them to opposite ends of the globe...*Miss Saigon* is surely going to amaze a lot of people for years to come" (*New York Times*, 4.21.91).

In *Theater Week*, Ken Mandelbaum made some perceptive comments: "The reasons why *Miss Saigon* is such an effective piece of musical theatre are quite simple. First, *Miss Saigon* was a very good idea. Many musicals have foundered because of a fundamentally unsound or dubious concept or source. But resetting the *Madama Butterfly* story during the final weeks of the Vietnam War and the years that followed immediately thereafter was an inspiration...the story of *Miss Saigon* had already been made into an opera, and one with a great score. But that does not detract from the story's power when recycled...and the libretto for *Miss Saigon* actually improves on that of *Madama Butterfly* in several respects. The opera's Pinkerton was a callous boor who never loved Cio-Cio-San...Chris falls in love at first sight with Kim, and leaves only when Saigon falls to the North Vietnamese and all Americans are evacuated. Their doomed affair has greater resonance than that of Pinkerton and Butterfly, and Chris's subsequent guilt over leaving Kim is symbolic of America's guilt for the disaster it wrought in a country where it didn't belong. The second reason for *Saigon's* effectiveness is its surprising intimacy...*Miss Saigon* tends to focus on scenes involving two or three principal characters...Most pop operas of the '80s have been epic with characters no one could really mistake for fully-dimensional human beings...*Miss Saigon* is the first pop opera about simple, real characters, and it tells a straightforward story, setting its intimate scenes against a spectacle that is always integral to the action and that serves to emphasize the theme of ordinary people in the grip of chaotic events beyond their control...it never forgets an element present in the best musical: genuine emotion, the kind with which an audience can identify...the ultimate trump card...is the figure of the Engineer...the first character in a pop opera who's genuinely funny...The *Saigon* score uses repetition with more subtlety and integrity than any other pop opera; the themes that are repeated actually stand for characters (i.e. Tam) or ideas (i.e. Uncle Sam), and they rarely occur without a reason. The score is invariably reflective of the dramatic situation, ranging from raucous rock'n'roll of a sleazy bar to the ethereal Oriental strains of Kim's wedding scene...*Saigon* makes perhaps the best case yet for the validity of the pop opera form; if its individual components may be equalled or bettered by other examples of the genre, *Saigon* is the most dramatically coherent and satisfying of them all" (4.22.91).

Frank Rich frankly summed up the mood and background in which *Miss Saigon* opened, before coming out in praise of the musical: "There may never have been a musical that made more people angry before its Broadway debut than *Miss Saigon*. Here is a show with something for everyone to resent—in principle, at least. Its imported stars, the English actor Jonathan Pryce and the Filipino actress Lea Salonga, are playing roles that neglected Asian-American performers feel are rightly theirs. Its top-ticket price of $100 is a new Broadway high, sprung by an English producer, if you please, on a recession-straightened American public. More incendiary still is the musical's content...*Miss Saigon* insists on revisiting the most calamitous and morally dubious military adventure in American history and, through an unfortunate accident of timing, arrives in New York even as the jingoistic celebrations of a successful war are going full blast. So take your rage with you to the Broadway Theatre, where *Miss Saigon* opened last night, and hold on tight. Then see just how long you can cling to the anger when confronted by the work itself...this musical is a gripping entertainment of the old school...it offers lush melodies, spectacular performances by Mr. Pryce, Miss Salonga, and the American actor Hinton Battle, and a good cry...If *Miss Saigon* is the most exciting of the so-called English musicals—and I feel it is, easily—that may be because it is the most American...*Miss Saigon* is escapist entertainment in style and in the sense that it finally even makes one forget about all the hype and protests that greeted its arrival. But this musical is more than that, too, because the one thing it will not allow an American audience to escape is the lost war that, like its tragic heroine, even now defiantly refuses to be left behind"* (*New York Times*, 4.12.91).

WORLDWIDE PRODUCTIONS

Miss Saigon has been opened by 26 companies worldwide: London, Broadway, Tokyo, US National Tour 1, Toronto, Budapest, Stuttgart, US National Tour 2, Sydney, Copenhagen, Scheveningen, Stockholm, Manila, Warsaw, Asian Tour, Danish Tour, UK Tour, US Troika Tour, Malmo, Tallinn, St.Gallen, Helsinki, UK Tam Tour, Gothenburg, Prague, and Gyor.

---

* © 1991, *The New York Times Co.* Reprinted with permission.

These productions have played in 23 countries: England, United States of America, Japan, Canada, Hungary, N. Ireland, Germany, Australia, Denmark, Holland, Sweden, The Philippines, Poland, Hong Kong, Singapore, Ireland, Scotland, Estonia, Luxemburg, Switzerland, Finland, the Czech Republic, and Wales.

Miss Saigon has been translated into 11 different languages: English, Japanese, Hungarian, German, Danish, Dutch, Swedish, Polish, Estonian, Finnish, and Czech.

CITIES WHERE THE SHOW HAS PLAYED

UK: England: London, Bradford, Bristol, Birmingham, Liverpool, Manchester, Milton Keynes, Norwich, Nottingham, Oxford, Plymouth, Southampton, Sunderland, Woking. **N. Ireland:** Belfast. **Scotland:** Edinburgh, Glasgow. **Wales:** Cardiff. **U.S.:** New York, Akron, Albuquerque, Amarillo, Ames, Amherst, Anchorage, Athens, Atlanta, Austin, Bakersfield, Baltimore, Baton Rouge, Benton Harbour, Beverly, Binghamton, Birmingham, Bismarck, Bloomington, Boise, Boston, Brunswick, Buffalo, Cedar Falls, Cedar Rapids, Champaign, Charleston, Charlotte, Chatanooga, Chicago, Chicoutimi, Cincinnati, Clarksville, Clearwater, Cleveland, Clinton Township, College Station, Colorado Springs, Columbia, Columbus, Coral Springs, Corpus Christi, Costa Mesa, Cupertino, Dallas, Davenport, Dayton, Daytona Beach, Denver, Des Moines, Detroit, Duluth, East Lansing, East Peoria, Elmira, Erie, Evansville, Fayetteville, Flint, Forestburgh, Fort Collins, Fort Lauderdale, Fort Myers, Fort Shafter, Fort Worth, Fort Wayne, Fresno, Fullerton, Gainesville, Galveston, Grand Rapids, Green Bay, Greensboro, Greenville, Hartford, Honolulu, Houghton, Houston, Huntsville, Indiana, Indianapolis, Iowa City, Jackson, Jacksonville, Kalamazoo, Kansas City, Knoxville, Lafayette, Las Vegas, Lawrence, Lexington, Lincoln, Lincolnshire, Little Rock, London, Long Beach, Los Angeles, Louisville, Lubbock, Macon, Madison, Mansfield, Marlton, Melbourne, Memphis, Miami, Millburn, Milwaukee, Minneapolis, Monroe, Morgantown, Muncie, Nashville, Newark, New Brunswick, New Orleans, Newport News, Newton, Niceville, Norfolk, North Charleston, Oklahoma, Omaha, Orange, Orlando, Owensboro, Paducah, Palm Desert, Pasadena, Pensacola, Peoria, Philadelphia, Phoenix, Pittsburgh, Portland, Providence, Raleigh, Rapid City, Reno, Richmond, Roanoke, Rochester, Rockford, Sacramento, Saginaw, Salt Lake City, San Antonio, San Bernardino, San Diego, San Francisco, San Jose, Savannah, Schenectady, Scranton, Seattle, Shreveport, Sioux City, Sioux Falls, South Bend,

Spokane, Springfield, St. Louis, St. Paul, Stamford, State College, Syracuse, Tallahassee, Tampa Bay, Temecula, Tempe, Thousand Oaks, Toledo, Tucson, Tulsa, Tyler, University Park, Utica, Wallingford, Walnut Creek, Washington, Waterbury, Wausau, West Lafayette, West Palm Beach, West Point, Wichita, Wilkes-Barre, Williamsport, Wilmington, Worcester, York, Youngstown. **Canada:** Calgary, Edmonton, Montreal, Ottawa, Regina, Saskatoon, Toronto, Vancouver, Winnipeg. **Australia:** Sydney. **Czech Republic:** Prague. **Denmark:** Copenhagen, Aarhus, Odense, Herning. **Ireland:** Dublin. **Estonia:** Tallinn. **Finland:** Helsinki. **Germany:** Stuttgart, Xanten. **Holland:** Scheveningen. **Hong Kong. Hungary:** Szeged, Budapest, Gyor. **Japan:** Tokyo. **Luxemburg. The Philippines:** Manila. **Poland:** Warsaw. **Singapore. Sweden:** Gothenburg, Malmo, Stockholm. **Switzerland:** St. Gallen.

AWARDS RECEIVED BY *MISS SAIGON*
UK
London
EVENING STANDARD AWARDS, 1989
Best Musical
Best Director: Nicholas Hytner
(shared with *Ghetto*)
THE CRITICS CIRCLE
Best Musical
Best Director: Nicholas Hytner
Best Designer: John Napier
VARIETY CLUB AWARDS
Best Actor: Jonathan Pryce—Engineer
OLIVIER AWARDS, 1990
Best Actress in a Musical: Lea Salonga—Kim
Best Actor in a Musical: Jonathan Pryce—Engineer

RECORDINGS
ORIGINAL LONDON CAST RECORDING
Gold Disc 1990
Awarded for selling 150,000 copies within 3 days
Platinum Disc

U.S.
Broadway
TONY AWARDS, 1991

Best Actor in a Musical: Jonathan Pryce—Engineer
Best Actress in a Musical: Lea Salonga—Kim
 Best Featured Actor in a Musical: Hinton Battle—John
DRAMA DESK AWARDS, 1991
Best Actor in a Musical: Jonathan Pryce—Engineer
 Best Actress in a Musical: Lea Salonga—Kim
Best Lighting: David Hersey
Best Orchestrations: William D. Brohn
OUTER CRITICS CIRCLE AWARDS, 1991
Best Musical
Best Actress in a Musical: Lea Salonga—Kim
Best Actor in a Musical: Jonathan Pryce—Engineer
THEATRE WORLD AWARD, 1991
Outstanding Debut: Lea Salonga

JAPAN
THE 47th GEIJUTSA-SAI AWARDS 1992
Arts Festival Awards:
Masachicka Ichimura—Engineer
THE GOLDEN ARROW AWARDS 1992
Best New Star in the Theatre Category: Minako Honda—Kim
THE GEKKAN MUSICAL AWARDS 1992
Best Musical
Best Actor: Massachika Ichimura—Engineer
THE PIE TEN 1992
Best Musical in a Theatrical Category
THE KIKUTA KAZUO AWARDS 1992
Theatrical Grand Prix: Masachika Ichimura—Engineer
THE KIKUTA KAZUO AWARDS 2005
Theatrical Grand Prix: Best Staging

GERMANY
Stuttgart
GOLDENE EUROPA AWARD 1995
Musical of the Year
GOLDENE CD—1998
250,000 copies sold

SWEDEN
Stockholm

GULDMASKEN 1998
Best Male Leading Role in a Musical: Stefan Sauk—Engineer
Best Female Supporting Role: Sofia Kallgren—Ellen
Best Male Supporting Role: Johan Boding—Chris

DISCOGRAPHY

MISS SAIGON—**Original London Recording (double album)**
Released in the UK by First Night Records
©1990 The David Geffen Company
Encore MC 5
Encore CD 5
Awarded Gold Disc for selling 150,000 copies within 3 days of its release and subsequently went platinum
1990
MISS SAIGON—**Highlights from the Original London Recording**
released in the UK by First Night Records ©1993 Exallshow Ltd.
CAST MC 38
CAST CD 38
1993
MISS SAIGON—**Japanese Cast Recording**
©1993 Toshiba EMI
TOCT-8008 (Act 1)
TOCT-8009 (Act 2)
1993
LES MISÉRABLES and *MISS SAIGON*—**Symphonic Pieces**
First Night Records © 1993 Exallshow Ltd.
CAST CD 39
C 39 (Cassette)
1993
MISS SAIGON—**Hungarian Cast Recording**
©1994 Polygram Hungary Kft.
068098-4 (cassette)
068098-2 (CD)
1994
MISS SAIGON—**The Complete Recording**
First Night Records ©1995 Exallshow
KIM MC 1
KIM CD 1
released in the U.S. by Angel Records and in Australia by Festival Records

1995
MISS SAIGON—Highlights from The Complete Recording
First Night Records ©1995 Exallshow
CAST MC 60
CAST CD 60
1995
MISS SAIGON—German Cast Recording
1995 Polydor GmbH
CD 527 705-2
MC 527 705-4
Awarded Gold Disc (Goldene CD), July 1998, for selling 250,000
   copies
1995
MISS SAIGON—Dutch Cast Recording (double album)
1997 Endemol Home Entertainment
ENCD 7103
1997
MISS SAIGON—Highlights from the Dutch Cast Recording
1997 Endemol Home Entertainment
ENCD 7113
1997
MISS SAIGON—Danish Cast recording
1997 Østre Gasværk og Focus Recording
ØG 6000
1997

VIDEO
THE HEAT IS ON: The Making of *Miss Saigon*
1989 First Night FNVPI PAL
VHS 1 hour 15 minutes

SYNOPSIS
ACT ONE
Saigon—April 1975
The show opens in Dreamland, a sleazy bar for American G.I.s, owned by the scheming Engineer. The bargirls sell themselves, not just for money but for the hope of gaining a better life in America with one of the G.I.s. Chris is utterly disillusioned with this way of life and ready to go home to America but, after a fake beauty contest to elect Miss Saigon, his friend John tries to lift his spirits by buying Kim, the beau-

tiful new girl, for him. Chris is attracted to her and, recognizing her innocence, he tries to persuade her to leave alone, but the Engineer interrupts and Kim leads Chris away. During their night together, they fall deeply in love. Kim tells Chris that her parents have been killed and her village burned, so that she had no choice but to come to the city and seek a living any way she could. Not wanting her to return to work in the bar, Chris asks her to live with him. Although Saigon is about to fall, they hold a blessing ceremony with the other girls attending. The celebrations are interrupted by Thuy, to whom Kim's father had promised her in marriage. Kim refuses to leave with him, guns are pulled, and Thuy leaves cursing Kim for breaking her father's word. Kim fears Chris will leave her now, but instead he promises to take her back to America.

Ho Chi Minh City—April 1978

Three years have passed, and Thuy, now a powerful commissar, orders the Engineer to find Kim for him. Kim keeps faith that Chris will return, not knowing that he is now married to an American wife, Ellen. Chris, back in America, is deeply troubled by nightmares about Kim. The Engineer finds Kim, and Thuy insists that she leaves with him, but she refuses. When she shows him her little son Tam, Thuy claims that the child will blight their new life together. He is about to kill Tam, but Kim shoots Thuy first. Kim goes to the Engineer for help to get to America to be with Chris, and when he realizes that Tam is the son of an American Marine he agrees. He quickly realizes that if he poses as Tam's uncle, he will at last be able to get the American visa he has long dreamed of. While the Engineer goes off to arrange a passage, Kim dreams of the chance of a better life for her son in America, all the time knowing that, if necessary, she would give her life for her child. They leave the city with all the other people in search of a new life and hope for the future.

ACT TWO
Atlanta—September 1978

John holds a concert to raise money for the Bui-Doi, the children of the Vietnamese bargirls, and is engaged in helping to unite them with their American fathers. He informs Chris that he has a son and that Kim is alive, and Chris remembers how hard he tried to get back to her in the face of impossible odds. Chris then decides to go to Bangkok with Ellen and John to find them.

Bangkok—October 1978

The Engineer and Kim are now working at a bar in Bangkok. It was the Engineer who had filled in the appropriate forms, and it is John who arrives to tell them that Chris is there, too. But seeing how much Kim still loves Chris, John is unable to tell her about Ellen. As Kim gets ready to meet Chris, a flashback sequence shows how they became separated during the fall of Saigon. The sequence is initiated nightmarishly by the ghost of Thuy, who claims to be the guilt inside Kim's head. The scene clearly shows that Chris intended to marry Kim when they got to America. As the nightmare fades, the Engineer rushes in with the address of Chris's hotel. He wants to control the situation and sends Kim to find Chris first. But the plan misfires, and it is Ellen that Kim finds in the hotel room. Devastated to find that Chris has "another" wife when she believed herself to be married to him, Kim's only thoughts now are for her son. She begs Ellen to take Tam back to America, but Ellen refuses to take a child from his mother. After Kim has left, Chris and John return. Ellen feels she has been misled about Chris and Kim's relationship, and he tries to explain with great honesty what he has been through. They both agree that it would be best to support Kim and Tam in Bangkok, and only John realizes that this will not satisfy Kim's dreams for her son. The Engineer, believing that everything has gone to plan, fantasises about his new life in America where he can fulfil his own American Dream. The heartbroken Kim prepares Tam for a new life with his father. As she hears Chris arriving, she kisses Tam goodbye and sends him out to meet his father. Realizing that she is the only obstacle to Tam's future with his father, she takes her own life using the very gun that Chris had left for her protection. Chris finds her, and as she lies dying in his arms, Ellen now accepts her role with Tam.

THEMES

The principal themes in *Miss Saigon* are Impossible Love, Destiny, Illusion and Reality, and Personal Identity. The theme of Impossible Love is played out against the backdrop of political and historical events, which largely govern the destiny of the characters and negate many of the freedoms of personal choice. The sense of destiny and the opposition of Eastern mysticism with Western materialism is interwoven throughout, for while Chris puts his faith in American power Kim believes that her life is determined by the gods and she makes frequent reference to their influence. The East/West opposition is aptly shown in the imagery that symbolizes Chris and Kim's love: "You are sunlight, and I, moon/Joined by the gods of fortune/Midnight and high noon/Sharing the sky." Sun and moon are the perfect metaphors for two people who have a passionate but fleeting relationship, but who ultimately belong on opposite sides of the earth, their destiny being determined by fate as surely as that of the sun and moon. Sun and moon represent not only the polarity of East and West but also that of male and female, as the moon traditionally symbolizes the eternal feminine while the sun and sun gods have always represented the male. The image of the moon is a persistent and cohesive reference to Kim in the show. But if her love for Chris is doomed Kim takes matters into her own hands to ensure the future for her son: "They think they will decide your life/No it will be me." However, even as she lies dying by her own hand, Kim still believes that the gods are ultimately responsible: "The gods have guided you to your son." It is a fascinating interplay between the idea of a destiny laid out for you and free will, showing that they are not polar opposites, not mutually exclusive beliefs, but that free will can operate in a deterministic world if a person is strong willed enough.

The themes of Illusion and Reality are worked out chiefly through the motif of the dream. The bargirls, whose conception of reality is based on celluloid fantasy rather than reality, dream of the kind of life they've seen in American movies; they even work in a bar called Dreamland. Kim's dreams of true love appear as if they will be realized until they are thwarted by the American evacuation when John claims: "And if some dreams get smashed, perhaps it's best they were." Back in America, Chris has dreams too, but his dreams are nightmares: "You don't know, John, these nightmares/The things that I've seen/I have seen her face burned/ Seen her shot with my gun/I have chased her through streets/And only heard screams." Chris also dreams that he has a son, and his dreams do in fact show him some reality and foreshadow Kim's death when she is indeed shot with his gun. When Chris arrives in Bangkok, Kim believes her dreams have been fulfilled only to be bitterly disillusioned by the reality. And, instead, her dreams are transferred to her son's life with his father: "All I dreamed for you/He'll do." This is a dream that she is able to turn into reality by her own sacrifice.

The theme of Illusion and Reality is also worked out through the character of the Engineer, who is the ultimate illusionist, conning the G.I.s into paying for things he then claims they can get for free and handing out fake Rolex watches. The so-called eleven o'clock number "The American Dream" epitomizes the illusion, for this seeming celebration of American materialism is undercut by the emptiness of its capitalist values, and the Engineer's fantasy soon disappears into his world of hard reality.

The theme of Personal Identity is worked out through several characters. Chris's meeting with Kim leads to a sense of disorientation, and in the song "Why God Why?" he asks, "But why does nothing here make sense?" His love for Kim, however, has a pivotal effect; it changes him, and he says to John, "Do I sound diff'rent?/How else could I be." In the confrontation scene with Ellen, he acknowledges that back in Vietnam, "I didn't know who I am." But he takes full responsibility for his actions, despite his good intentions: "So I wanted to save and protect her/Christ, I'm an American/How could I fail to do good?" He then admits: "All I made was a mess, just like everyone else/In a place full of mystery/That I never once understood." It is at this point in the musical, in particular, that we see how the personal is related to the political and historical, for Chris's statement directly reflects America's involvement and failure in Vietnam. In *Miss Saigon*, the idea of personal identity is closely linked with that of national identity, of what it means to be an American. Kim wants her son to be an American, believing only then will he have the freedom to choose his own identity: "You will be who you want to be—you/Can choose whatever heaven grants/As long as you can have your chance." But intriguingly, the choice is still set within the limits set by the gods: "Whatever heaven grants." The Engineer has no doubt he is a true American at heart, and after three years under the Viet Cong he can still claim: "They washed out my brain/I'm still what I am/Deep inside, I know what I know/Wherever I go/I speak Uncle Ho/And think Uncle Sam." Ultimately, he pretends to be Tam's Uncle in the hope that he can indeed reinvent himself as a true American.

FACTS AND TRIVIA

Miss Saigon is one of the most spectacular and technically complex productions ever staged. Of the 266 people who worked on the London production at each performance, only 47 appeared in front of the audience.

Many of the artists appearing in *Miss Saigon* have come from the Philippines. There is a *Miss Saigon* school in Manila, and in London a special school was set up to help train young performers in the singing and dancing skills required.

The Bui Doi Fund was set up by the trustees of The Mackintosh Foundation in January 1990 for the relief of refugees. It expanded its objective to help the poor and sick of Southeast Asia resulting from war,

Schönberg at the *Miss Saigon* School in Manila.

its aftermath, and oppression. A part of the proceeds from performances of *Miss Saigon* was allocated to the funds, which together with other private and public donations amounted to a sum of over £1.2 million ($2.3 million) over a period of eleven years.

In July 2005, Joanna Ampil released a CD, *Reach For The Stars* with music by Thomas Schönberg (Claude-Michel's son). All the proceeds are donated to Sun and Moon, Home for Children, which Claude-Michel opened in Manila in the Philippines and which celebrated its tenth anniversary also in 2005.

The helicopter is a masterstroke of illusion. The "blades" in reality are thin cords with centrifugal force giving the impression of a completely realistic, whirling blade motion. It is suspended from two huge cables on a gimbal, which allows it to rotate in any direction, and it is operated manually by remote control joysticks. The realistic helicopter sounds, perhaps more than anything, add to the illusion of total authenticity. When not in use it is stored high up near the roof of the theatre.

The oriental instruments used in *Miss Saigon* are not specifically Vietnamese but a blend of instruments from the Far East. Claude-Michel used gamelan sounds from Indonesia, the shamisan, a three-stringed guitar from Japan, which sounds like the moon guitar from Vietnam, and the odaïko drum from Japan, while some of the violins were written like Chinese violins, all of which gives a broadly Asian flavor. Some of the sounds were programmed into a synthesiser. But perhaps the most significant instrument, which Claude-Michel loved and insisted was played live in the pit, was the shakuhachi. This is a Japanese bamboo flute with a paper membrane which gives a striking purity of sound, and so it was used to characterize Kim and only played when she was singing or when someone was thinking or singing about her.

A Gala Performance of *Miss Saigon*, the night before the official opening, was attended by Princess Diana, wearing an ice-blue Catherine Walker silk chiffon dress. Jonathan Pryce, fighting a throat infection, had been instructed by his singing teacher not to speak to anyone, as speaking is so much harder on the voice than singing. But, of course, he made an exception when Princess Diana went on stage to meet the cast after the performance. Alain and Claude-Michel shared the Royal box with the Princess, and the performance raised £100,000 ($190,000) for Relate Marriage Guidance and the Prince's Trust.

The most unusual production to date was an open-air production in Szeged, Hungary where a real helicopter was used to recreate the evacuation of Saigon by the American forces. This production later transferred to the Operetta Theatre in Budapest.

The first German-language production of *Miss Saigon* opened on December 2, 1994 in the Music Hall, Stuttgart, which was built especially for the show.

The Princess of Wales Theatre in Toronto was designed and built to accommodate the technical requirements of its opening production, *Miss Saigon*.

Miss Saigon marked the culmination of the opening season of the newly refurbished Capitol Theatre in Sydney in 1995.

THE ENGINEER'S TOUR OF *MISS SAIGON*

This production, which opened in Manchester on November 22, 2001, was the first UK touring production of *Miss Saigon*, and it has some intriguing facts, figures, and trivia. While the look of the production was the same as that which played the Theatre Royal Drury Lane, some elements were smaller and had been redesigned in order to make touring the show easier and quicker.

Twenty-six 44-foot trailers moved the set between venues. From the final performance in one venue it took 12 days to strike, move, and rebuild the set, then retech it with a new crew before the first preview in the next venue.

An additional crew of approximately 24 production carpenters, riggers, sound engineers, production electricians, and programers were responsible for moving the show.

The Ho Chi Minh statue was 18 feet high and weighed approx 397 lbs. The hotel set weighed approximately 1 ton.

The helicopter was computer-controlled and was life-size. It weighed 1,764 lbs. and was so large it needed a 8.2 cubic foot box to hold it. Six hydraulic devices were responsible for the helicopter rotas and the pilots' movements.

The Cadillac was designed especially for the production. It weighed 23 lbs. and folded in half for easy storage.

There were 32 motors used throughout the set. Fifteen alone were needed to move the enormous Venetian blinds.

Each performance used 6 follow-spots, 20 vari-lights (special moving lights), 30 moving light curtains, 8 fog and smoke machines, 298 lbs. of dry ice, 25 radio microphones, and 94 winches.

The lighting rig to buy new would have cost in the region of £5 million ($9.5 million). Relamping the lamps in the moving lights, which took place every 700 hours, cost approx. £7,500 ($14,200).

19,700 feet of cable and 52 electronic circuit boards were used to send data and power around the set.

There were 44 members of the cast, 19 members of the orchestra, and with other company members and crew, a total of 136 people were required for each performance.

It was also thirsty work. The company, crew, and orchestra drank just over 90 gallons of water a week.

The company used, on average, 3 boxes of tissues and 3 boxes of wet wipes per performance.

For the props there were 816 bottles of Budweiser/Schwarz Beer, 450 bottles of Coke, 8 handguns (3 of which fired blank bullets), 17 G.I. rifles, 33 Vietnam flags, 19 Ho Chi Minh flags, 29 Red Army flags, and 26 Ribbon sticks. For each performance 35 cigarettes, 19 roll ups/spliffs, and 300 dollar bills were needed.

The wig department consisted of 3 Touring wig staff. The company wore 10 American Dream wigs, which were acrylic-backed and had real hairlines, 1 Miss Chinatown wig and 2 Engineer wigs. The principal understudies also had their own wigs.

The wardrobe department consisted of 5 Touring Wardrobe staff plus 15 local dressers and freelancers who moved the show. There were 380 different costumes in the show plus those for swings and covers, as well as 360 pairs of shoes and 176 hats. Sixty-five different kinds of beads were used for the American Dream and the Bangkok costumes. The daily laundry included 102 pairs of socks, 52 underpants, 33 bras and pants, and 48 shirts, needing 8 large boxes of detergent and 4 gallons of fabric softener per week. To move the wardrobe department from venue to venue required one 44-foot truck.

THE TROIKA AND TAM TOURS OF *MISS SAIGON*

After *Miss Saigon* had been successfully touring in the UK and the U.S. for some time, it was decided to develop a new production to suit many more theatres that would never have been able to accommodate the original production. The Troika Tour in the U.S., which was named after the US Entertainment Company, took off first and opened at the Victoria Theatre in Dayton on September 5, 2002. It went on to tour over 150 cities. The Tam Tour, named after Kim's child, opened at the Theatre Royal in Plymouth, England on July 21, 2004 and toured extensively in the U.K. This production had a breathtaking new design and used cutting-edge visual techniques to vividly recreate the streets of Vietnam and Bangkok, including the memorable final helicopter flight from the roof of the American Embassy, which seemed incredibly real. The production was directed by Mitchell Lemsky and the set was designed by Adrian Vaux with the famous illustrator Gerald Scarfe joining the design team to create his own inimitable take on the "American Dream" number. The Tam Tour was further developed from the experience gained in the Troika Tour, and Totie Driver joined the creative team as an Associate Designer.

MARTIN GUERRE

LONDON PRODUCTION

Martin Guerre premiered in London at the Prince Edward Theatre on July 10, 1996. It was a spectacular production, but not only were the reviews mixed, there were also some major concerns expressed by the public and the creative team alike. In the early weeks, the creative team worked hard and quickly to clarify the narrative, rearrange some of the material, and remove one pretty, but nonessential song. In order to make more radical changes, the show was closed from October 28–31, 1996, and the production was completely revised. This revised version opened after a week of previews on November 11, 1996. The critical response was significantly improved, and the revised show went on to win the

1997 Laurence Olivier Awards for Best Musical and Best Choreography
before finally closing on February 28, 1998 after 675 performances.

LONDON CREATIVE TEAM
The creative credits are:
Book   Alain Boublil and Claude-Michel Schönberg
Music   Claude-Michel Schönberg
English Lyrics   Edward Hardy
Original French Text   Alain Boublil
Additional Lyrics   Herbert Kretzmer and Alain Boublil
Director & Co-Adapter   Declan Donnellan
Musical Supervisor   David White
Musical Director   David Charles Abell
Orchestrator   Jonathan Tunick
Choreographer   Bob Avian
Production Designer   Nick Ormerod
Lighting   David Hersey
Sound   Andrew Bruce
Creative Team change Autumn 1996:
English Lyrics: Edward Hardy & Stephen Clark

ORIGINAL LONDON CAST
Arnaud du Thil   Iain Glen
Bertrande de Rols   Juliette Caton
Guillaume   Jerome Pradon
Martin Guerre   Matt Rawle
Benoit   Michael Matus
Madame de Rols   Susan Jane Tanner
Pierre Guerre   Martin Turner
Father Dominic   Marcus Cunningham
Judge Coras   Paul Leonard

LONDON CAST CHANGE JUNE 16, 1997
Arnaud du Thil   Hal Fowler
Bertrande de Rols   Jenna Russell
Martin Guerre   Michael Cahill
Guillaume   David Shannon
Benoit   Sebastien Torkia
Madame de Rols   Susan Fay
Pierre Guerre   Don Gallagher

Father Dominic   Nigel Richards
Judge Coras   Julian Forsyth

MUSICAL NUMBERS

The musical numbers on opening night were:
ACT I
Prologue   Orchestral
Artigat   Madame de Rols, Pierre Guerre, The Notary, Company
A Year Later
Over A Year   Celestine, Ernestine, Hortense
Charivari   Martin, Bertrande, Guillaume, Cronies
Why Won't You Love Me   Bertrande
The Rejection   Martin, Pierre Guerre, Madame de Rols
Martin Guerre   Martin
Seven Years Later
A Battlefield in Flanders
Here Comes the Morning   Arnaud, Martin
A Life For A Life   Arnaud
Artigat
Sleeping On Our Own   Celestine, Ernestine, Hortense
The Confession   Bertrande, Father Dominic, Catherine, Company
Louison/Now You've Come Home   Benoit, Arnaud, Company
Tell me To Go   Bertrande, Arnaud
The Seasons   Company
All I Know   Bertrand, Arnaud
The Conversion   Arnaud, Bertrande, Andre, Catherine
Bethlehem   Andre, Catherine, Company
The Dinner   Guillaume, Pierre Guerre, Arnaud, Madame de Rols,
   Bertrande, Company
Louison (Reprise)   Benoit, Soldier
One by One   Guillaume, Cronies
The Capture   Bertrande, Arnaud, Benoit, Guillaume, Cronies
All I Know (Reprise)   Bertrande, Arnaud
ACT II
Entr'acte   Orchestral
Hallelujah   Guillaume, Benoit, Madame de Rols, Pierre Guerre,
   Company
Bethlehem (Reprise)   Andre, Catherine, Company
The Courtroom
Me   Benoit, Company

Martin Guerre (Reprise)   Arnaud
Someone   Bertrande, Arnaud
The Imposters   Company
The Last Witness   Judge, Martin, Arnaud, Pierre Guerre, Madame
    de Rols, Bertrande, Company
Here Comes The Morning (Reprise)   Arnaud, Martin, Bertrande,
    Guillaume
The Sentence   Judge
I Will Make You Proud   Guillaume, Company
The Madness   Benoit, Company
The Jail
All I Know/A Life For A Life (Reprise)   Bertrande, Arnaud, Martin
The Escape   Bertrande, Arnaud, Martin, Benoit, Guillaume
The Reckoning   Bertrande, Arnaud, Martin, Benoit, Guillaume
The Land Of The Fathers   Father Dominic, Martin, Bertrande,
    Company

LONDON REVIEWS
The reviews for the original London production were generally very poor:
"Its book lacks real narrative thrust and excitement" (Nicholas de Jongh,
Evening Standard, 7.11.96); "*Les Miz* and *Miss Saigon* had a melodic sweep
and emotional clarity signally absent from *Martin Guerre*" (Michael Coveney, *Observer*, 7.14.96); "In Declan Donnellan's stylistically-insecure production the dramatic metronome has stopped ticking" (Robert Butler,
Independent on Sunday, 7.14.96); "*Martin Guerre* is a bore, and a surprisingly inefficient bore" (Alistair Macaulay, *Financial Times*, 7.11.96). A few
reviews were more favorable: "*Martin Guerre* is an admirable, high-quality
company creation … a beautifully produced addition to London's the-
atreland" (Steve Grant, *Time Out*, 7.17.96); "For the third time in little
more than a decade, or so it would seem from all but about two of the first
dozen reviews, Alain Boublil and Claude-Michel Schönberg have written
a great and classic musical which nobody likes except the public…*Martin
Guerre* is as much a masterpiece of musical magic and mystery as that
earlier score [*Les Misérables*]" (Sheridan Morley, *Spectator*, 7.20.96).

REVISED LONDON PRODUCTION
MUSICAL NUMBERS
The musical numbers for the revised London opening night were:
ACT I
Prologue   Orchestra, Company

Pray For The Day   Bertrande, Benoit
Working On The Land   Pierre Guerre, Martin, Bertrande, Madame de Rols, Guillaume, Father Dominic, Company
A Year Later
Where's The Child   Guillaume, Father Dominic, Bertrande, Martin, Celestine, Hortense, Ernestine, Madame de Rols, Pierre Guerre, Andre, Catherine, Company
The Rejection   Martin, Pierre Guerre, Madame de Rols
Martin Guerre   Martin
Seven Years Later
A Battlefield in Flanders
The Battlefield/Here Comes The Morning   Arnaud, Martin, Bertrande
Artigat
Sleeping On Our Own   Celestine, Ernestine, Hortense
Duty   Father Dominic, Guillaume, Pierre Guerre, Bertrande, Company
When Will Someone Hear   Bertrande, Catherine, Andre, Company
Louison/Welcome Home   Benoit, Arnaud, Father Dominic, Pierre Guerre, Madame de Rols, Celestine, Hortense, Ernestine, Company
Tell Me To Go   Bertrande, Arnaud
Louison (Reprise)   Benoit
The Seasons   Arnaud, Bertrande, Company
All I Know   Bertrande, Arnaud
Bethlehem   Andre, Catherine, Arnaud, Bertrande, Company
The Dinner   Guillaume, Pierre Guerre, Arnaud, Madame de Rols, Bertrande, Company
One By One   Guillaume, Father Dominic, Celestine, Hortense, Ernestine, Benoit, Company
All I Know (Reprise)   Bertrande, Arnaud, Guillaume
ACT II
Entr'acte   Orchestral
Courtroom
The Courtroom   Judge, Pierre Guerre, Arnaud, Hortense, Guillaume, Company
Me   Benoit, Judge, Company
Martin Guerre (Reprise)   Arnaud
Someone   Bertrande, Arnaud

The Imposters   Father Dominic, Madame de Rols, Pierre Guerre, Guillaume, Arnaud, Bertrande, Company

The Last Witness   Judge, Arnaud, Bertrande, Martin, Madame de Rols, Company

Here Comes The Morning (Reprise)   Arnaud, Bertrande, Martin, Guillaume

The Sentence   Judge

I Will Make You Proud   Guillaume, Company

The Madness   Benoit, Company

Jail

The Jail   Bertrande, Arnaud, Martin, Benoit, Company

The Reckoning   Guillaume, Martin, Arnaud, Bertrande, Benoit, Company

The Land Of The Fathers/Working On The Land   Madame de Rols, Pierre Guerre, Father Dominic, Martin, Bertrande, Company

REVIEWS OF THE REVISED LONDON PRODUCTION

When *Martin Guerre* reopened at the Prince Edward, the reviews were a great deal better: "The narrative is clear and full of suspense, there are some sharper lyrics (by Stephen Clark), and the emotional volume has been dramatically turned up" (Georgina Brown, *Mail on Sunday*, 11.17.96); "The relaunched version at the Prince Edward at least has a narrative drive and coherence missing from the original" (Michael Billington, *Guardian*, 11.13.96); "The piece has now been rejigged and, in my view, significantly improved" (Benedict Nightingale, *The Times*, 11.13.96); "The show has been restructured to make it both clearer and more plausible...it now has scenes of real power and passion, while its achingly romantic melodies linger resonantly in the memory" (Charles Spencer, *Daily Telegraph*, 11.12.96).

WEST YORKSHIRE PLAYHOUSE PRODUCTION/ UK TOUR

The West Yorkshire Playhouse in Leeds was the new, nurturing home for a completely rewritten version of *Martin Guerre*. The Artistic Director Jude Kelly invited Alain and Claude-Michel to rework their musical there, and in a co-production between The West Yorkshire Playhouse and Cameron Mackintosh *Martin Guerre* opened on December 8, 1998. It then embarked on a national tour, which ended in Bristol on August 7, 1999, after 227 performances.

WEST YORKSHIRE PLAYHOUSE/UK TOUR CREATIVE TEAM

The creative credits are:

Book   Alain Boublil and Claude-Michel Schönberg
Music   Claude-Michel Schönberg
Lyrics   Alain Boublil and Stephen Clark
Director   Conall Morrison
Musical Supervisor   Martin Koch
Musical Director   David Shrubsole
Orchestrator   William David Brohn
Musical Staging & Choreography   David Bolger
Designer   John Napier
Costume Designer   Andreane Neofitou
Lighting Designer   Howard Harrison
Sound Designer   Andrew Bruce

WEST YORKSHIRE PLAYHOUSE/UK TOUR CAST

Arnaud du Thil   Mathew Cammelle
Bertrande de Rols   Joanna Riding
Martin Guerre   Stephen Weller
Guillaume   Maurice Clark
Benoit   Terry Kelly
Madame de Rols   Kerry Washington
Pierre Guerre   Michael Bauer
Father Dominic   Gareth Snook
Judge Coras   Geoffrey Abbott

MUSICAL NUMBERS

The musical numbers on opening night were:
ACT I
On the BATTLEFIELD—1560
Live With Somebody You Love   Martin, Arnaud
In Artigat—Seven Years Later
Your Wedding Day   Pierre Guerre, Madame de Rols, Martin,
   Bertrande, Guillaume, Company
The Deluge   Martin, Bertrande, Madame de Rols, Pierre Guerre,
   Father Dominic, Guillaume, Company
I'm Martin Guerre   Martin
On the Battlefield—1560
Without You As A Friend   Martin, Arnaud

In Artigat—1560
How Many Tears   Bertrande
The Conversion   Catherine, André, Bertrande, Protestants
God's Anger   Father Dominic, Catherine, Guillaume. Pierre
   Guerre, Bertrand, Company
In Artigat—Three Months Later
Dear Louison   Benoit, Arnaud
Welcome to The Land   Guillaume, Benoit, Arnaud, Madame de
   Rols, Pierre Guerre, André, Catherine, Company
The Confession   Bertrande, Arnaud
The Seasons Turn   Catherine, Arnaud, Pierre Guerre, André,
   Guillaume, Madame de Rols, Company
Don't   Arnaud, Bertrande
All The Years   Arnaud, Bertrande
The Holy Fight   André, Catherine, Protestants
The Dinner   Guillaume, Pierre Guerre, Arnaud, Bertrande,
   Madame de Rols, Company
The Revelation   Guillaume, Father Dominic, Madame de Rols,
   Benoit, André, Catherine, Pierre Guerre, Company
The Day Has Come   Bertrande, Arnaud, Guillaume, Pierre
   Guerre, André, Father Dominic, Company
ACT II
In Artigat—One Week Later
Entr'acte   Orchestra
If You Still Love Me   Arnaud, Martin
The Courtroom   Guillaume, André, Pierre Guerre, Usher,
   Catherine, Judge, Arnaud, Madame de Rols, Benoit, Company
Who?   Benoit, Judge, Company
I'm Martin Guerre (Reprise)   Arnaud, Judge, Pierre Guerre,
   Madame de Rols, Company
All That I Love   Bertrande, Arnaud, Judge
The Imposter Is Here   Judge, Guillaume, André, Pierre Guerre,
   Benoit, Father Dominic, Arnaud, Bertrande, Madame de Rols,
   Company
The Final Witness   Usher, Judge, Martin, Father Dominic, Arnaud,
   Guillaume, Bertrande, Madame de Rols, Company
The Verdict   Judge
Justice Will Be Done   Guillaume, Martin, Pierre Guerre, Company
Benoit's Lament   Benoit
At the Jail

Why?   Arnaud, Bertrande, Martin
In the Village Square
You Will Be Mine   Guillaume, Arnaud, Martin, Bertrande
How Many Tears (Reprise)   Bertrande, Arnaud
Live With Somebody You Love (Reprise)   Martin, Bertrande,
  Company

WEST YORKSHIRE PLAYHOUSE REVIEWS

The critical reviews for this production genuinely seemed to appreciate all the hard work and dedication that went into this completely new production, and aside from a few whinges, it received generally good reviews: "Everything about this version, and its staging, is sharper and more focused…The love story and the theme of religious division are, for the first time, tightly integrated" (Paul Taylor, *Independent*, 12.10.98); "This is now a tighter, more compact and dynamic musical, with a smaller cast and a more integrated narrative" (John Peter, *Sunday Times*, 12.13.98); "My original objection was the show had no center. Now the focus is clear, posing the Brechtian question of ownership. To whom does Bertrande belong: to Arnaud whom she loves, or to Martin who is still her legal husband? The show has a palpable narrative urgency and a strong sense of an unresolvable emotional triangle" (Michael Billington, *Guardian*, 12.10.98); "It's essentially a brand new show. What's immediately most noticeable is the improved clarity and context it brings to the story…Staged simply but with great visual flair, the love story gripped me, thanks to gutsy, fullblooded performances from the two romantic leads, Joanna Riding and Mathew Cammelle" (Georgina Brown, *Mail on Sunday*, 12.13.98).

CITIES WHERE UK TOUR PLAYED

Leeds, Newcastle, Glasgow, Aberdeen, Norwich, Edinburgh, Manchester, Birmingham, Llandudno, Nottingham, Plymouth, Bristol.

GUTHRIE THEATER PRODUCTION/US TOUR

The North American premiere of *Martin Guerre* was at the renowned Guthrie Theater in Minneapolis on September 29, 1999. The Artistic Director Joe Dowling welcomed the opportunity for a co-production between the Guthrie Theater and Cameron Mackintosh so that *Martin Guerre* could be fine-tuned for its first American audience. There was some more reworking of the show for this production. Some musical numbers were moved, and there was a general softening of the village characters to make them more likeable and more individualized.

GUTHRIE THEATER/US TOUR CREATIVE TEAM

The creative team remained the same as the West Yorkshire Playhouse except for:

Musical Supervisor   David Caddick
Musical Director   Kevin Stiles
Sound Designers   Andrew Bruce/Mark Menard

GUTHRIE THEATER/US TOUR CAST

Arnaud du Thil   Stephen R. Buntrock
Bertrande de Rols   Erin Dilly
Martin Guerre   Hugh Panaro
Guillaume   Jose Llana
Benoit   Michael Arnold
Madame de Rols   Kathy Taylor
Pierre Guerre   John Leslie Wolf
Father Dominic   John Herrera
Judge Coras   D.C. Anderson

MUSICAL NUMBERS

The musicals numbers on opening night were:
ACT I
On the Battlefield—1564
Prologue   Arnaud, Martin
Without You As A Friend   Arnaud, Martin
In Artigat—Seven Years Later
Your Wedding Day   The Company
The Coming Storm   The Company
The Exorcism   The Company
Someone I Could Trust   Martin, Bertrande
I'm Martin Guerre   Martin
On the Battlefield—1564
Live With Somebody You Love   Martin, Arnaud
Artigat—1564
Back In Artigat   Guillaume, Victor, Bertrande, Pierre Guerre,
    Father Dominic, Madame de Rols
The Conversion   Catherine, André, Bertrande, Protestants
God's Anger   The Company
How Many Tears   Bertrande
From this point the musical numbers were the same as in the West
    Yorkshire Playhouse Production.

GUTHRIE THEATER/US TOUR REVIEWS

The reviews for the American production of *Martin Guerre* were varied, to say the least. Many of the critics were aware of the British critical responses to the various re-workings of the show, and it certainly arrived carrying plenty of critical baggage. In Minneapolis the reviews were generally good: "*Guerre* is on its way to being a winner. Besides, there are at least two songs to hum on the way out…though the musical will engage the intellect only lightly, it speaks loudly, earnestly, and passionately to the heart…questions of identity and romantic love roar like jet engines through the musical" (Rohan Preston, *Star Tribune*, 10.1.99); "The show evokes the 16th-century story with luscious music and a bold spirit. While its sensibility is decidedly modern and its emotional rhythms are occasionally flawed, at its core it is as captivating as the original story—a tale as well known in France as Robin Hood is in England. As a love story, as an attack on superstition, and the rich details of village life, it is largely a delight…it is never boring" (M. S. Mason, *Christian Science Monitor*, 10.1.99); "There's no question that this latest incarnation of the long-troubled tuner *Martin Guerre* is a vast improvement over the production that first underwhelmed the public at London's Prince Edward Theatre in 1996…In this new leaner version, we're far more focused on the themes that Boublil and Schönberg say they have always wanted to emphasize: a trio torn apart by the religious wars and the agony of striving for passion and friendship in a world of denominational hatred" (Chris Jones, *Variety*, 10.4.99). Despite some dismissive reviews of the show in Washington, D.C., Roy Proctor of *The Richmond Times Dispatch* was more enthusiastic: "What not many people are likely to expect, given the checkered production history of *Martin Guerre*, is that this show is as effective, moving and gloriously melodic as it is. It adds up to much more than the pyrotechnics that frame it…This show is in mint condition…it looks *Les Miz* great" (12.31.99). However, by the time the show reached Los Angeles the baggage had accelerated, and it was announced that as there was no medium-sized theatre available on Broadway, the show would not have the spring opening that had been planned. There were a few good reviews in Los Angeles such as that in *The Beverly Hills Courier*: "The show is extraordinary theatre…*Martin Guerre* is crammed with beautiful music and voices…It has remarkable spirit and tenderness. It has twists and turns—good and evil—beauty and ugliness. It has everything that makes great theatre…*Martin Guerre* is a winner—first rate all the way" (Candy Carststensen, 2.25.00). But mostly the reviews were poor: "They've added a new dimension to the story but also drained it of its original suspense and, perhaps, made the story too complex for its own good…At times the show feels operatic, at times soap operatic" (Jay Reiner, *The Hollywood Reporter*, 2.25.00); "This is a team with operatic ambitions, but without the skills needed to achieve opera's emotional amplitude or communicative abilities" (Paul Hodgkins, *Orange County Register*, 2.25.00); "It's not really musicalized since technically it's a sung-through opera. But it's not an opera Puccini would recognize. It's more pop music. Which I guess makes it a 'popera' and its creators 'poperazzi'" (S. Farler, *Daily Breeze*, 2.25.00); "After all the revisions…no one wants the result to be drab. But it is. *Martin Guerre* is not thrilling, nor (despite its most feverish power ballads) is it drenched in flop sweat" (Michael Phillips, *Los Angeles Times*, 2.25.00). Such reviews prompted letters of support for the show in *The Los Angeles Times* and a perceptive comment in *LA Weekly*: "For this American tour, forty percent of the music, and almost all of the lyrics, have been replaced. This widely-reported news appears to have had such a toxic effect, *Martin Guerre* might as well have arrived in a coffin. I can't remember another show pulling into town with such an uncharitable and unfair disposition against it…But…*Martin Guerre* is a strange and wonderful musical" (Steven Leigh Morris, 3.3.00).

CITIES WHERE US TOUR PLAYED
Minneapolis, Detroit, Washington, Seattle, Los Angeles.

WORLDWIDE PRODUCTIONS
A licensed production of *Martin Guerre* opened at the Odense Teater, in Denmark on December 30, 1999 and it ran until March 6, 2000.

AWARDS RECEIVED BY MARTIN GUERRE
UK
London
OLIVIER AWARDS, 1997
Best Musical
Best Choreography
GROUP LEISURE, 1997
Best Theatre Production

DISCOGRAPHY
MARTIN GUERRE—**Original London Recording (single album)**
Released in the UK by First Night Records
©1995 Exallshow Ltd

CAST CD 59
CAST C 59
MARTIN GUERRE—The 1999 Cast Recording (single album)
Released in the UK by First Night Records
©1999 Exallshow Ltd
CAST CD 70
CAST C70

VIDEO

MARTIN GUERRE: A Musical Journey
Video about the making of the show including excerpts from the
   London production
1997 VCI VC6614
VHS 70 minutes

SYNOPSIS

ACT ONE
On the Battlefield, 1564
After a fierce battle, Martin and Arnaud reflect on the futility of their lives as soldiers and on their close friendship, and Martin reveals that he was married at fourteen.

In Artigat, seven years earlier
Bertrande, Guillaume, and Martin are playing childishly together when the scene merges into the wedding of Bertrande and Martin, with Guillaume watching jealously. Martin's Uncle Pierre and the other villagers forcefully impress upon the young couple the need for a child, an important heir for Catholic Artigat. Protestants briefly appear, and are treated with hostility. Martin's failure to consummate the marriage is seen as the work of the devil and the cause of the continuing deluge the village is suffering from. Father Dominic publicly whips Martin to release the demons in him. Martin, totally humiliated, rejects Bertrande's sympathy and love and decides to leave in search of a new life.

On the Battlefield, 1564
Arnaud persuades Martin that it is time to return to Artigat, and they decide to go together. But the Protestants attack, and Martin is badly wounded saving Arnaud's life. As he lies dying he asks Arnaud to tell Bertrande he is sorry.

Artigat, 1564

Artigat is suffering from a drought now, and again it is Bertrande's barren state that is held to blame. In her despair she turns to the more sympathetic covert Protestants and becomes one of them. Father Dominic insists that Bertrande marry Guillaume, but she hates him and refuses, always hoping that Martin will return.

Artigat, three months later

Benoit, the village fool, is out in the fields with Louison, his beloved scarecrow, when Arnaud arrives looking for Bertrande. He tells Benoit his name, but when Benoit rushes into the village to tell them a stranger is looking for Bertrande they don't give him the chance to say who it is and immediately jump to the conclusion that Martin has returned. Bertrande does realize that it is not Martin, but when Arnaud tells her that Martin is dead she decides to let Arnaud stay, which is what the village wants, rather than be forced into marriage with Guillaume. Arnaud takes up village life with gusto, and when the harvest is good they believe it is because of him. Arnaud worries about the deception, but by now he and Bertrande have fallen deeply in love and eventually they allow themselves to make love. Bertrande confesses to him that she is now a Protestant, and Arnaud accompanies her to the Protestant service held secretly in the woods. At the feast Arnaud announces that Bertrande is carrying their child, but Guillaume denounces Martin Guerre as a Protestant and draws a knife on him. In order to save him, Benoit stuns everyone by saying that it is not Martin, and Arnaud is arrested so that he can stand trial. As the curtain falls there is a dramatic glimpse of Martin, alive and on his way back to Artigat.

ACT TWO

Artigat, a week later

Martin is seen wondering if Bertrande still loves him, while Arnaud is in jail believing he is going to die. The court case begins, and the Judge calls for witnesses to identify who the prisoner really is. Nothing is clear, the Catholics and Protestants cause uproar, and the judge has just ruled that there is no case to answer when Martin appears. Bertrande is called to identify the real Martin, but Arnaud then confesses and Bertrande admits that she knew all the time that he was not Martin. The judge sends Arnaud to jail, leaving it up to Martin to decide his fate. Guillaume whips up hatred for the Protestants, inciting violence and ripping Louison apart.

At the Jail

Arnaud tries to explain to Martin that he believed him dead, and although Martin feels betrayed he unselfishly sets him free so that Arnaud and Bertrande can continue to live their lives together.

In the Village Square

Guillaume and the Catholics attack the Protestants and burn the village, many of the villagers dying in the fighting. Guillaume holds a knife to Bertrande's throat, and Martin and Arnaud both try to distract his attention away from her. As Guillaume is about to stab Martin, Arnaud intervenes and is stabbed instead, saving Martin's life. Benoit then kills Guillaume with the heavy wooden post that supported Louison. As Arnaud lies dying in Bertrande's arms, he asks Martin to forgive him and to care for his child. While still proclaiming her love for Arnaud, Bertrande reaches out for Martin's hand.

THEMES

The overriding theme in *Martin Guerre* is, of course, that of Personal Identity, but other significant themes are: Friendship and Trust, Justice and Truth, and Impossible Love. Friendship and Trust are focal issues introduced right at the beginning of the show. Martin leaves Artigat because he feels his trust has been betrayed: "First I trusted Pierre/I was sold at the shrine/Then I trusted the Priest/Now my blood runs like wine/And then there was Bertrande/It seems all love must turn to dust/There must be someone I can trust." On the battlefield, Martin does indeed find someone to trust through his friendship with Arnaud, and he asks, "Where would I be/Without you as a friend." But ultimately, when Martin discovers that Arnaud has taken on his identity he again feels betrayed: "You were someone I trusted." Now there is an irony to the earlier lines, for as he leaves Bertrande and Arnaud to live their lives together he ends with: "So it seems/We have come to the end/I'll live my life/Without you as a friend," and the final phrase resonates back, but now with a contrary meaning.

The themes of Justice and Truth are also prominent, but as in *Les Misérables*, justice is shown to be a concept that varies with the individual. For the judge, justice is bound up with truth and fairness: "All I want is the truth/To above all be fair." But for the villagers, justice is not so much connected to truth as to religious bigotry, and they each want the case resolved differently according to whether they are Catholic or Protestant. For Guillaume, justice is bound up with his desire for

Bertrande, and Marie claims: "It's not justice you want…it's Bertrande." Guillaume's idea of justice can only be achieved by a bloody wiping out of the Protestants: "In the heat of battle/Justice will be done." Benoit also takes justice into his own hands, killing Guillaume in revenge for Louison and Arnaud. Benoit's justice is a natural justice, an "eye for an eye" kind of justice.

One of the intriguing things about *Martin Guerre* is the way it questions the nature of truth. Is there only one absolute truth, or are there different kinds of truths, and do some truths matter more than others? If Arnaud is living a lie as Martin, then he does so with village complicity, at least when they want him to be Martin. Benoit is the only one of the villagers to know the truth, and in two senses, for he knows that "Martin" is Arnaud di Thil and he recognises the fact that Martin Guerre is whoever the village want him to be: "Yes! he's who you all want him to be for you." Arnaud and Bertrande are uneasy with their deception of the village, but they are always truthful to each other, and for Bertrande the only truth that matters is her love for Arnaud. When Martin turns up in court, Bertrande shows the paradox of the truth: "The truth is not enough. The truth cannot explain/The truth…what is the truth?" and "The only truth I know—I love him/I knew from the start he was not Martin Guerre."

The theme of Love and Impossible Love is worked out with several strands and is fully integrated into the historical context of religious intolerance. Guillaume's love for Bertrande is unrequited, Bertrande's early love for Martin is never fulfilled, and although Bertrande and Arnaud love each other deeply, his death separates them. The song "Live with Somebody You Love" embodies this central theme, and its reprise ends the show with the hope that, despite their sadness at Arnaud's death, Bertrande and Martin can live the rest of their lives together with Arnaud's child in a loving relationship.

In *Martin Guerre*, the issue of personal identity is a fascinating one because it is a very modern issue. While forensic science can now unquestioningly establish physical identity, personal and moral identity is a separate issue. We constantly hear of people reinventing themselves, whether they are well-known stars or ordinary people. It is something that seems to be generally approved of—if you don't like who you are, then you can become someone else, with a different job, partner, lifestyle, appearance, or even sexuality. It is also true that society still imposes identity on us; we are so often categorized by job, clothes, accent, age, sexuality, and so on, and we are labeled doctor, dustman, wife, father, old, gay, feminist, or unemployed, or by any number of identifying labels.

Martin Guerre examines exactly what it is that constitutes personal identity, how society tries to impose identity, and the moral dilemmas implicit in establishing identity. In those medieval times, identity could be confirmed by various means: by name, by physical appearance, by moral character, by religious belief, and by the perceptions of one's self and the sometimes unreliable perceptions of others. Martin Guerre is whoever the village need him to be at a given moment. Identity is primarily signified by name, and when Martin has been humiliated, he seeks to reaffirm his own sense of identity: "But I swear it aloud, I will be proud that/Martin Guerre is my name." When Arnaud turns up and the villagers take him to be Martin, Guillaume questions him: "Tell me Martin/If you're Martin/Can you tell me my name?" Arnaud can easily guess that it's Guillaume from what Martin has told him, and, ironically, it is by identifying Guillaume correctly by name that Arnaud's identity as Martin is confirmed. Benoit shows up the inadequacy of naming as a means of identification: "You call me fool/I know that's not my name/See, it's strange/Names can always change/But I'm still the same." Physical appearance is also used to establish identity, and if overall appearance can be misleading then evidence rests on certain distinguishing features: a wart, a mark, boot size, and scars. Religious identity is a key issue, too, along with the idea of imposters. There is more than one kind of imposter, for all of them are living a lie of one kind or another, whether they are undercover Protestants or couples living together without love. The moral implications for Arnaud as an imposter are overcome by the belief that Martin is dead and by his love for Bertrande: "I bear his name yet feel no shame." Arnaud wants there to be no confusion of identity for his child, and as he is dying he asks Martin, "Let him bear my name." But the ultimate theme of *Martin Guerre* is that true identity is concerned with being true to yourself and true in love.

FACTS AND TRIVIA

For the *Martin Guerre* London production, the set was influenced by the real French village of Artigat and the paintings of Breughal.

The striking red poster for the London production offered an intriguing clue to the theme of ambiguous identity, as the outline of what appears to be a man's face from one angle becomes a standing man when viewed from the reverse angle, while on the other hand the name, Martin Guerre, appears to be hewn immutably from stone. The poster from the second version shows what looks like a slash of flame, but is in fact the background to the black silhouettes of two faces, facing each other closely.

Early preview goers to the London production wrote numerous letters to Cameron Mackintosh saying what they did and didn't like, and, even more importantly, what they didn't understand. These comments were taken seriously and had some influence on the subsequent reworkings.

On receiving the 1997 Laurence Olivier Award for Best Musical, Claude-Michel made, to the accompaniment of much laughter, the following comic reference to their previous lack of success with this award:

CMS: For the 1986 Laurence Olivier Awards, our first show lost to *Me and My Girl*, so the following morning Alain and me, we decided to write for the next show a 1930s, very funny, comic, uplifting work, and we did *Miss Saigon*! But for the 1990 Laurence Olivier Award, *Saigon* lost to *Forbidden Planet*, so we decided to write a very rock-and-roll show with a lot of compilation and heavy metal work, and we did *Martin Guerre*! So receiving tonight this wonderful award, we think that we took the right decision. Thank you very much everyone.

The second version of *Martin Guerre* was very advanced in its use of pyrotechnic effects. It opened with a huge cannon on stage firing directly out toward the audience, so that a perfect ring of smoke rolled upward and out over the auditorium. The end of the show was even more spectacular, as the set appeared to burn down every night before the audience's eyes. (See *Martin Guerre* photo insert 10.) This was achieved by covering the big dividing sections of the set and the whole back wall with an inflammable paste that would burn fiercely. Inside the wall were metal prongs that carried most of the flames, and as the wall rose the prongs would go down to create a greater sense of scale. Of course it was all very strictly tested so that only the things that were meant to burn could burn, and nothing else would be able to burn even if you took a blowtorch to it. This was not only an amazingly striking visual effect, but it had the appropriately symbolic resonance of religious hellfire.

WUTHERING HEIGHTS

Claude-Michel's first ballet, *Wuthering Heights*, premiered at the Alhambra Theatre, Bradford on September 21, 2002 before going on a UK tour and being performed at Sadler's Wells Theatre in London in March

2003. *Wuthering Heights* is ballet *theatre*, which endeavors to capture the spirit and soul of Emily Brontë's heartbreaking story, while telling the story with music so clearly that there is absolutely no need to consult the program to find out what's happening. With haunting orchestrations by William Brohn, it is a work heavy with emotion and power, and one that evokes the stark beauty and spirit of the wind-blasted moors and hills of Yorkshire. And it works well because dance is about emotion, getting complex emotions across, and capturing the feelings of the people portrayed. It is, of course, a local story, as Bradford is not far from Haworth where the Brontë family lived.

Originally, Derek Deane of the English National Ballet commissioned Claude-Michel to write the music. However, shortly after the score was completed, Deane left ENB. The UK's Northern Ballet Theatre has a good reputation for successful, narrative-led productions, and so Claude-Michel contacted their new artistic director David Nixon. Nixon was "blown away" by the fact that he'd never previously had the chance to work with a composer in devising a piece and had always had to pick existing music. He was inspired, almost seduced, by Claude-Michel's music and his passion for it, although at times a little intimidated by the challenge of living up to it. But it was a genuine meeting of minds, and Claude-Michel was thrilled to be working with a choreographer who so loved the music.

CREATIVE TEAM
The creative credits are:
Choreography   David Nixon
Music   Claude-Michel Schönberg
Orchestration   William David Brohn
Theatre Associate and Dramaturge   Patricia Doyle
Set Design   Ali Allen
Costume Design   David Nixon
Lighting design   David Grill

CAST
Heathcliff   Jonathan Oliver
Cathy   Charlotte Talbot
Child/Young Cathy   Pollyanna Th'ng
Young Heathcliff   Simon Kidd
Child Heathcliff   Robert White
Hindly   Jonathan Renna

Joseph   Jeremy Kerridge
Mr Earnshaw   Steven Wheeler
Edgar   Hironao Takahashi
Isabella   Desiré Samaai

REVIEWS

The reviews were mostly good with a few exceptions: "Nixon's chore-ography is just not inventive enough...none of it is memorable" (David Dougill, *Sunday Times*, 9.29.02); "Claude-Michel Schönberg's soupy and derivative score conjures visions of a glove-compartment filled with bal-let tapes" (Louise Levene, *Sunday Telegraph*, 9.29.02). However, there were many more enthusiastic reviews: "Let's start with the music for once...it is very effective and evocative, infusing the dancers' torrid emo-tions with exuberant romanticism and rising to some splendid melo-dramatic climaxes...David Nixon's choreography goes with Schönberg's flow...what lifts the evening to another plane is the superb performance of Charlotte Talbot as Cathy...she proves herself a powerful dance ac-tress" (Rupert Christiansen, *The Mail On Sunday*, 9.29.02); "Nixon and Schönberg share the popular touch. Their artistic choices might not al-ways be the subtlest, but as storytelling the two acts are admirably clean and clear" (Donald Hutera, *The Times*, 9.25.02); "Pitched at the perfect length, this production glides along smoothly at all times, accompanied by Claude-Michel's excellent score...the music achieves that rare trick of being both subtle and memorable...*Wuthering Heights* is the NBT doing what the NBT does best—making ballet more accessible thanks to a powerful shot of theatre. Traditionalists may sniff, but this brave production deserves every bit of box office success that comes its way" (*What's On Stage*, 27.9.02); "Composer Claude-Michel's simple themes help take the audience on a magical mystery tour of the moors above Haworth—ready to watch the tragedy unfold...this is truly culture at its best" (Damian Bates, *Telegraph & Argus*, 9.24.02); "Claude-Michel's schizophrenic score switches from light to brooding dark in an instant, matching both the frippery of Thrushcross Grange and the choking brooding of Heathcliff" (Karen Joyner, *Metro Life*, 9.25.02); "Schön-berg's idea seems to have paid off triumphantly. There was never a dull moment, with both music and dance driving the story along to its inevi-table climax. And the Bradford audience seemed captivated throughout, with more than a few wet eyes at the end of the evening" (*BBC Bradford and West Yorkshire*, 9.24.02).

CITIES WHERE *WUTHERING HEIGHTS* PLAYED

Wuthering Heights played a total of 70 performances in the following UK cities: Bradford, Nottingham, Sheffield, Norwich, Canterbury, London, Milton Keynes, Leeds, Cardiff.

DISCOGRAPHY
WUTHERING HEIGHTS: The Ballet
1st Night Records ©2003 Exallshow Ltd.

ONE DAY MORE

One Day More, a symphonic concert celebrating the work of Boublil and Schönberg, premiered at the NEC Symphony Hall in Birmingham on September 16, 2004 and played to packed houses for two nights. The Midland Symphony Choir opened the evening with "At The End of the Day" from *Les Misérables*, and this was followed by "It's a Frog's Life," a humorous introduction to the works of Alain and Claude-Michel and to the vocalists: Joanna Ampil, Hadley Fraser, Claire Moore, Jerome Pradon, Stephen Tate, and Marie Zamora. The concert featured their five existing works: *La Révolution Française, Les Misérables, Miss Saigon, Martin Guerre,* and the ballet *Wuthering Heights,* along with a preview of their new show *The Pirate Queen.* The concert was directed by Fiona Laird, and the BBC Concert Orchestra was conducted by Adrian Jackson. Stephen Tate hosted the evening, and between each section of the concert he read out witty postcards supposedly sent by Alain and Claude-Michel, which either introduced the next section or commented on the previous number. This gave the evening a truly informal, light-hearted, and even personal atmosphere.

A section of six songs from *Miss Saigon* was followed by four songs from their very first musical, *La Révolution Française.* The first three were sung by the two talented French performers Jerome Pradon and Marie Zamora (Alain's wife), who were the original Marius and Cosette from the Paris *Les Misérables* in 1991. The English lyrics were shown on a large screen at the back of the orchestra filled stage. The last song, a duet titled "A World to Come: Quatre Saisons Pour un Amour," was sung by Joanna and Hadley, and had been translated into English especially for the concert by Herbert Kretzmer. The first act concluded with a section of "The Songs That Might Have Been," which was a presentation of songs that had been rewritten or removed from the shows and included

"Sacred Bird" from *Miss Saigon* and "Five Bullets/Little People" from *Les Misérables*, beautifully performed by seven young boys.

The second act opened with music from Claude-Michel's ballet *Wuthering Heights*, followed by songs from *Martin Guerre*. Next came a highly entertaining look at "How The Songs Might Have Been." The haunting "Empty Chairs at Empty Tables" from *Les Misérables* was sung by Hadley and turned into a sensual tango that the other performers danced to. Javert's "Suicide" was turned into "Javert Rap," sung by Stephen while wearing appropriate dark shades, and with the rest of the cast engaged in wacky rap dance movements. The last song in this section turned Eponine's moody "On My Own" into a swinging big band number, "On My Own Swing," sung engagingly by Claire, Joanna, and Marie. *The Pirate Queen* was next in line with a beautiful love duet from Joanna and Hadley, "I Never Want This Dream To End." The concert ended, as all good concerts of musical theatre seem to, with songs from *Les Misérables*, culminating naturally with the concert's unforgettable title song, "One Day More." The encore, demanded by the audience, was "Do You Hear The People Sing?," which met with a roaring standing ovation as Alain and Claude-Michel appeared briefly on stage and took their bows.

CREATIVE TEAM
Evening Devised by   Alain Boublil, John Caird, Claude-Michel Schönberg
Additional Orchestrations   Simon Hale, Mike Townend, Adrian Jackson
Director   Fiona Laird
Musical Director   Adrian Jackson
Lighting Design   Alistair Grant
Sound Design   Richard Brooker Design

MUSICAL NUMBERS
ACT I
At The End Of The Day   Midland Symphony Choir
It's a Frog's Life   Company
Miss Saigon
Bui Doi   Stephen Tate, Jerome Pradon, Choir
The Movie In My Mind   Joanna Ampil, Claire Moore, Marie Zamora
The American Dream   Stephen Tate, Choir

Last Night Of The World   Joanna Ampil, Hadley Fraser
Fall Of Saigon   BBC Concert Orchestra
I'd Give My Life For You   Joanna Ampil
La Révolution Française
Retour de la Bastille: Français, Française   Jerome Pradon, Choir
Au Petit Matin   Marie Zamora
Declaration Des Droits De L'Homme Et Du Citoyen   Jerome
    Pradon, Choir
A World To Come: Quatre Saisons Pour un Amour   Joanna
    Ampil, Hadley Fraser, Choir
The Songs That Might Have Been
What If He Doesn't Come Back Tonight (*Miss Saigon*)   Claire
    Moore
When Will Someone Hear (*Martin Guerre*)   Marie Zamora
Five Bullets/Little People (*Les Misérables*)   Alex Gibbs, James
    Hudson, Isaak Rushton, Alick Draper, Stuart Bacon, Kieran
    Forbes, Matthew McNutty
Sacred Bird (*Miss Saigon*)   Joanna Ampil
Land Of The Fathers (*Martin Guerre*)   Company
ACT II
Wuthering Heights (From the ballet)
The Wind/Entr'acte/The Wind Reprise   BBC Concert Orchestra
Martin Guerre
Martin Guerre   Hadley Fraser
Bethlehem   Choir
Live With Somebody You Love   Jerome Pradon, Marie Zamora
All I know   BBC Concert Orchestra
The Imposters   Company
How The Songs Might Have Been
Empty Chairs Tango   Hadley Fraser
Javert Rap   Stephen Tate
On My Own Swing   Claire Moore, Joanna, Ampil, Marie Zamora
The Pirate Queen
I Never Want This Dream To End   Joanna Ampil, Hadley Fraser
Les Misérables
Back At The Barricades   BBC Concert Orchestra
Stars   Jerome Pradon
Love Montage—I Saw Him Once/   Marie Zamora, Hadley Fraser,
    Joanna Ampil
In My Life/A Heart Full Of Love

Master Of The House   Stephen Tate, Marie Zamora
Bring Him Home   Claire Moore, Jerome Pradon
One Day More!   Company

REVIEWS

The local reviews for the concert were excellent: "Bringing together the outstanding show tunes of *Les Misérables, Miss Saigon*, and *Martin Guerre* in one concert couldn't have got much better for fans of the musicals" (Alison Dayani, *Evening Mail*, 9.20.04); "Delight over the magical musical and...the superb performance of this symphonic concert of their West End hits, with new music" (Derek Weekes, *Express & Star*, 9.17.04). *Musical Stages*, the "parish magazine of the West End" that has a worldwide circulation, devoted a full-page review to the concert: "Those who had been expecting a straightforward concert received a very pleasant surprise...the team did themselves proud...though still very powerful, some of the songs were incomprehensible when taken out of their context and placed in a concert. However, this caused no real problem, as most of the audience knew the shows and lyrics by heart anyway. It was a pleasure watching these excellent and versatile performers giving their all at a most memorable musical feast" (Melly, Winter 04).

More concerts of *One Day More* are planned for 2007 in the UK.

THE PIRATE QUEEN

The Pirate Queen began its pre-Broadway, World Premiere engagement at the Chicago Cadillac Palace Theatre with previews from October 3, 2006. It played there until November 26, with the opening night on October 29. It previews on Broadway at the Hilton Theatre from March 6, 2007 and opens on April 5. This section is accurate as of the Chicago opening. Richard Maltby (co-lyricist) and Graciela Daniele (musical staging) have joined the creative team and some changes are being made before the show opens in New York.

CREATIVE TEAM

The creative credits are:
Book   Alain Boublil & Claude-Michel Schönberg
Music   Claude-Michel Schönberg
Lyrics   Alain Boublil & John Dempsey
Orchestrator   Julian Kelly

Director   Frank Galati
Artistic Director   John McColgan
Choreographer   Mark Dendy
Irish Dance Choreographer   Carol Leavy Joyce
Scenic Design   Eugene Lee
Costume Design   Martin Pakledinaz
Lighting Design   Kenneth Posner
Sound Design   Jonathan Deans

CAST
Grania   Stephanie J. Block
Tiernan   Hadley Fraser
Dubhdara   Jeff McCarthy
Queen Elizabeth I   Linda Balgord
Donal   Marcus Chait
Bingham   William Youmans
Evleen   Áine Uí Cheallaigh
Majella   Brooke Elliott
Eoin   Chase Krepp, Brooks Marks

MUSICAL NUMBERS
The musical numbers at the Chicago Premiere were:
ACT ONE
Overture
All Aboard the "Ceol Na Mara"   Dubhdara, Tiernan, Grania,
    Oarsmen, Company
My Grace   Dubhdara
Here On This Night   Grania, Tiernan, Oarsmen, Company
Battle At Sea   Grania, Tiernan, Dubhdara, Company
The Waking Of The Queen   Elizabeth, Ladies in Waiting
Rah-Rah, Tip-Top   Elizabeth, Bingham, Lords, Ladies in Waiting
The Choice Is Yours   Grania, Bingham, Dubhdara, Company
Boys'll Be Boys   Donal, Mates
The Wedding Ring   Grania, Tiernan, Donal, Dubhdara, Evleen,
    Company
I'll Be There   Tiernan
Boys'll Be Boys Reprise   Donal, Mates
Because I'm A Wife   Grania
Trouble At Rockfleet   Grania, Majella, Tiernan, Donal, Bingham,
    Company

A Day Beyond Belclare   Grania, Tiernan, Donal, Company
Go Serve Your Queen   Elizabeth, Bingham
Dubhdara's Farewell   Dubhdara, Grania
Sail to the Stars   Dubhdara, Grania, Tiernan, Donal, Evleen,
Company
ACT TWO
Entr'acte
Son Of The Irish Seas   Grania, Tiernan, Donal, Evleen, Majella,
Company
Enemy At Port Side   Grania, Tiernan, Donal, Evleen, O'Malley
Apprentice, Company
I Dismiss You   Grania, Donal, Oarsman
If I said I Loved You   Tiernan, Grania
The Role Of The Queen   Elizabeth, Bingham, Company
The Christening   Evleen, Grania, Tiernan, Company
Let A Father Stand By His Son   Donal, Grania, Bingham, Tiernan,
Evleen, Company
Surrender/Each In Time   Bingham, Tiernan, Elizabeth, Company
She, Who Has All   Elizabeth, Grania, Tiernan, Bingham, Company
Lament   Grania, Company
The Sea Of Life   Grania, Company
The Queen Will See You Now   Company
Woman To Woman   Elizabeth, Grania, Company
Grania And Elizabeth In Private   Company
Grania'a Exit   Elizabeth, Grania, Bingham, Company
May Long We Sail The Sea   Grania, Tiernan, Evleen, Company

SYNOPSIS
(Based on Chicago Première)

ACT ONE
Clew Bay
Dubhdara, the Chieftain of the Clan O'Malley, prepares to set sail on
his ship, the Ceol Na Mara (Music of the Ocean). His young daughter
Grania is desperate to accompany her father and her childhood companion Tiernan. But not only are these dangerous times at sea, they are
also times when it was considered bad luck to have a woman aboard.
Grania, still determined to go, disguises herself as a boy and secretly
joins them.

Onboard the Ceol Na Mara
During a fierce storm, Grania bravely climbs up to the mainsail spar and cuts down the sail to prevent the ship from capsizing. Fondly lamenting his daughter's tomboyish-ness, Dubhdara agrees to let Grania stay, and she swears she will serve both him and Ireland without fail. Aboard the ship, Grania and Tiernan's relationship alters from childhood fondness to adult love. During a battle at sea wherein the English are defeated, Grania fights fiercely, proving her courage and her swordsmanship. She saves her father's life, and he pronounces her Queen of the Pirates.

Queen Elizabeth's Bedroom
In England, Elizabeth has just been crowned queen and is eager to prove her statesmanship to the men at court. The courtiers try to convince her that all is well, but her confidante Lord Bingham is forced to admit that they have lost a ship to the Irish and, what's more, to a female captain. Elizabeth is outraged at this and demands that Grace O'Malley be defeated.

Clew Bay
Back in Ireland, there is turmoil as English oppression grows. Dubhdara believes that their cause would be strengthened if the warring clans were united through the marriage of his daughter Grania with Donal, son of the chieftain of the neighboring Clan O'Flaherty. He does not demand this of Grania but leaves her to choose. Grania, although very much in love with Tiernan, puts duty and her country first and agrees to the marriage.

The Shebeen at Rockfleet
Donal, however, is a womanizer and a drunk who most enjoys visiting the shebeen, where there are women of loose morals and plenty to drink, with his mates. He sees no reason why this should change after the marriage.

Clew Bay
In accordance with Irish laws, the couple initially are bound together for three years. The clans are united at the wedding and celebrate with much dancing. As Grania and Donal set off for Rockfleet, Tiernan mourns his loss but pledges his constancy to her.

Rockfleet

Grania's marriage proves to be a stormy affair due to Donal's continued womanizing and drinking. When the English attack, it is Grania who leads the women in fighting them off. In the process, she wounds Lord Bingham, ensuring he becomes an even more bitter enemy. She has won the respect of the Clan O'Flaherty, and when Tiernan arrives to tell her that her father is dying, they accompany her back to Clew Bay.

Clew Bay

Grania arrives in time to hear her father's last words and promises him that she and Donal will have a child. With Dubhdara's death, Grania becomes the chieftain, most probably the first and only woman to hold this position in Ireland.

ACT TWO
Onboard the Ceol Na Mara

Grania, now captain of the ship, gives birth to a son, Eoin, on board. Shortly after, they are attacked by the English, and Grania, still weak from giving birth, leads the battle to defeat them. Donal has shown himself to be a cowardly, drunken traitor, wishing to surrender at the first hint of trouble. Grania is outraged at his behavior and, in the tradition of the Brehon Law, she dismisses him publicly, officially dissolving their marriage. Tiernan and Grania are now free to declare their love, but they both hold back from doing so.

The Queen's Court

Elizabeth is enraged at Bingham's failure to defeat Grania, but he has colluded with the treacherous scoundrel Donal to ensure Grania's downfall.

Clew Bay

Donal turns up at the baby's Christening and demands to see his son. Just as Grania agrees to this, English troops burst in and seize her. Donal reveals his betrayal and tries to take his son. Tiernan attempts to stop him, and in the fight Donal is killed. Tiernan takes the child in accordance with Grania's wishes.

Dublin

Grania has been in jail for some years, and the English have won supremacy in Ireland. The Irish chieftains come to surrender unconditionally.

Tiernan offers the English a trade—his freedom for Grania's—and the queen agrees. Elizabeth finds herself affected by this turn of events and reflects on her own life as a woman. Tiernan is imprisoned and Grania set free to care for her child, now a young boy.

Clew Bay

Grania's joy at being reunited with her son is tempered by the realization of how Ireland has changed during her imprisonment. The country has grown desolate, her lands are ravaged, her people are hungry, and injustice reigns. Grania decides to go to England and seek an audience with the queen.

The Queen's Court

These two powerful women, one a reigning queen and the other without a crown, find themselves face to face, woman to woman, in a private conversation unheard by eager courtiers. The most unexpected truce is hammered out between them, freeing Clew Bay from the worst of English rule. Tiernan is granted his freedom, and Lord Bingham falls into disgrace.

Onboard the Ceol Na Mara

Grania and Tiernan are reunited at last. Unencumbered now by war and previous alliances, they can finally pledge themselves to each other.

THEMES

The main themes dealt with in *The Pirate Queen* are Love and Thwarted Love, Patriotism and Betrayal, Destiny, and Personal Identity. The theme of Love is worked out not only through romantic love, but also through parent-child relationships. Grania and her father have a very loving, touching relationship. She clearly respects and adores her father with an affinity that goes beyond the grave. And in turn, it is her love for her son that motivates her to reverse the situation she finds in Ireland when she is released from jail by seeking an audience with the queen. Tiernan and Grania's love is initially thwarted by outside circumstance, but they never lose their feelings for each other. Tiernan's constancy is proved beyond doubt as he cares for Grania's child and finally goes to jail in her place. When Grania is in jail, Elizabeth comes to realize that although in material terms she has everything and Grania nothing, in real terms it is the reverse: "Only now do I see/That a woman in love, it is she/Who has all."

The themes of Patriotism and Betrayal are paramount in the musical. Grania has a fierce national loyalty and pride, and is even prepared to sacrifice her own and Tiernan's happiness by marrying a man she doesn't know and doesn't love for the sake of her country. She believes that "Two small lives/Matter not in war" and feels she has no real choice: "My heart? My land?/My choice/Is clear." Throughout, Grania fights for the freedom of Ireland to retain its traditions and its culture, both of which she holds so dear. Donal, on the other hand, betrays not only Grania with his womanizing, but, more importantly, he betrays his country with his cowardice and his collusion with the enemy.

The theme of Destiny is closely linked with that of Personal Identity. *The Pirate Queen* is the story of two unique women. Grania takes everything that fate throws at her, and she never succumbs but fights to reverse the situation. She acts instead of allowing herself to be acted upon, and she determines her own fate. Elizabeth too determines her own destiny, refusing to act by men's standards and demonstrating her political acumen to her courtiers right from the start: "'Difficult,' your father said,/'This business of the King.'/One day out, already/You've a handle on the thing." Bingham may mistakenly believe that he defines her identity: "I alone shall be seen/As defining the role of the queen.'" But Elizabeth leaves no doubt that it is she herself who defines her role and her sovereign identity.

Grania refuses the limits that define a sixteenth-century woman in Ireland and breaks the mold that tradition had set on female identity by becoming the captain of her ship, the chieftain of her clan, and a powerful political leader. She has the ability to reinvent herself as, and when necessary. She readily adapts herself to life at sea, acting with courage and fortitude, winning the respect of all the crew, and overturning traditional notions of what a woman can do. When she marries Donal for the sake of Ireland, she reinvents herself as a wife, leaving behind her true self: "I now leave behind/The woman that I am." It is only when her father dies that she can re-establish her old life back at sea, now as chieftain of her clan: "And so it is I must reclaim myself." When she leaves prison and her people tell her of the devastation and turmoil ("Ev'ry day a war/Fortune's rearranged"), she refuses to submit to this state of affairs: "No, my boy, I can't allow this world/I'll change it for you/I'll do as I know I must do." The "Sea of Life" is an apt metaphor for the destiny in which she trusts, while at the same time taking her own positive actions: "I'll do what I believe, and pray, prevail/I'll stay fast to my course, succeed or fail/And give my fate this night/ To this, the sea we sail."

FACTS AND TRIVIA

Musical Instruments

The musical instruments in *The Pirate Queen* are the typical Irish Band instruments: the uilleann pipes, whistles, fiddle, Gaelic harp, and bodhrán. These are played alongside the more traditional violin, clarinet, saxophone, French horn, harp, guitars, banjo, bass, drums, percussion instruments, and keyboards.

A Factual History of Grace O'Malley

Granuaile (Grace O'Malley) was born in 1530 to Owen "Dubhdara" (Black Oak) and Margaret O'Malley. Her father was the chieftain of the Barony of Murrisk, and the O'Malley clan were renowned mariners, traders, and sometimes pirates.

In 1546, when she was 16, she was married to Donal O'Flaherty, who was many years her senior. Hotheaded and ill-tempered, Donal's nickname was Donal-an-Chogaidh (Donal of the Battles). By the time Donal was killed in 1560, fourteen years after their marriage, Grace had borne him three children: Owen, Murrough, and Margaret.

Grace had been sailing since her youth and was an accomplished mariner. When her father died, she inherited both his title and his fleet, and commanded three large ships of about three hundred men. She also employed the terrifying Scottish Gallowglass mercenaries and, on one occasion, a thousand Gallowglass travelled to the West of Ireland seeking employment with the Pirate Queen.

Grace and her crew traded as far south as Spain and Portugal and north into the Baltic, bringing back wine, port, silks, weapons, and amber to Ireland. They were also not above a little piracy; a common tactic was to waylay a merchant ship and levy a fee for its safe passage.

Grace married her second husband, Richard-an-Iarainn (Iron Richard), in 1566. One year later, she promptly divorced him under the ancient Irish legal system known as the Brehon Laws. She did keep his strategic castle, however. They nonetheless remained good friends until his death in 1583.

She had one son by Richard in 1567, called Tibbot-na-Long, or Theobald of the Ships. She was pregnant with the child before she divorced Richard, and was 37 when Tibbot was born.

Traditional accounts record Tibbot as having been born on the high seas while Grace was returning from a trading mission. The day after the birth, Grace's ship was attacked by Turkish corsairs. When Grace's captain told her that the corsairs were about to take the ship, Grace strapped on her weapons and stormed into the battle, a blunderbuss in one hand and a sword in the other. The sight of the wild woman is said to have terrified the Turks, who were quickly defeated. Turkish and Algerian pirates raided the south and west coast of Ireland regularly throughout this period. They also raided Iceland for slaves.

The great love of her life was Hugh de Lacy, who was washed ashore following a shipwreck. Hugh was of French or Norman extraction, and the couple fell deeply in love. Their passionate relationship ended when Hugh was killed by a rival clan. Grace's revenge was terrible. She personally killed those responsible and then captured their castle.

Grace was a dangerous and wily enemy. When the English captain William Martin laid siege to her castle at Rockfleet, she turned the tables and attacked and defeated him. But Grace knew she would have to accommodate England. In 1577, she did a deal with Sir Henry Sidney, Queen Elizabeth's representative in Ireland, offering him her ships and men. But less than a year later, she ended up in jail, charged with being "a great spoiler, and chief commander and director of thieves and murders at sea."

She spent a year in the notorious Limerick Jail before being transferred to the dungeons of Dublin castle. A year later, she was released and allowed to return to Connaught on a promise of good behavior.

In 1584, Grace's nemesis, the ruthless Sir Richard Bingham, became the Governor of Connaught. He and Grace quickly became sworn enemies. It took him two years before he captured her. In the same year, Grace's eldest son Owen was stabbed to death while in custody, and two of her nephews were hanged. Surprisingly, Bingham did not hang Grace; he robbed her of all her wealth before releasing her.

Grace went on the offensive. She brought in Scottish mercenaries to fight Bingham's English troops, and in one battle over fourteen hundred men were killed. Knowing that if she continued she would be ruined, Grace adopted an extraordinarily daring tactic. In the early summer of 1593, she wrote to Queen Elizabeth. Before there could have been any reply from the queen, Bingham arrested both her son and her brother. Grace realized she had to act swiftly before they were either executed or "accidentally" died in custody. So in June 1593, Grace sailed her own ship to London to stand before the queen and plead for the lives of her family.

The two women met in July 1593. They could not have been more different, one pale and delicate and the other dark and strong. They conversed in Latin. At one point, Grace sneezed and was handed a lace handkerchief by a lady-in-waiting. Grace blew her nose loudly and then flung the handkerchief into the fire. The court was aghast. Elizabeth suggested that one did not throw away such valuable linen; Grace responded that the Irish did not keep their soiled cloth about their person. The English queen was obviously impressed by Grace. In September, the queen wrote to Bingham effectively telling him to release Grace's family and leave her alone.

Grace died in 1603, the same year as Elizabeth. She was 73 years old. Legend has it that she is buried in the ruins of the Cistercian Abbey on Clare Island.

Why was Grace O'Malley written out of Irish history?

Grace O'Malley's extraordinary life was completely ignored by Irish historians, although her life was documented in Elizabethan State Papers. In her fascinating book, *Granuaile, Ireland's Pirate Queen*, Anne Chambers explains: "To the sixteenth-century English administrators and military men who firstly by persuasion and later by the sword came to conquer the land of her birth, this 'notorious woman' provoked awe, anger, revulsion, and admiration. But in Ireland for over 400 years she was destined to remain a prisoner of indifference, as Irish history chose to ignore her unique contribution to the social, political, and maritime history of her time. But folklore, poetry, and fiction showed no such bias and must be congratulated for preserving the memory of one of the most remarkable women of history, Gráinne (Grace) O'Malley, or as she is more familiarly known in Ireland, Granuaile."

"Like her sisters, Granuaile was a victim of the mainly male orientation of historical record and analyses. But in her case more than male chauvinism ensured her dismissal from the pages of history. By not fitting the mold demanded by later generations of Irish historians, Granuaile committed an additional transgression. Until relatively recently, Irish heroes and heroines were required to be suitably adorned in the green cloak of patriotism, their personal lives untainted, their religious beliefs fervently Roman Catholic, with an occasional allowance made for rebel Protestants. Granuaile was, as one of her male detractors wrote of her, 'a woman who overstepped the part of womanhood,' who allowed neither religious, social, nor political convention to deter her during her lifetime, and did not really fit the required mold. Granuaile, the 'chief commander and director of thieves and murders at sea,' hardly fitted the rose-hued picture of Gaelic womanhood painted by latter-day male and often clerical historians."

"However, it is a measure of Granuaile's greatness that her memory at least was preserved by legend and by folklore. Legends are not created about insignificant people. To be remembered in folk history is as much a tribute to the impact she made in her life as any academic treatise. As to the factual evidence, it was left to the English administrators and generals, who came to conquer Ireland during her lifetime, to record aspects of the extraordinary role she played. These Elizabethan documents are now faded and brittle, their age-darkened, spider-like handwriting evidence of the passage of four hundred years since their authors put quill to parchment. From the swirls and flourishes of these sixteenth-century scribes, the story of Gráinne O'Malley springs to life" (Anne Chambers, *Granuaile, Ireland's Pirate Queen*, Dublin: Wolfhound Press, 2003).

From the Elizabethan State Papers

"There came to me also a most feminine sea captain called Granny Imallye and offered her services unto me, wheresoever I would command her, with three galleys and two hundred fighting men, either in Scotland or Ireland. She brought with her her husband, for she was as well by sea as by land well more than Mrs. Mate with him…This was a notorious woman in all the coasts of Ireland."

—*Sir Henry Sidney, Lord Deputy of Ireland, 1576*

"A notable traitoress and nurse to all rebellions in the Province for 40 years."

—*Sir Richard Bingham, Governor of Connaught, 1586*

INDEX